Physical Chara[cteristics]
Japanes[e]
(from The Kennel C[lub])

Body: Withers high and well developed. Short loin, level back. Deep chest. Moderate spring of rib. Belly moderately tucked up.

Tail: Set on high. Thick and carried curled or curved as in a sickle.

Hindquarters: Long upper thigh, short strong second thigh. Hocks strong and parallel when seen from the rear. Turning neither in nor out. Well developed. Slight but definite bend to stifle.

Colour:

Red: Intense, clear red. White markings restricted to eye spots, cheeks, underjaw, forechest, underparts and underside of tail and legs. No white above elbows or hock. The white markings on the chest resembling the shape of a bow-tie.

Size: Height: Dogs 39.5 cms (15.5. ins). Bitches 36.5 cms (14.5 ins) with allowance of 1.5 cms (.75 ins) either way.

Feet: Cat-like, with firm, well-knuckled toes. Pads firm and elastic. Dark nails preferred.

Japanese Shiba

By Andrew De Prisco

Contents

Japanese Shiba

PUBLISHED IN THE UNITED KINGDOM BY:

INTERPET
PUBLISHING
Vincent Lane, Dorking Surrey RH4 3YX England

ISBN 1-903098-65-3

PHOTO CREDITS:
Norvia Behling, Mary Bloom, TJ Calhoun, Carolina Biological Society, Doskocil, Isabelle Français, James Hayden-Yoav, James R Hayden, RBP, Carol Ann Johnson, Bill Jonas, Dwight R Kuhn, Dr Dennis Kunkel, Mikki Pet Products, Phototake, Jean Claude Revy, Dr Andrew Spielman, Karen Taylor and Alice van Kempen.

The Japanese Shiba Inu was named as one of Japan's Natural Monuments, protected by the government. The enigmatic Shiba is one of Japan's most ancient breeds as well as its most recent phenomenon. Perhaps the nation's best kept secret, the Shiba fits well into the crowded living conditions in large cities and in the past decade has become an in-vogue breed in the West.

History of the

JAPANESE SHIBA

Isolated from intruders from across the sea, Japan basked in virtual independence for centuries. This highly ritualistic society, rather primitive compared to the Western world, with which it had not contact until the latter half of the 19th century, was content to pass on its history and culture without interruption. The nation's indigenous dogs, regarded today as 'Natural Monuments,' are mostly members of the spitz family, including the Japanese Akita, Shiba, Tosa and many others. Spitz dogs derive from the colder climates and possess characteristic features that facilitate their survival in sub-zero conditions. Well-furred, erect and small ears protect the dog from wind and snow; a dense double coat provides insulation from the cold as well as coolness from heat, should the need arise; a well-furnished, tightly curled tail covers the dog's nose when he is sleeping in his typical circular position; a wolf-like muzzle warms the air through the long passages before entering the animal's lungs. From the tiny Shiba to the giant Akita, all the Japanese spitz breeds share these essential physical characteristics.

The Japanese Shiba, the smallest of Japan's spitz breeds, possesses all of these traits, plus a tonne of personality and attitude. Among the Shiba's cousins are the Japanese Akita, the largest and most popular of these indigenous spitzes; the Ainu or Hokkaido, a fearless guard dog; and three middle-sized dogs, the Shikoku, Kai and Kishu. Of these six Japanese breeds, only the Shiba and Akita have established followings outside Japan, although the other four are recognised by the Fédération Cynologique Internationale (FCI), the world kennel club association. The breed known as the Japanese Spitz is not related to the Shiba but to the Samoyed, in whose image the breed was created. Americans recognise the similarities between the Japanese Spitz and the Miniature American Eskimo Dog, also a solid white, abundantly coated Nordic dog.

To Westerners, the notion of

TEN BREEDS OF JAPAN

The six Japanese spitz breeds are divided by size, namely the Akita as the large breed; the Shiba as the small breed, and four medium size breeds, Kai, Kishu, Shikoku and Hokkaido (or Ainu). Only the Akita and Shiba have established significant followings outside Japan. There are four other recognised Japanese breeds, including the giant mastiff breed known as the Tosa, the lovely toy breed known as the Chin, the solid white Japanese Spitz and the diminutive Japanese Terrier. Of course, the Chin is the most popular of these breeds worldwide. In Japan, the Shiba is the most popular Japanese breed, followed by the Japanese Spitz, Chin and Akita.

The largest spitz breed of Japan, the Akita enjoys world-wide popularity, despite the unfortunate politics that has divided the breed into the Japanese Akita and the American Akita, also recognised as the Great Japanese Dog.

a small, efficiently built dynamo from Japan is an apparently modern one. However, history reveals that the Shiba-Inu is much older than the Toyota Corolla or the Honda Accord, and goes even further per litre of petrol! Archaeologists in Japan have unearthed the remains of small dogs with curled tails dating back to 8000 BC. Experts assert that these diminutive but sturdily-built skeletons represent the ancestors of the Shiba-Inu. Based on pottery from the Jomon Period (8000 to 200 BC), these small dogs were used by men to hunt deer, boar and bear. Most scholars agree that the Shiba-Inu is the oldest and purest of the Japanese spitz breeds.

Shibas could be found in various regions of Japan, differing slightly in coloration, coat length and density, bone and maturation. These variations can still be seen in Shibas today, though breeders have strived to agree upon and establish one correct type. From the mountainous regions, the Shibas bred for hunting possessed heavier bone and coarser type. Colours varied from region to region: the intense red coloration of the San-In region dogs, compared to the mottled black coloration of the Yamanashi region dogs. The

Shin-Shu and Mino type dogs were smaller in size and lighter in bone, prized for their hunting prowess and boundless energy. The Mino Shibas possessed the darkest red coloration, the colour preferred by most Shiba fanciers today, as well as dark brown triangular eyes, thick ears and a sickle tail (compared to the curled tail of the other Shiba types).

COLOURS IN JAPANESE SHIBAS

Burning with the fire of the Japanese sun, the red Shiba-Inu has become the most prized of the Shiba colours, though it is by no means the only recognised or desirable Shiba colour. There are three colours in the Shiba: red, red sesame and black and tan. Some controversy existed over other colours, including white (which is acceptable in other Japanese breeds but not Shibas) as well as grey and brindle (both of which are seen in other Japanese breeds but do not exist in Shibas). The sesame colour is

GENUS *CANIS*

Dogs and wolves are members of the genus *Canis*. Wolves are known scientifically as *Canis lupus* while dogs are known as *Canis domesticus*. Dogs and wolves are known to interbreed. The term *canine* derives from the Latin derived word *Canis*. The term 'dog' has no scientific basis but has been used for thousands of years. The origin of the word 'dog' has never been authoritatively ascertained.

created by a combination of black and white hairs with the principal colour red. The term 'Urajiro' describes the desirable white coat markings on the Shiba's muzzle, neck and lower jaw, cheeks, chest, stomach, underside of tail and inside of legs. All three coat colours should have white in these areas.

To confuse matters, The Kennel Club's interim standard lists 'red, black, black and tan or brindle. White with red or grey tinge' as the list of Shiba colours. The brindle pattern is associated not with the Shiba

The Ainu or Hokkaido originated in the northern Japanese island called Hokkaido. The breed is somewhat larger than the Shiba and used as a hunting and companion dog.

but with its cousin the Kai, 'the Tiger Dog,' which can be found in red, black and grey brindles. White is frowned upon in the breed's native Japan and is associated with the Kishu, not the Shiba. There is no mention of the red sesame coloration—a pity! As for a solid black Shiba?...perhaps some club member owned a black and tan without the tan and lobbied for its inclusion in the standard. A puzzlement, to say the least! A later version of The Kennel Club standard lists red, red

The Shikoku is one of the Japanese native spitz breeds that is medium in size. Like fellow medium-sized spitz breeds, the Hokkaido and Kai, the breed is rarely seen outside Japan.

A black and tan Japanese Shiba bitch, showing ideal markings and an alert stance.

sesame, black and tan, and white, with descriptions of each.

Colour prejudice and politics abound in many breeds. It is sad to see that the show scene in the UK and US has become so partial to red Shibas that black and tan and red sesame exhibits are practically non-existent. The Shiba has never been a one-colour breed and this author, who favours the truly unique Japanese colour—red sesame, patiently awaits the turn of the trend when exhibitors can enter the ring with a red sesame (or black and tan!) and have an equal chance at the blue ribbons.

BREED NAME

In the Japanese language, words have various meanings, similar to the concept of homonyms in the English language. Thus the word *shiba* in Japanese has a variety of meanings. Some say that *shiba* refers to the red coloration of dried brushwood (called shiba), recognising that the Shiba has also been called the Brushwood Dog. Others state that *shiba* simply means 'small,' as the breed has been called the Japanese Small Dog in some English text books.

Unlike the Shiba, the other Japanese breeds have been named for their regions, such as the Akita, Sanshu and Hokkaido, all of which are named for the locality in which the breed originated. Because the Shiba is associated with

A solid-white Japanese Akita is not commonly seen in the UK, though they are perfectly acceptable and handsome.

The Hokkaido comes in colours similar to the Shiba, including this black and tan pattern. This Hokkaido is being shown at the World Dog Show in Milan, 2000.

'Urajiro' refers to the white markings on the Shiba's coat, seen on this red sesame on its neck, muzzle, cheeks and chest.

WESTERN INFLUENCE ON JAPAN

In the mid-1850s, Commodore Perry and the US Navy pried open Japanese ports and forced the Japanese to see how 'behind the times' their semi-feudal society indeed was. Among the Western imports that helped 'modernise' Japan were the popular European dog breeds, including German Shepherd Dogs, Poodles and Dachshunds as well as many gundog breeds, such as Pointers and English Setters, igniting a new trend for hunting in Japan. Among the upper-class fanciers, these Western breeds were prized for their specialised skills and 'foreignness,' and the native Japanese breeds were neglected for decades or crossbred

numerous regions, various names for Shiba types have evolved. The Shin-Shu Shiba derived from Nagano, the central mountainous area of Honshu, and is perhaps the most famous of the Shiba types. Other names include the Mino Shiba (from the Gifu Prefecture) and the San-In Shiba (from Tottori and Shimane Prefectures and the northwestern part of Honshu).

The word *inu* or *ken* in Japanese simply translates as 'dog.' It is not uncommon for the breed to be called Shiba-Inu or Shiba-Ken. This suffix can be used with any of the Japanese breed names, such as Sanshu-Inu or Akita-Ken.

This black and tan Japanese Shiba is smiling about its newfound popularity in the Western World, even if its red brethren are favoured by most fanciers (and judges!).

NATIVE BREEDS OF JAPAN

BREED	SIZE	COLOURS	UTILITY
Shiba	14.5-15.5 ins	Red, red sesame, black and tan	Small bird hunting/companion
Shikoku	17-22 ins	White, fawn, tan, grey, pied	Deer hunting/companion
Kai	18-23 ins	Black brindle, red brindle, brindle	Deer hunting
Kishu	17-22 ins	White	Herding/guarding
Hokkaido/Ainu	18-22 ins	Red, fawn, black & tan	Bear and deer hunting/guarding
Akita	24-28 ins	Any including brindle or pinto	Bear and boar hunting/guarding

haphazardly to the imported dogs.

This influx of Western breeds nearly caused the extinction of the pure Japanese breeds, including the Shiba. It was not until 1928 when Dr Hiroyoshi Saito formed a club dedicated to the preservation of these native Japanese breeds that the situation began to rectify itself. The new organisation known as the Nihon Ken Kozonkai (for short, Nippo) was successful in persuading the Japanese government to designate the six native breeds as 'Natural Monuments' in the 1930s under the Cultural Properties Act. The Shiba breed was designated in 1936.

Nippo draughted breed standards for the six native breeds, held shows for native breeds and registered dogs. Tako was the first Shiba to be registered and was the only Shiba of the 15 entered in the first Nippo show to be

'URAJIRO'

This Japanese word refers to the white (or cream) coloration on the coat of the Shiba. These markings are on the side of the nose, cheeks, beneath the jaw and neck, chest, abdomen and insides of the legs. Some Shibas also have white markings on their legs, giving the impression of boots, though these are not desirable according to most standards.

'recommended' for type. Of course, breed type in all six breeds was variable at best, as there were few good examples of the breeds left in most areas. Interest in the breeds grew in Japan, though not overseas, and more shows and clubs were formed in Japan. The national Nippo show of 1939 saw Aka of Fugoku, a ten-month-old Shiba dog, winning the major award, which had previously only been won by the larger breeds. Aka and his offspring would survive the oncoming Second World War and become the foundation of the modern Shiba.

Due to the breed's recognition as a 'Natural Monument,' the FCI recognised the Shiba and dogs were shown in major shows in Tokyo. World War II dealt a devastating blow to all dog activities in Japan, and the Shiba nearly became extinct. The San-In and Mino Shibas were harder hit than the Shin-Shu Shibas. Following the war, an outbreak of distemper in 1959 caused further damage to the surviving Shiba strains. Breeders had to rescue the breed by recreating breeding programmes, transporting dogs from the montane regions to urban centres. The remaining dogs from various lines were combined to create the foundation of today's Shibas. Breeders were forced to select sires and dams from the dwindling Shiba population—dogs of known and pure origins—or to crossbreed

MOST INFLUENTIAL RESTORATION SHIBAS

NAME	SIRE	DAM
Ishi	Hisahara	Kochi
Koro	Unknown	Unknown
Aka of Fugoku	Ishi	Koro
Naka of Akaishiso	Akani	Beniko
Nakaichi of Akaishiso	Naka	Beniko
Tenko of Jonenso	Senko	Tamahime
Matsumaru of Shinshu	Benisachi	Aka Fusame
Meiho of Shimamura	Koronaka	Eienme
Kuratanoishi of Kurataso	Ichiroku	Korohime
Hideyoshi of Shinshu Kirinso	Benisachi	Umehime
Taketoyo of Hokoso	Meiho Kenikomo no Tetsu	Kuro Yakko

to a similar Japanese dog known as the Mikawa. The Mikawa (also known as the Sanshu) has been discredited for being crossbred with the Shiba to recreate the breed. Some Mikawas were even passed off as Shibas. The Mikawa possessed uncharacteristic round eyes and lacked the desired 'Urajiro' markings, sure signs of mixed breeding with Western breeds. The Mikawa lost favour in Japan and is no longer registered by the JKC or FCI. Most breeders opted not to include the Mikawa in their programmes, and resultant health problems ensued due to the limited gene pool. The occurrence of slipped kneecaps and missing teeth still plagues Shiba breeders today.

JAPANESE DEVELOPMENT IN THE 20TH CENTURY
Following the devastation of the Second World War, Japanese society was unstable and anxious, in part due to the change in the recognised value system of the nation. Many Japanese families sought the protection of German Shepherds or other guard-dog-type breeds that they encountered from the occupational forces living in Japan. In time, the Japanese realised that they needed an organisation to help regulate the breeding of these dogs, and the All Japan Guard Dog Association (AJGDA) was formed in 1948 with Kijuro Shidehara serving as honourary chairman and Tanzan Ishibashi as chairman. This organisation was the predecessor of the Japan Kennel Club. The first show for the AJGDA was held on 23 November 1949 at Ueno

The modern Japanese Shiba is a typy, noble small dog with characteristic almond-shaped eyes, small ears and a spitz tail.

BRAIN AND BRAWN
Since dogs have been inbred for centuries, their physical and mental characteristics are constantly being changed to suit man's desires for hunting, retrieving, scenting, guarding and warming their masters' laps. During the past 150 years, dogs have been judged according to physical characteristics as well as functional abilities. Few breeds can boast a genuine balance between physique, working ability and temperament.

Ikenohata Park and attracted 240 dogs. In 1950, the first issue of the AJGDA's gazette was published; in 1957 the gazette would be renamed *The Companion Dog.*

A second Japanese organisation known as the Japan Dog Federation was established in 1963 and became an associate member of FCI, the first such gesture toward Japan's interest in the international dog scene. Around this time, the first international judges from the UK and US were invited to judge at Japanese dog shows. By 1971, the newly formed Asia Kennel Union, established to promote quality pure-breds in Asian dog world, accepted Japan as its chair. In 1976, the AJGDA became known as the Japan Kennel Club (JKC), and

Toyosaku Kariyabu, the third president of the organisation, initiated major changes to modernise the organisation. In 1982, the first FCI World Dog Show ever to be held in Japan took place in Tokyo. In 1992, the JKC established mutual recognition with the American Kennel Club and Canadian Kennel Club.

According to JKC statistics, the Shiba ranks number 12 in the nation's breed registrations, though Japan's most popular breed is the Dachshund! By the end of the 20th century, the Shiba-Inu accounted for about 80 percent of Nippo's total registrations and, due to its convenient flat-size, is one of Japan's most popular breeds. Pure-bred dog registrations have skyrocketed in Japan: in 1992, there were over 300,000 dogs registered and in 1996, there were over 400,000.

MODERN SHIBA HISTORY
We can trace our modern Shiba to less than a dozen influential ancestors, which were first identified by breeder and Japanese dog scholar, Mr Ishikawa, who studied the pedigrees of winning dogs to determine which foundation Shibas have had the most lasting influence. Among the two most important were Aka of Fugoku and Naka of Akaishiso.

Aka of Fugoku, a red male, passed on his good bone, dense coat, proper angulation and ideal temperament to over 200 litters. Naka of Akaishiso lived in the Nagano Prefecture and has been called the father of the Shiba restoration because of his many excellent offspring found throughout Japan.

SHIBAS COME TO AMERICA
Although the Akita made its way to the US in the 1950s, the Shiba did not whistle 'Yankee Doodle' until the early 1970s. Some records show that a stray Shiba or two found their way to the US after World War II, but none of these dogs contributed to the establishment of the breed on American soil. The first show in which the Shiba was exhibited was a rare breed show in California, judged by visiting Japanese breeder, Mr Kaiji Katsumoto. The first national speciality of the Shiba

In the UK and around the world, the Japanese Shiba has become a consistent winner at shows, due to the breed's elegant appearance, sparkling personality and natural beauty.

The first American Japanese Shiba Inu to win an all-breed Best in Show was Ch Katuranishiki of Oikawa House, owned by Richard Tomita, one of the first Americans to import the breed into the US. Quite unintentionally, Mr Tomita called this great dog 'Chibi,' which loosely translates to 'runt.'

Club of America (SCA) took place in October 1981, with Mr Keiche Jige as judge. The SCA followed the Nippo standard and encouraged others to do so. As is the case with most new breeds, dissension and disagreement reigned supreme and a new club on the East Coast was founded, the National Shiba Club of America (NSCA). The new club's goal was to seek the acceptance of the American Kennel Club (AKC), a goal that the SCA did not embrace. The NSCA was attempting to follow in the steps of the Akita Club of America, which as history would tell us would be a foolhardy path at best! (Consider the problems of the current Japanese versus American Akita situation, where the American Akita is now called the Great Japanese Dog at FCI shows!). Nevertheless, by 1991, the AKC accepted the Shiba into its Miscellaneous Class, and into the Non-Sporting Group by June 1993.

The first Shibas to be imported to the US belong to

Kaiji and Toshiko Katsumoto of the Kenwaso kennel. Later Julia Cadwell became involved with the breed and imported some dogs. Merry and Frank Atkinson, Akita people, imported Shibas with the help of Mr Katsumoto. Other breeders include Frank and Alice Sakayeda, Joan Harper Young, also an Akita person, Janice Cowen, Kathleen Brown-Truax and Bruce Truax, Jane Chalfant, Dorothy Warren, Gretchen Haskett and Evelyn Behren.

In the mid-1980s, world-respected Boxer breeder, Richard Tomita, of Jacquet Boxers, imported 15 Shibas from Japan, with the help of Dr Nakazawa, a vet and show judge. Five of these excellent

dogs were from the Oikawa House kennel, including the famous Ch Katsuranishiki of Oikawa House, known to all on the East coast as 'Chibi.' Chibi was a top sire and Best in Show-winning dog, not the least of his progeny being the author's beloved house dog, Jacquet's Tengu, whom Tomita has called an improvement on his father. Progeny of Chibi have the prized feature of improving with age, and Tengu at ten years of age is still in his physical prime. Mr Tomita's Shiba programme was continued by handler Don Robinder and his sister Christine Tomita-Eicher.

Famous American sire, Ryutaro of Yamazakisow Kensha, owned by Richard Tomita, was a multi-Best of Breed winner and sire to many great Shibas in the early 1990s. One of Ryutaro's daughters is the author's lovely bitch, Maikohime of Akatani ('Kabuki').

Am Ch Katuranishiki of Oikawa House, or 'Chibi' for short, is a top American sire who passed on his exquisite head, type and movement to many great dogs. Chibi is the sire of the author's dog, Jacquet's Tengu, bred by Richard Tomita.

SHIBAS IN THE UK

Hailing from the US, not Japan, the first Shibas were sent by Ed and Terry Arndt of Jade-Shogun kennels, Arizona, to the UK in 1985. These three Shibas arrived at Kiskas Akita kennels, owned by Gerald and Kath Mitchell. Among the three dogs was Shogun Hisui Megami, the foundation bitch for Brian and Kath Hindley's Yorlands kennel, an established Rottweiler kennel. The other two Shibas were Shogun Hisui Yukita-mahime (Dixie) and Shogun Hisue Yukihikari (Yen), who would produce the second litter on British soil in October 1986. The three original imported Shibas began their campaign in Britain upon being released from quarantine, starting with a promotional programme for Crufts in February 1986. The Hindleys later imported Ogan No Takame Ogon Taiyo So of Kiskas, who was carrying a litter sired by Beni Washi-go. She whelped two pups in quarantine.

The honour of 'first litter produced in England' goes to Shogun Hisui Tukihikari Kiskas and Shogun Hisui Megami of Yorlands, who produced two pups on 7 September 1986. The breeder was Kath Hindley. Maureen Atchinson acquired one of Dixie and Yen's pups for her Madason kennel and later imported the first Japanese-born male into the UK, again from the Arndts in the US. He was called Taka for short (his formal name was Tamawakamaru of Madason) and was bred by Mr Yaichiro Watatsu of Japan.

Only red Shibas had been imported into England thus far, but that was rectified by a few imports. The first red sesame dog to be imported into the UK was a bitch named Camboalijo Ujahjme, called Suki. She was owned by John and Dana Ogilvie. The first black and tan was Minimeadows Summer Dream, imported by Joe and Betty Neath. Although these dogs and others were imported, the reds continue to predomi-nate on the British Shiba scene.

Once the Shiba was accepted into the Utility Group, it began turning heads of fanciers and judges alike. The first Shiba to win a Group and Best in Show was Wellshim Blackjack Is Vormund, who did so in 1991. The first Junior Warrant winner was Tony Walker's Farmbrook Hot Gossip, bred by Chris Thomas, also in 1991. The first Shibas partici-pated in classes at Crufts in 1992, judged by Mrs Jo Gibbs. Best of Breed and Best Dog on this momentous occasion was Wellshim Black Jack of Vormund, owned by Liz Dunhill; the Best Bitch award went to Madason Toya, daughter of Japanese-born Taka, owned by Maureen Atchinson.

Author Andrew DePrisco, a prolific writer and editor of dog books, with his ever-smiling, ever-loving bitch Kabuki.

Challenge Certificates were not on offer until 1996, when the first champions were made up. The first Shiba champion was the male Kerrilands Total Majic, bred by Bill and Jenny Cowland, and the first bitch champion was Vormund I'm Smartie, bred by Liz Dunhill.

At the Japanese Shiba Inu Club of Great Britain, this Shiba was judged Best Puppy in Show.

Established in 1987, the Japanese Shiba Inu Club of Great Britain has been

With the support of many experienced British breeders, the Japanese Shiba has done well in the show rings in the UK.

promoting the Shiba steadily since its inception. Its fortune has been the devoted interest of experienced dog breeders and judges, who have led the way for the Shiba in Britain. Thanks to these breeders and their years of experience in various breeds, the Shiba has taken successful steps toward a healthy and enthusiastic following in the UK. Each year, Shiba registrations increase with The Kennel Club and the quality of dogs bred and imported continues to rise.

WORLD DOMINATION

The Shiba has begun its campaign of 'world domination' and fanciers around the globe unite in their admiration for this Nipponese treasure chest! Down Under, breeder, judge and author Arthur Lane was cast under the Shiba's spell in the mid-1970s and since has founded a successful Shiba kennel in Australia. Many Shibas have been imported from Japan and the UK to establish bloodlines in Australia.

The first Shibas on Continental Europe entered Sweden in 1972. Credit is given to the Manloten kennels of Mr and Mrs Carolsson. European neighbours soon followed, and imports from England, Japan and America went to Holland, Denmark, France, Italy and Norway. At most FCI shows on the Continent, a strong Shiba entry is present to represent the breed.

This class of Japanese Shibas is competing at the famous Crufts Dog Show.

Dancing on her twos, Kabuki is quite an entertaining Shiba. The Japanese Shiba's balance and agility, like the breed's spirit and good nature, are impressive.

Characteristics of the
JAPANESE SHIBA

The essence of the Japanese Shiba is quite ineffable... like translating and paraphrasing an ancient haiku into English... or describing the knowing glint in your Shiba's deep brown eyes. In the Japanese Shiba, there is a purity, a nobility, an essence that is remarkably perfect, remarkably Japanese. Like a tiny sculpture or painting rendered by a skilled Asian craftsman, like an impeccably pruned bonsai tree cultivated by a Japanese gardener, so too is the miniature Japanese wonder we call Shiba-Inu.

That the Shiba is a pure-bred dog of ancient lineage cannot be challenged. When an uninformed onlooker first eyes the Shiba, it is clear to even him that this is a special and wondrous canine. As the standard begins, the Shiba is 'small' and 'well balanced.' Balance and harmony, in all great art as in Japanese dogs, are absolute essentials, and the Shiba must be properly proportioned, in head and in expression, in body and in spirit.

The Japanese describe the Shiba's essence with some very interesting words that are difficult to translate, particularly for the Westerner who does not know the Shiba. *Kan-i* means 'spirited boldness,' a phrase that has been incorporated in the American standard to describe the temperament of the Shiba—'brave, bold, alert, calm and controlled'. The Japanese word *ryosei* translates as 'good-natured,' also words used in the American standard, as the Shiba is first and foremost a companion dog. *Soboku* refers to the Shiba's gentleness and modesty, both qualities that underlie the breed's natural sense of dignity.

The breed standard, which is a written description of the ideal representative of the breed, is eye-opening indeed regarding the character of the Shiba. The American standard suits the author's needs more so than the English standard, which defines characteristics as 'bright, active, keen and alert, also docile and faithful.' (Unfortunately The Kennel Club standard could be describing any breed of dog, mongrel, or perhaps even a cat or rabbit.) The AKC standard defines the Shiba's temperament: 'A spirited boldness, a good nature, and an unaffected forthrightness, which together yield dignity and natural beauty. The Shiba has an independent nature and can be reserved toward strangers but is loyal and affectionate to those who earn his respect. At times aggressive toward other dogs, the Shiba is always under the control of his handler.'

'Unaffected forthrightness' strikes a resonant chord with the Shiba owner. The breed's nobility and dignity are as natural as his primitive dog behaviour. There is nothing affected or superficial about the Shiba's character. The breed is natural both in spirit and in physique. Nothing is exaggerated about the Shiba's canine structure, which is comparable to that of the wolf or fox—natural—or perhaps a feral dog like the Australian dingo, an animal that appears Shiba-like in some respects but lacks the refinement and subtle balance of the Japanese dog.

ARE YOU A SHIBA PERSON?

Having lived with Shibas for over ten years, this author feels as qualified as any to recommend the Japanese Shiba to the right owner. You could not find a more delightful, life-loving, appealing dog anywhere in the world. Shibas, by and large, are healthy and long-lived and relatively undemanding of their owners. Their size is perfect: not so small that they can be misplaced and sat upon, as could a toy breed, and not so large that an owner can't

The author wholeheartedly recommends the Shiba to the right person. These are delightful, energetic and intelligent dogs that demand commitment and patience from their owners...on an hourly basis!

whisk them into his arms and be on his way. Temperamentally, Shibas are trustworthy and loyal, alert, charismatic and intelligent. Shibas are clean, resourceful and great fun for children.

However, no breed of dog is for everyone, and the Shiba is no exception. The Shiba is an independent dog that has a mind that rivals that of the smartest owner. Training a Shiba is a test of wills, and Shibas despise repetition. These are intense and serious dogs that can find a way to solve any problem. Yet, in true Japanese style, Shibas are as stubborn as they are independent and smart. Shibas can concentrate on a problem for hours and then work a way out of the dilemma. (Can Shibas think?—don't let them hear

you say that!) A Shiba's training (teaching session, please!) must begin as early as six to eight weeks. For other breeds, this may be too young, but the Shiba will start to work things out before you do and then convince you that you are doing them wrong. Case in point, lead training! Don't wait or you will have a life-long struggle at the other end of the lead.

THE CAT'S MEOW
The quality that originally attracted me to the Shiba was their 'cat-like behaviour.' Like felines, Shibas are very clean and will spend hours grooming themselves. (Shibas know that they are beauties, just as cats do.) If you live in a flat on the tenth floor, you can even train your Shiba to use a

Shibas welcome the company of well-behaved children who don't mind a little affection. Here Alyse Badal receives a wet hello from Kabuki.

DOGS, DOGS, GOOD FOR YOUR HEART!
People usually purchase dogs for companionship, but studies show that dogs can help to improve their owners' health and level of activity, as well as lower a human's risk of coronary heart disease. Without even realising it, when a person puts time into exercising, grooming and feeding a dog, he also puts more time into his own personal health care. Dog owners establish a more routine schedule for their dogs to follow, which can have positive effects on a human's health. Dogs also teach us patience, offer unconditional love and provide the joy of having a furry friend to pet!

DO YOU WANT TO LIVE LONGER?

If you like to volunteer, it is wonderful if you can take your dog to a nursing home once a week for several hours. The elder community loves to have a dog to visit with and often your dog will bring a bit of companionship to someone who is lonely or somewhat detached from the world. You will be not only bringing happiness to someone else but keeping your little dog busy—and we haven't even mentioned the fact that it has been discovered that volunteering helps to increase your own longevity!

litter box, though it's not wholeheartedly recommended. Shibas use their paws in cleaning themselves and in playing the same way cats do. My female Kabuki even climbs into windowsills to watch over the garden. Their intensity and concentration are as feline as a metaphysical poem. Shibas are also catlike in their love of chasing small animals, such as mice or birds. They are reckless is their pursuit of a furry or feathered foe. I have seen my Kabuki leap into the air after a bird on the wing. Also like cats, Shibas are indecipherably smart and therefore are difficult to train.

One last word about cats. Shibas don't particularly like cats, perhaps because they are too much like themselves. With proper introductions and close supervision, an owner can trust a Shiba and a cat. The author's two Shibas live with three Bengal cats....quite willingly. Kabuki rather likes them and will groom them (when the cats permit), though my male, Tengu, defiantly acts as the 'Bengal Warden' and will attempt to bully them (especially when they're sleeping!). Tengu is a typical Shiba male, brimming with self-importance.

OPERATION HOUDINI

Shiba owners are forewarned! Keeping Shibas is more difficult than just keeping Shibas! No

Kabuki and one of her Bengal cats, Jazzman, have a very open relationship. Kabuki met Jazzman as a kitten when she was five years old and accepted him as part of the family. Socialisation and confident instruction are key in introducing a new pet into one's household.

matter how perfect a home you provide for your Shiba, it is the Shiba's nature to treat a human abode as a prison and his only goal in life is to escape! Freedom is the sweetest reward and every Shiba is devoted to tasting it. It seems as if the 'call of the wild' or the allure of the Japanese Mainland is so strong in the Shiba that they must run free. Combined with the Shiba's intelligence, craftiness, small size, agility and intensity, this need to escape is a concern for all owners.

I have witnessed adult Shibas in crates at dog shows unhook the locks on their crates just to have a look-see about the show grounds. My own Shibas have found ways to open the front gates to the garden so that they can roam the neighbourhood. A fence is no security against the Shiba obsessed with escaping. Shibas are remarkable diggers, able to burrow under a fence with their catlike feet and claws and strong forequarters. While they are small, they are still agile enough to climb a fence, using the paws and teeth to effect the escape!

'SELECTIVE HEARING'

Shibas have keen senses, as they were bred to hunt by sight and smell. Although the Shiba has perfectly normal ears, they don't work as well as an owner might expect. This phenomenon is known as 'selective hearing disorder.' Shibas choose not to hear their owners when they use certain commands, especially 'come' or 'no.' (Mysteriously, they can always hear words like 'eat,' 'walk,' and 'playtime.') For a dog that lives to run away, this selective hearing is a real problem for Shiba owners.

By the grace of God and pure luck, the author has been able to keep both his Shibas for over ten years. One trick that the author has relied on is related to the Shiba's sensitivity to scolding and correction. Shibas are independent but do not like to fail or disappoint. When my Kabuki starts to bolt, I immediately hurl reprimands her way (the neighbours love this!). 'Bad dog!' 'Bad girl!' (be creative here). Fortunately, she is so overwhelmed by my disappointment and scolding that she stops dead in her tracks and rolls over! She waits for me to pick her up and carry her home. In true Shiba fashion, her ears are folded back and she shows just enough of her gums to paint a pathetic portrait.

THE MIGHTY HUNTER

Every book written on the Shiba claims that this is a superb hunting dog, blessed with astute instincts and skill. If the new owner is selecting a Shiba for hunting, he might wish to rethink his strategy. Choosing a Shiba to hunt is akin to choosing an Italian Greyhound to race! We have all read romantic stories of Shibas carrying home 50 quails or 8 dozen hares, but such dogs are rare indeed.

Historically in Japan, the Shiba has been employed by hunters for pheasants and ducks as well as small wild animals, such as rabbits, badgers and weasels. The Shiba trained to hunt pheasants does not, in fact, retrieve or flush the bird, as would a gundog, but trees the bird, as would a coon dog in pursuit of a raccoon. The hunter is then able to locate the bird from the Shiba's barking and then shoot the pheasant. Japanese hunters have trained Shibas as decoys for duck hunting as well. The Shibas lure the ducks to the shore, intrigued by the Shiba's wagging tail and barking enthusiasm. Shibas are traditionally used for either bird hunting or small-mammal hunting, rarely both. Once the Shiba has a taste for catching a rabbit, it will always be distracted by any twitching in the grass and thereby forget about luring or treeing the birds.

Although Shibas may not get much 'on the field' experience today, their chase instincts are surely intact. Most Shibas will pursue and catch small mammals with little to no effort, particularly rodents and rabbits. The Shiba's nose is extremely sensitive and able to detect a burrowing rodent with the precision of a terrier. Swift and animated, the Shiba can outrun a rabbit and kill it with

TAKING CARE
Science is showing that as people take care of their pets, the pets are taking care of their owners. A study in 1998, published in the *American Journal of Cardiology,* found that having a pet can prolong his owner's life. Pet owners have lower blood pressure, and pets help their owners to relax and keep them more physically fit. It was also found that pets help to keep the elderly connected to their community.

grace and dexterity. While most Shiba owners don't relish such gifts of their dogs, it is not uncommon for the Shiba to deliver a rat or a rabbit to his owner's feet—and always with that unmistakable Shiba smile!

KABUKI THEATRICS

Japan has two original theatrical forms, the Kabuki theatre and the Nōh theatre. The former is known for its highly ritualistic movement and exaggerated vocal style and the latter is known for its more subtle classical pageantry. Without a doubt, the Shiba subscribes to the Kabuki approach to life (and doesn't even recognise the word 'no'). The author's bitch was thus named Kabuki because of her broad theatrical mannerisms. Like a true Shiba, she dances on her hindfeet to express her delight; she screams, screeches and squeaks to vocalise her dismay and her discontent; she jumps, leaps, twists and rolls to convey her various moods and desires. There is nothing subtle about Kabuki.

Shibas are very expressive with their voices and are capable of making many unusual canine sounds, including monkey-like squealing, parrot-like honking and earth-shattering screams. Despite this impressive vocabulary, Shibas are not necessarily vocal dogs and use their barks most discreetly. For some Shibas, barking is a last resort (when the more interesting squeaking and squawking fail to get the desired response). Shibas will bark when a stranger approaches the front door, though they will not bark for the sake of barking and have no interest in repeating such a mundane utterance.

MALE VS FEMALE

There are positive and negative aspects of both sexes when selecting a Shiba. The female is naturally maternal, making a loving and demonstrative companion for both adults and children. Females are easier to toilet train, though lead training is not necessarily any easier. Males tend to be more stubborn, especially where matters of the bladder are concerned. Both male and female Shibas are territorial, though females tend to be more aggressive than males. Bitches are more likely to engage in a fight than are males, which is not necessarily so with most breeds. Two bitches will fight as sure as the Japanese sun will rise! Females tend to be more straightforward with their emotions while males seem more reserved, though once the love of a male Shiba is earned, it is steadfast and true. Females tend to be more flighty and fun-loving. Males may be more adventure-seeking than females, a result of their need to spray the whole neighbourhood every day. In general, females are more outgoing and friendly, while males are more reserved with people they don't know.

HEALTH CONCERNS FOR SHIBA OWNERS

Compared to many other pure-bred dogs, Shibas are graced with good health and relative freedom from hereditary problems. The most common problem in Shibas is slipped kneecaps, more properly called luxated patellas. This condition can either be hereditary or caused by an accident. As a result of the kneecap slipping out of position, it is weaker from the distress.

More stressful for Shibas are hot spots, which are a form of moist dermatitis that occurs on the Shiba's rear quarters, usually on the back under the tail or on the tail itself. Other locations include the thighs, ears or around the mouth. The dog will bite and scratch the spot until it is raw and irritated. Seek veterinary assistance, as an injection of antihistamine and clipping the affected area will provide relief.

Monorchids and cryptorchids are a concern in every breed, and the Shiba is no exception. These conditions, marked by one or both testicles not descending properly in the scrotum, are cause for disqualification in the show ring and are hereditary. Such animals should be excluded from breeding programmes. Male Shibas mature

slowly and may require up to ten months for both testicles to descend.

Ear problems are also common in Shibas, usually caused by mites. Suffering dogs will shake their heads and scratch at their ears. Proper cleaning of the ears and drops prescribed by your vet will alleviate the problem. Shibas hate to have their ears fussed with, so check the ears regularly to be certain that no residue or odour is detectable.

Eye concerns include progressive retinal atrophy, an hereditary condition that can lead to blindness in many breeds, as well as entropion and trichiasis, both of which are disorders of the eyelashes. Breeders should screen for these eye problems in their dogs to keep the Shiba free of such debilitating problems. Likewise, breeders are screening their Shibas for hip dysplasia, which has been a horrible problem in larger breeds, rendering the dogs crippled and unworthy of breeding and showing.

An informed new owner will recognise a well-bred, healthy litter of Shiba puppies. Discuss breed health with your chosen breeder.

Breed Standard for the
JAPANESE SHIBA

A breed standard is a written description of the ideal representative of a breed. This description is used by judges, breeders and exhibitors to guide them in their selection, breeding and promotion of the best dogs. At dog shows, the judges compare each dog entered to the dog described in the breed standard. The Shiba that most closely 'conforms' to the standard is selected as the winner. For this reason, dog shows are sometimes called 'conformation competitions.' Breed standards are draughted by a kennel organisation, either a governing registrar (like The Kennel Club) or a parent club (like the National Shiba Club of America or Nippo).

In discussing the Shiba standard, there are four standards of importance: 1. The original Japanese standard (Nippo); 2. The Kennel Club standard (the current English standard); 3. The FCI standard (used throughout Europe and beyond); 4. The American Kennel Club standard. In essence, all four standards describe the same dog, though they vary in wording, content and completeness. First we present The Kennel Club standard and then we will discuss differences between it and the others.

THE KENNEL CLUB STANDARD FOR THE JAPANESE SHIBA INU

General Appearance: Small, well balanced, sturdy dog of Spitz type. Very slightly longer than height at the withers.

Characteristics: Bright, active, keen and alert, also docile and faithful.

Temperament: Bright, active, keen and alert.

Head and Skull: Head appears as a blunt triangle when viewed from above. Broad flat skull, cheeks well developed. Definite stop with slight furrow. Muzzle straight of good depth, tapering gradually. Lips tight. Black nose preferred but flesh coloured accepted in white dogs.

Eyes: Relatively small, almond, obliquely set well apart and dark brown.

Ears: Small triangular, pricked and inclining slightly forward.

Mouth: Jaws strong with a perfect regular and complete scissor bite, i.e. upper teeth closely overlapping lower teeth and set square to the jaws.

Neck: Slightly arched. Medium length, thick and muscular.

Forequarters: Shoulders moderately sloping. Elbows set close to the body. Forechest well developed. Forearms straight. Pasterns slightly sloping.

Body: Withers high and well developed. Short loin, level back. Deep chest. Moderate spring of rib. Belly moderately tucked up.

Hindquarters: Long upper thigh, short strong second thigh. Hocks

strong and parallel when seen from the rear. Turning neither in nor out. Well developed. Slight but definite bend to stifle.

Feet: Cat-like, with firm, well-knuckled toes. Pads firm and elastic. Dark nails preferred.

Tail: Set on high. Thick and carried curled or curved as in a sickle.

Gait/Movement: Light, quick and energetic.

Coat: Hard, straight outer coat with soft, dense undercoat. Hair on tail slightly longer.

Colour:
Red: Intense, clear red.
Red sesame: Red with an even overlay of black guard hairs, black to be not less than 25 per cent or more than 60 per cent of normal red area.
White markings in Red and Red sesame restricted to eye spots, cheeks, underjaw, forechest,

The Shiba should be a small, well balanced, sturdy dog with a keen and alert temperament.

The correct Shiba head has a black nose, tight lips and a straight muzzle of good depth. The bitch has a decidedly feminine appeal.

underparts and underside of tail and legs. No white above elbows or hock. The white markings on the chest resembling the shape of a bow-tie. Eye spots in red sesame may be tan.

Black and tan: Dull black with a bronze cast. Tan markings restricted to eye spots, cheeks, inside of ears, legs and tail. White markings as in Red and Red sesame. Tan markings only occur between black and white areas.

White: White coat with red or grey tinges. White undercoat.

Size: Height: Dogs 39.5 cms (15.5. ins). Bitches 36.5 cms (14.5 ins) with allowance of 1.5 cms (.75 ins) either way.

Faults: Any departure from the foregoing points should be considered a fault and the seriousness with which the fault should be regarded should be in exact proportion to its degree.

White markings in red dogs are restricted to eye spots, cheeks, underjaw, forechest, underparts, and underside of tail and legs.

Note: Male animals should have two apparently normal testicles fully descended into the scrotum.

DISCUSSION AND COMPARISON OF THE BREED STANDARDS

The AKC standard describes the general appearance of the Shiba similarly but adds the following: 'His frame is compact with well-developed muscles. Males and females are distinctly different in appearance: males are masculine without coarseness, females are feminine without weakness of structure.' The original Nippo standard supports this notion, recognising that refined species should show apparent differences in the sexes: 'Males and females are obviously distinct, with

proportioned bodies.' Males are more vigorous, stocky and muscular, always moving with confidence. The male's head is wide and flat, slightly longer than the female's head, which is finer and slightly narrower.

The FCI standard adds: 'Constitution strong. Action quick, free and beautiful' as well as a section on 'Utilisation' that reads 'Hunting dog for birds and small animals. Companion dog.'

While the English standard is rather bland in its description of the Shiba's temperament, the American standard commits to a more concise portrait: 'A spirited boldness, a good nature and an unaffected forthrightness, which together yield dignity and natural beauty. The Shiba has an independent nature and can be reserved towards strangers but is loyal and affectionate to those who can earn his respect. At times aggressive

THE IDEAL SPECIMEN
According to The Kennel Club, 'The Breed Standard is the "Blueprint" of the ideal specimen in each breed approved by a governing body, e.g. The Kennel Club, the Fédération Cynologique International (FCI) and the American Kennel Club.

'The Kennel Club writes and revises Breed Standards taking account of the advice of Breed Councils/Clubs. Breed Standards are not changed lightly to avoid "changing the standard to fit the current dogs" and the health and well-being of future dogs is always taken into account when new standards are prepared or existing ones altered.'

towards other dogs, the Shiba is always under control of his handler.' Similarly, the Nippo standard states: 'The dog has a spirited boldness with a good nature and a feeling of artlessness. It is alert and able to move quickly with nimble, elastic steps.'

The Shiba is considered to be a 'head breed,' meaning that the correct head is crucial to correct type. In profile, the forehead appears flat and broad, 'wide,' according to the Nippo standard. The cheeks are very full and 'well developed.' The stop is moderate in profile, with a hardly visible furrow. The Shiba's muzzle is firm, thick, full and round, projecting from the full cheeks.

The shape and colour of the eyes also contribute to the correct Shiba expression. The AKC describes them thus: 'Eyes are somewhat triangular in shape, deep set, and upward slanting toward the outside base of the ear. Iris is dark brown. Eye rims are black.' The Shiba's eyes are small, though in the female's more refined head, they may appear slightly larger than those of the male. The eyes are the windows to the Shiba's soul, and his gaze conveys intelligence, worldliness and confidence.

The placement, size and shape of the Shiba's ears also affect expression and correct balance. The ears are small and

The judge uses the mental picture conjured by the breed standard when he accesses each Japanese Shiba entered in competition. Dog shows revolve around the judge's interpretation of the written standard.

BREEDING CONSIDERATIONS

The decision to breed your dog is one that must be considered carefully and researched thoroughly before moving into action. Some people believe that breeding will make their bitch happier or that it is an easy way to make money. Unfortunately, indiscriminate breeding only worsens the rampant problem of pet overpopulation, as well as putting a considerable dent in your pocketbook. As for the bitch, the entire process from mating through whelping is not an easy one and puts your pet under considerable stress. Last, but not least, consider whether or not you have the means to care for an entire litter of pups. Without a reputation in the field, your attempts to sell the pups may be unsuccessful.

have two equal sides (isosceles), each side extending slightly down the side of the Shiba's head.

Teeth have always been a 'sore point' in the Shiba standard, as the breed is notorious for missing teeth. The Nippo standard indicates that 'A Shiba with more than four minus marks will not be ranked.' The standard sets up deductions for each missing teeth: First premolars equal one minus mark; second premolars equal three minus marks; any other missing tooth equals five minus marks. Judges and breeders must concentrate on awarding Shibas with full dentitions—42 teeth, to be exact. By and large, the Shiba mouth is strong and sturdy with sizeable teeth, unlike many Toy breeds that suffer similar problems. Ignoring the need for a full dentition can only do harm to the breed.

well furred, creating a desirable hooded effect. The AKC standard has this to say in terms of position: 'Ears are set well apart and tilt directly forward with the slant of the back of the ear following the arch of the neck.' The Nippo standard indicates some common Shiba ear faults that are believed to be inherent in certain lines and to be avoided: 'Thin ear leather, ears that are narrow at the bottom, high ear-set, long ears, flapping of the ear tip, incorrect ear lines, and lack of forward slant are all strongly hereditary and are faults.' The desired triangular shape should

The shape, size and colour of the eyes contribute to the Shiba's expression, which, to some, is Oriental and feline.

The neck is well developed and in males appears more well-muscled than the female's refined neck. The neck is crucial to the harmony of the Shiba's outline. The body, according to the AKC standard, 'is dry and well muscled without the appearance of sluggishness or coarseness.' The Shiba's chest is well developed and powerful; it appears to be the centre of the body, contrasting with the well-tucked belly. Both the AKC and Nippo standards add that the Shiba's topline is straight. Angulation is key to the overall balance of the dog, and the AKC standard states: 'Forequarters: Shoulder blade and upper arm are moderately angulated and approximately equal in length' and 'Hindquarters: The angulation of the hindquarters is moderate and in balance with the angulation of the forequarters.' Breeders consider a 30-degree layback of the shoulders ideal for the Shiba when moving. The rear legs must be strong and flexible, the driving force for Shiba locomotion. Over-angulated stifles are a detriment to proper Shiba gait, as is too wide or narrow a stance.

The Shiba's coat is typical of the spitz dogs, a hard outer coat and a soft undercoat. Depending on the dog's heritage, the Shiba coat can appear full with a generous undercoat and straight guard hairs or thick and dense, appearing somewhat flatter. The former style coat can be compared to 'fur' or a 'pelt' while the latter style has a more resilient uniform quality. Note also that the Shiba's coat is not a long coat, but rather medium in length. Just as in Akitas, longcoat puppies do occur. These dogs make fine pets, requiring a little extra grooming, though they should not be bred or exhibited.

Colours in Shibas have also been debated in breed circles. Although The Kennel Club standard still permits four colours to be exhibited, the Japanese and American standards only permit three colours. The AKC standard states that 'Cream, white, pinto or any other colour or marking not specified is a very serious fault and must be penalized.' The English standard permits white dogs even though the Nippo standard states that white coat colour is not desirable. In Japanese dogs, white can be seen on breeds other than the Shiba, including the Kishu (which is usually white) as well as the Akita. In respect to the Japanese homeland of the Shiba, the white coloration should not be promoted in the UK or elsewhere. The interim Kennel Club standard referred also to brindles and greys being acceptable in Shibas—these fortunately do not exist, so the issue passed without debate.

The red Shiba has become the most popular colour and far outnumbers the red sesames and black and tans.

A lovely red Shiba's head, showing exquisite expression, a well-padded muzzle, small, well-furred ears and white marks over the eyes, on the cheeks and on the neck and chest.

The AKC, FCI and Nippo use a term in their standards to describe the cream to white ventral colours—*Urajiro*. These markings are required on all coat colours as follows: 'on the sides of the muzzle, on the cheeks, inside the ears, on the underjaw and upper throat, inside of legs, on the abdomen, around the vent and the ventral side of the tail. On reds: commonly on the throat, forechest and chest. On blacks and sesames: commonly as a triangular mark on both sides of the forechest. White spots above the eyes permitted on all colors but not required.' (AKC)

Gait in the Shiba is tantamount to the dog's whole being. AKC states that 'Movement is nimble, light and elastic. At the trot, the legs angle in towards a center line while the topline remains level and firm. Forward reach and rear extension are moderate and efficient.'

The Shiba tail, last but not least, is a hallmark of the breed, held in curl or curved in a sickle. It should be thickly furred and (when straightened out) reach nearly to the hock joint. Like the head, the correct tail balances the overall Shiba picture. The tail is strong and expressive, essential for the breed's quick movement and balance. The hair on the tail is longer than anywhere else on the body.

The FCI standard includes the following faults: shyness, bitchy dogs, doggy bitches,

The standard requires that the forechest is well developed and the forearms straight.

malocclusion (overshot or undershot mouth), and numerous missing teeth. FCI disqualifications include: ears not pricked and hanging or short tail. The AKC standard disqualifies overshot or undershot bites as well as males over 16.5 ins and under 14.5 ins and females over 15.5 ins and under 13.5 ins. The Nippo standard faults developmental defects and nutritional deficiency, disharmony between the colour of the body and the colour of the nose, white spots in coloured areas of the coat and short tail caused by genetic defect. Nippo disqualifies any dog lacking the quality of a Japanese dog and any dog with an overshot or undershot bite.

THE INTERROGATION

So you perceive yourself as Shiba material? You feel worthy of owning one of the Shiba breed...how well do you satisfy the Shiba's expectations? Please consider the following:

1. How much time do you have to devote to a Shiba each day? Do you work all day? Is your evening schedule bustling with social activities?

2. What kind of home can you provide for your Shiba? Although Shibas do quite well in cities, flats that are too small may be too confining for the Shiba.

3. Do you have a garden in which the Shiba can run and play? Is the garden securely fenced?

4. Do all members of the family welcome the arrival of this energetic ball of spitz fur?

5. Do you have allergies? Shibas cast their coat twice a year and may aggravate an existing allergy.

6. Are you a cleaning fanatic? Shibas are tidy but they do cover their surroundings with fur at least twice a year. Bitches in season may blow coat an additional time as well.

7. Are you fit and lively?

Keeping up with a Shiba on the other end of a lead requires considerable physical fitness. Chasing a Shiba requires even more! Shibas are always on the go—ready to explore and ready to run. Are you physically up to the Shiba challenge?

8. Do you have the time and patience required by the grooming and training of a Shiba puppy? Shibas learn very fast—when they want to. They can be very stubborn. Grooming chores are not too time-consuming, though a weekly session is advisable. Baths

INSURANCE

Many good breeders will offer you insurance with your new puppy, which is an excellent idea. The first few weeks of insurance will probably be covered free of charge or with only minimal cost, allowing you to take up the policy when this expires. If you own a pet dog, it is sensible to take out such a policy as veterinary fees can be high, although routine vaccinations and boosters are not covered. Look carefully at the many options open to you before deciding which suits you best.

are the real chore, as most Shibas don't welcome time in the bath.

9. Do you have children in the family? While Shibas are reasonably fond of children (depending on their behaviour), they are still quite small dogs and will only tolerate a limited amount of rough play and mishandling.

10. Do you plan frequent holidays? Shibas prefer to be home or with their owners. Boarding a Shiba frequently will

Breeder Richard Tomita with a young Shiba pup ready for a new pet home. Find a breeder who cares for his dogs and is willing to make you a part of his extended 'dog family.'

be stressful to the dog.

11. Are you willing to devote 12 to 16 years to the life of your Shiba? Thankfully, the Shiba is a long-lived little dog that remains active for most of its years.

12. Do you have the financial ability to provide your Shiba with proper veterinary care, food and upkeep for the whole of his life?

If you have passed this test, then you are ready to consider how to go about locating a Shiba puppy. Admittedly it is difficult for the potential owner to contain his excitement about adopting a Shiba pup. Few breeds have the 'puppy appeal' of the Shiba...with their plush cuteness, tiny ears, dark eyes and curvy tail...plus the Shiba puppy swish...racing around the floor or trying to mount steps. The author implores

PREPARING FOR PUP

Unfortunately, when a puppy is bought by someone who does not take into consideration the time and attention that dog ownership requires, it is the puppy who suffers when he is either abandoned or placed in a shelter by a frustrated owner. So all of the 'homework' you do in preparation for your pup's arrival will benefit you both. The more informed you are, the more you will know what to expect and the better equipped you will be to handle the ups and downs of raising a puppy. Hopefully, everyone in the household is willing to do his part in raising and caring for the pup. The anticipation of owning a dog often brings a lot of promises from excited family members: 'I will walk him every day,' 'I will feed him,' 'I will housetrain him,' etc., but these things take time and effort, and promises can easily be forgotten once the novelty of the new pet has worn off.

DOCUMENTATION

Two important documents you will get from the breeder are the pup's pedigree and registration certificate. The breeder should register the litter and each pup with The Kennel Club, and it is necessary for you to have the paperwork if you plan on showing or breeding in the future.

Make sure you know the breeder's intentions on which type of registration he will obtain for the pup. There are limited registrations which may prohibit the dog from being shown, bred or from competing in non-conformation trials such as Working or Agility if the breeder feels that the pup is not of sufficient quality to do so. There is also a type of registration that will permit the dog in non-conformation competition only.

On the reverse side of the registration certificate, the new owner can find the transfer section which must be signed by the breeder.

new owners to do their homework before venturing into ownership. New owners must find the right breeder and the right puppy. Shiba breeders in the UK are a growing clan, though there aren't too many breeders who have as many years' experience as the German Shepherd or Collie breeders whom a new owner might encounter in looking for

those more popular breeds. For the owner who is serious about acquiring a top-quality, potentially showable Shiba, a visit to a dog show and a perusal of the catalogue is time well spent. The dogs in the catalogue are listed by their full Kennel Club names, which usually include a kennel prefix (such as Kerriland, Madason, Sparskip, Kiskas and Merryn). Finding the quality breeders attached to these kennels is an obvious first step. Foundation breeders like Maureen Atchinson, Bill and Jenny Cowland, Lynn Lane and Liz Dunhill have established 'Shiba families,' fanciers who have their bloodlines and expand to create 'sublines.'

Since the Shiba is still a relatively new breed in the UK, it is quite easy to meet 'the right people' in the breed to get started. If you approach owners at a dog show when they are not busy grooming or handling the dog, most Shiba fanciers are willing to talk to you about their favourite topic: Shibas! These folk are ideal for recommending breeders who are expecting a litter and teaching you the ins and outs of the Shiba world. You may also contact The Kennel Club for a list of qualified Shiba breeders in your area.

There is a tremendous difference between buying a puppy and purchasing a car or a bedroom suite. Breeders are not

49

salespeople. They are not looking to 'unload' their litter on any anxious puppy buyer who has the money. You will not get a discount, and in the dog world you get what you pay for! Expect the breeder to ask you many questions about your intentions, experience with dog ownership, time constraints, accommodations, etc. The questions at the beginning of this chapter will be on the breeder's list as well.

Breeders do not feel that you are their customers; they feel that you are adopting one of their children. Since Shibas have relatively small litters (from two to six puppies), selection at a kennel will not be great. Breeders often retain a puppy for show purposes and have a waiting list of potential owners who have passed their interview process. Be wary of the breeder who asks no questions and sells you a pup on the spot without any hesitation. Owners should always enquire of the breeder about health screening, problems in their lines, including behavioural, and ask to meet the sire and dam (and possible other relatives) of the puppy.

Consider how the breeder relates to his dogs. Is he familiar with all of them? Do the dogs crave his attention? Is there obvious admiration in the dogs' eyes when they look at the breeder? These are all subtle signs

that the breeder is a responsible, caring individual who wants to see his progeny go to proper homes where they will stay for their whole lives. Responsible breeders will also take back any puppy that an owner decides is not right for his lifestyle. Dog breeders rarely care about the money, as the dogs and the breed

PUPPY PERSONALITY
When a litter becomes available to you, choosing a pup out of all those adorable faces will not be an easy task! Sound temperament is of utmost importance, but each pup has its own personality and some may be better suited to you than others. A feisty, independent pup will do well in a home with older children and adults, while quiet, shy puppies will thrive in a home with minimum noise and distractions. Your breeder knows the pups best and should be able to guide you in the right direction.

PUPPY SELECTION
Your selection of a good puppy
can be determined by your needs.
A show potential or a good pet?
It is your choice. Every puppy,
however, should be of good
temperament. Although show-
quality puppies are bred and
raised with emphasis on physical
conformation, responsible
breeders strive for equally good
temperament. Do not buy from a
breeder who concentrates solely
on physical beauty at the
expense of personality.

SELECTING A SHIBA PUPPY

Shiba puppies are irresistible, no
matter what kind of dog you
prefer. Shibas look like tiny fox
pups with their jet black noses
and deep brown eyes. If you view
the litter at about three or four
weeks of age, the colours of the
puppies will be quite similar
(except the blacks and whites).
Red and red sesame puppies will
show a good deal of black hair,
which lightens in reds as the
undercoat grows in. All Shibas
have black masks that fade as the
puppy develops. The tiny ears
take a few weeks to become erect
and will be well furred by the
fifth or sixth week. The pigment
on the pup's nose, eye lids, paw
pads and lips should be jet black
(except in whites). Even as a
puppy, the Shiba has a blunt
triangular head shape and a well-
padded muzzle. White markings
(Urajiro) begin to emerge between
the fifth and sixth week on the
Shiba's face, underparts and chest.
Be sure that the Shiba puppy's
bite is neither undershot or
overshot. It's not prudent to count
teeth on a six-week-old puppy,
but you may ask the breeder to
show you the parents' bites if you
are serious about showing your
puppy.

The six-week-old puppy
should radiate its Shiba spirit.
These tiny puppies know that
they are a 'chosen race' and glow
with confidence and that

come first. By the same token, this
doesn't mean that you should not
pay top price for your puppy. The
breeder's programme is very
costly and it's necessary that
owners pay full price for every
puppy in the litter in order for the
kennel to remain operational.

celebrated sense of self-importance that Shiba fanciers adore. The litter should be energetic and happy-go-lucky, ready to overwhelm visitors with their antics. All Shiba puppies do not act the same. There may be a more reserved puppy in the litter, less inclined to greet visitors but nonetheless interested in his surroundings. Do not mistake this pup for a shy or 'spooky' puppy. This pup is a typical Shiba intellect, reserved in the usual 'Oriental' fashion. Shiba puppies by and large should look like miniature versions of adults and do not change too dramatically as they grow. As the breed is such a natural canine, its development is quite predictable.

Rely on your breeder to recommend which Shiba puppy is suited to your lifestyle. Shibas have unique personalities that emerge early on and the breeder will know which pup will be the clown, the intellect, the wanderer, the lover, etc. No matter what the personality of the Shiba puppy, all pups can make a smiling, loving addition to the right home. Shibas promise to perk up any household, and owners must be ready for that daily jolt of Shiba fun (like a double espresso at early dawn!).

COMMITMENT OF OWNERSHIP
After considering all of these factors, you have most likely already made some very important decisions about selecting your puppy. You have chosen a Shiba, which means that you have decided which characteristics you want in a dog and what type of dog will best fit into your family and lifestyle. If you have selected a breeder, you have gone a step further—you have done your research and found a responsible, conscientious person who breeds quality Shibas and who should be a reliable source of

DID YOU KNOW?
You should not even think about buying a puppy that looks sick, undernourished, overly frightened or nervous. Sometimes a timid puppy will warm up to you after a 30-minute 'let's-get-acquainted' session.

help as you and your puppy adjust to life together. If you have observed a litter in action, you have obtained a firsthand look at the dynamics of a puppy 'pack' and, thus, you should learn about each pup's individual personality—perhaps you have even found one that particularly appeals to you.

Researching your breed, selecting a responsible breeder and observing as many pups as possible are all important steps on the way to dog ownership. It may seem like a lot of effort...and you have not even taken the pup home yet! Remember, though, you cannot be too careful when it comes to deciding on the type of dog you want and finding out about your prospective pup's background. Buying a puppy is not—or should not be—just another whimsical purchase. This is one instance in which you actually do get to choose your own family! You may be thinking that buying a puppy should be fun—it should not be so serious and so much work. Keep in mind that your puppy is not a cuddly stuffed toy or decorative lawn ornament, but a creature that will become a real member of your family. You will come to realise that, while buying a puppy is a pleasurable and exciting endeavour, it is not something to be taken lightly. Relax...the fun will start when the pup comes home!

Always keep in mind that a puppy is nothing more than a baby in a furry disguise...a baby who is virtually helpless in a human world and who trusts his owner for fulfilment of his basic needs for survival. In addition to water and shelter, your pup needs care, protection, guidance and love. If you are not prepared to commit to this, then you are not prepared to own a dog.

Wait a minute, you say. How hard could this be? All of my

DO YOUR HOMEWORK!
In order to know whether or not a puppy will fit into your lifestyle, you need to assess his personality. A good way to do this is to interact with his parents. Your pup inherits not only his appearance but also his personality and temperament from the sire and dam. If the parents are fearful or overly aggressive, these same traits may likely show up in your puppy.

neighbours own dogs and they seem to be doing just fine. Why should I have to worry about all of this? Well, you should not worry about it; in fact, you will probably find that once your Shiba pup gets used to his new home, he will fall into his place in the family quite naturally. But it never hurts to emphasise the commitment of dog ownership. With some time and patience, it is really not too difficult to raise a curious and exuberant Shiba pup to be a well-adjusted and well-mannered adult dog—a dog that could be your most loyal friend.

PREPARING PUPPY'S PLACE IN YOUR HOME

Researching your breed and finding a breeder are only two aspects of the 'homework' you will have to do before taking your Shiba puppy home. You will also have to prepare your home and family for the new addition. Much as you would prepare a nursery for a newborn baby, you will need to designate a place in your home that will be the puppy's own. How you prepare your home will depend on how much freedom the dog will be allowed. Whatever you decide, you must ensure that he has a place that he can 'call his own.'

When you bring your new puppy into your home, you are bringing him into what will become his home as well.

PUPPY APPEARANCE
Your puppy should have a well-fed appearance but not a distended abdomen, which may indicate worms or incorrect feeding, or both. The body should be firm, with a solid feel. The skin of the abdomen should be pale pink and clean, without signs of scratching or rash. Check the hind legs to make certain that dewclaws were removed, if any were present at birth.

Obviously, you did not buy a puppy so that he could take over your house, but in order for a puppy to grow into a stable, well-adjusted dog, he has to feel comfortable in his surroundings. Remember, he is leaving the warmth and security of his mother and littermates, as well as the familiarity of the only place he has ever known, so it is important to make his transition

WHAT YOU SHOULD BUY

CRATE

To someone unfamiliar with the use of crates in dog training, it may seem like punishment to shut a dog in a crate, but this is not the case at all. Although all breeders do not advocate crate training, more and more breeders and trainers are recommending crates as preferred tools for show puppies as well as pet puppies. Crates are not cruel—crates have many humane and highly effective uses in dog care and training. For example, crate training is a very popular and very successful toileting method. A crate can keep your dog safe during travel and, perhaps most importantly, a crate provides your dog with a place of his own in

Meet the dam of your chosen Shiba puppy. Her physical appearance as well as temperament will be passed along to her pups.

as easy as possible. By preparing a place in your home for the puppy, you are making him feel as welcome as possible in a strange new place. It should not take him long to get used to it, but the sudden shock of being transplanted is somewhat traumatic for a young pup. Imagine how a small child would feel in the same situation—that is how your puppy must be feeling. It is up to you to reassure him and to let him know, 'Little chap, you are going to like it here!'

> **'YOU BETTER SHOP AROUND!'**
> Finding a reputable breeder that sells healthy pups is very important, but make sure that the breeder you choose is not only someone you respect but also with whom you feel comfortable. Your breeder will be a resource long after you buy your puppy, and you must be able to call with reasonable questions without being made to feel like a pest! If you don't connect on a personal level, investigate some other breeders before making a final decision.

CRATE TRAINING TIPS

During crate training, you should partition off the section of the crate in which the pup stays. If he is given too big an area, this will hinder your training efforts. Crate training is based on the fact that a dog does not like to soil his sleeping quarters, so it is ineffective to keep a pup in a crate that is so big that he can eliminate in one end and get far enough away from it to sleep. Also, you want to make the crate den-like for the pup. Blankets and a favourite toy will make the crate cosy for the small pup; as he grows, you may want to evict some of his 'roommates' to make more room.

It will take some coaxing at first, but be patient. Given some time to get used to it, your pup will adapt to his new home-within-a-home quite nicely.

your home. It serves as a 'doggie bedroom' of sorts—your Shiba can curl up in his crate when he wants to sleep or when he just needs a break. Many dogs sleep in their crates overnight. With soft bedding and his favourite toy, a crate becomes a cosy pseudo-den for your dog. Like his ancestors, he too will seek out the comfort and retreat of a den—you just happen to be providing him with something a little more luxurious than what his early ancestors enjoyed.

As far as purchasing a crate, a wire crate is the choice for the Shiba. It is more open, allowing

A wire crate is the only choice for your Shiba's crate. Shibas need to know what is going on around them and will feel 'trapped' in a fibreglass crate. When introduced to the crate as puppies, adult Shibas love to spend time in the comfort and security of their crates.

medium-size crate will be necessary for a fully-grown Shiba, who stands approximately 15 inches high.

BEDDING

Veterinary bedding in the dog's crate will help the dog feel more at home and you may also like to pop in a small blanket. This will take the place of the leaves, twigs, etc., that the pup would use in the wild to make a den; the pup can make his own 'burrow' in the crate. Although your pup is far removed from his den-making ancestors, the denning instinct is still a part of his genetic makeup. Second, until you take your pup home, he has been sleeping amidst the warmth of his mother and littermates, and while a blanket is not the same as a warm, breathing body, it still provides heat and something with which to snuggle. You will want to wash your pup's bedding frequently in case he has an accident in his crate, and replace or remove any blanket that becomes ragged and starts to fall apart.

TOYS

Toys are a must for dogs of all ages, especially for curious playful pups. Puppies are the 'children' of the dog world, and what child does not love toys? Chew toys provide enjoyment for both dog and owner—your dog will enjoy playing with his

FEEDING TIP

You will probably start feeding your pup the same food that he has been getting from the breeder; the breeder should give you a few days' supply to start you off. Although you should not give your pup too many treats, you will want to have puppy treats on hand for coaxing, training, rewards, etc. Be careful, though, as a small pup's calorie requirements are relatively low and a few treats can add up to almost a full day's worth of calories without the required nutrition.

the air to flow through and affording the dog a view of what is going on around him. Shibas hate fibreglass crates that are too confining and don't allow the dog to see what's going on. The size of the crate is another thing to consider. It is best to buy a crate that will accommodate your dog both as a pup and at full size. A

Veterinary bedding can make a Shiba's bed or crate more cosy for the pups. These pups also thinks it is fun to play with.

favourite toys, while you will enjoy the fact that they distract him from your expensive shoes and leather sofa. Puppies love to chew; in fact, chewing is a physical need for pups as they are teething, and everything looks appetising! The full range of your possessions—from old tea towel to Oriental carpet—are fair game in the eyes of a teething pup. Puppies are not all that discerning when it comes to finding something to literally 'sink their teeth into'—everything tastes great!

Some Shiba puppies are fairly aggressive chewers and only the strongest toys should be offered to them. Breeders advise owners to resist stuffed toys, because they can become de-stuffed in no time. The overly excited pup may ingest the stuffing, which can be harmful to the dog.

Similarly, squeaky toys are loved by Shibas and can be used as an aid in training, but not for free play. If a pup 'disembowels' one of these, the small plastic squeaker inside can be dangerous if swallowed. Monitor the condition of all your pup's toys carefully and get rid of any that

Shibas love squeaky and furry toys. Always supervise your pup whenever he has a toy that contains a plastic squeaker, which could be dangerous if removed from the toy.

PLAY'S THE THING

Teaching the puppy to play with his toys in running and fetching games is an ideal way to help the puppy develop muscle, learn motor skills and bond with you, his owner and master.

He also needs to learn how to inhibit his bite reflex and never to use his teeth on people, forbidden objects and other animals in play. Whenever you play with your puppy, you make the rules. This becomes an important message to your puppy in teaching him that you are the pack leader and control everything he does in life. Once your dog accepts you as his leader, your relationship with him will be cemented for life.

swallow and become a mushy mess on your carpet.

LEAD

A nylon lead is probably the best option as it is the most resistant to puppy teeth should your pup take a liking to chewing on his lead. Of course, this is a habit that should be nipped in the bud, but if your pup likes to chew on his lead he has a very slim chance of being able to chew through the strong nylon. Nylon leads are also lightweight, which is good for a young Shiba who is just getting used to the idea of walking on a lead.

For everyday walking and safety purposes, the nylon lead is

MENTAL AND DENTAL

Toys not only help your puppy get the physical and mental stimulation he needs but also provide a great way to keep his teeth clean. Hard rubber or nylon toys, especially those constructed with grooves, are designed to scrape away plaque, preventing bad breath and gum infection.

have been chewed to the point of becoming potentially dangerous.

Be careful of natural bones, which have a tendency to splinter into sharp, dangerous pieces. Also be careful of rawhide, which can turn into pieces that are easy to

a good choice. As your pup grows up and gets used to walking on the lead, you may want to purchase a flexible lead. These leads allow you to extend the length to give the dog a broader area to explore or to shorten the length to keep the dog near you. Of course there are special leads for training purposes, and specially made leather harnesses, but these are not necessary for routine walks.

COLLAR

Your pup should get used to wearing a collar all the time since you will want to attach his ID tags to it. Plus, you have to attach the lead to something! A lightweight nylon collar is a good choice; make sure that it fits snugly enough so that the pup cannot wriggle out of it, but is loose enough so that it will not be uncomfortably tight around the

TOYS, TOYS, TOYS!

With a big variety of dog toys available, and so many that look like they would be a lot of fun for a dog, be careful in your selection. It is amazing what a set of puppy teeth can do to an innocent-looking toy, so, obviously, safety is a major consideration. Be sure to choose the most durable products that you can find. Hard nylon bones and toys are a safe bet, and many of them are offered in different scents and flavours that will be sure to capture your dog's attention. It is always fun to play a game of catch with your dog, and there are balls and flying discs that are specially made to withstand dog teeth.

Your local pet shop will have a wide selection of leads from which you can choose the one that best suits your needs.

QUALITY FOOD
The cost of food must also be mentioned. All dogs need a good quality food with an adequate supply of protein to develop their bones and muscles properly. Most dogs are not picky eaters but unless fed properly they can quickly succumb to skin problems.

pup's neck. You should be able to fit a finger between the pup and the collar and keep in mind that your Shiba's neck size will change as he grows and his coat comes in. It may take some time for your pup to get used to wearing the collar, but soon he will not even notice that it is there. Never use a metal chain collar on your Shiba—it will destroy the dog's neck hair.

FOOD AND WATER BOWLS

Your pup will need two bowls, one for food and one for water. You may want two sets of bowls, one for inside and one for outside, depending on where the dog will be fed and where he will be

spending time. Stainless steel or sturdy plastic bowls are popular choices. Plastic bowls are more chewable. Dogs tend not to chew on the steel variety, which can be sterilised. It is important to buy sturdy bowls since anything is in danger of being chewed by puppy teeth and you do not want your dog to be constantly chewing apart his bowl (for his safety and for your purse!).

CLEANING SUPPLIES

Until a pup is housetrained you will be doing a lot of cleaning. Accidents will occur, which is acceptable in the beginning because the puppy does not know any better. All you can do is be prepared to clean up any 'accidents.' Old rags, towels,

FINANCIAL RESPONSIBILITY
Grooming tools, collars, leashes, dog beds and, of course, toys will be an expense to you when you first obtain your pup, and the cost will continue throughout your dog's lifetime. If your puppy damages or destroys your possessions (as most puppies surely will!) or something belonging to a neighbour, you can calculate additional expense. There is also flea and pest control, which every dog owner faces more than once. You must be able to handle the financial responsibility of owning a dog.

CHOOSE AN APPROPRIATE COLLAR

The **BUCKLE COLLAR** is the standard collar used for everyday purpose. Be sure that you adjust the buckle on growing puppies. Check it every day. It can become too tight overnight! These collars can be made of leather or nylon. Attach your dog's identification tags to this collar.

The **CHOKE COLLAR** is the usual collar recommended for training, though it is not ideal for coated breeds like the Shiba. It is constructed of highly polished steel so that it slides easily through the stainless steel loop. The idea is that the dog controls the pressure around its neck and he will stop pulling if the collar becomes uncomfortable. Never leave a choke collar on your dog when not training.

The **HALTER** is for a trained dog that has to be restrained to prevent running away, chasing a cat and the like. Considered the most humane of all collars, it is frequently used on smaller dogs for which collars are not comfortable.

Your local pet shop sells an array of dishes and bowls for water and food. Being a small dog, the Shiba does not require large dishes or bowls.

PHOTO COURTESY OF MIKKI PET PRODUCTS

newspapers and a safe disinfectant are good to have on hand.

BEYOND THE BASICS

The items previously discussed are the bare necessities. You will find out what else you need as you go along—grooming supplies, flea/tick protection, baby gates to partition a room, etc. These things will vary depending on your situation but it is important that you have everything you need to feed and make your Shiba comfortable in his first few days at home.

PUPPY-PROOFING YOUR HOME

Aside from making sure that your Shiba will be comfortable in your home, you also have to make sure that your home is safe for your Shiba. This means taking precautions that your pup will not get into anything he should not get into and that there is nothing within his reach that may harm him should he sniff it, chew it, inspect it, etc. This probably seems obvious since, while you are primarily concerned with your pup's safety, at the same time you do not want your belongings to be ruined. Breakables should be placed out of reach if your dog is to have full run of the house. If he is to be limited to certain places within the house, keep any potentially dangerous items in the 'off-limits' areas. An electrical cord can pose a danger should the puppy decide to taste it—and who is going to convince a pup that it would not make a great chew toy? Cords should be fastened tightly against the wall. If your dog is going to spend time in a crate, make sure that there is nothing near his crate that he can reach if he sticks his curious little nose or paws through the openings. Just as you would with a child, keep all household cleaners and chemicals where the pup cannot reach them.

It is also important to make sure that the outside of your home is safe. Of course your puppy should never be unsupervised, but a pup let loose in the garden will want to run and explore, and he should be granted that freedom. Do not let a fence give you a false sense of security; you would be surprised how crafty (and persis-

Your dog's droppings must be cleaned up and disposed of in a proper manner. Your local pet shop will have devices to aid you in the cleanup.

tent) a dog can be in working out how to dig under and squeeze his way through small holes, or to climb over a fence. Remember that Shibas are celebrated escape artists and live to practise their art. The remedy is to make the fence well embedded into the ground and high enough so that it really is impossible for your dog to get over it (about 3 metres should suffice). Be sure to repair or secure any gaps in the fence. Check the fence periodically to ensure that it is in good shape and make repairs as needed; a very determined pup may return to the same spot to 'work on it' until he is able to get through. Once a

NATURAL TOXINS
Examine your grass and garden landscaping before bringing your puppy home. Many varieties of plants have leaves, stems or flowers that are toxic if ingested, and you can depend on a curious puppy to investigate them. Ask your vet for information on poisonous plants or research them at your library.

Shiba decides that it's time to find a way out, he will devote his entire spirit to the pursuit of freedom. Owners must be ready to prevent this escape and always have your trainers handy!

FIRST TRIP TO THE VET
You have selected your puppy, and your home and family are ready. Now all you have to do is collect your Shiba from the breeder and the fun begins, right? Well...not so fast. Something else you need to prepare is your pup's first trip to the veterinary surgeon. Perhaps the breeder can recommend someone in the area

that specialises in Shibas, or maybe you know some other Shiba owners who can suggest a good vet. Either way, you should have an appointment arranged for your pup before you pick him up.

The pup's first visit will consist of an overall examination to make sure that the pup does not have any problems that are not apparent to the new owner. The veterinary surgeon will also set up a schedule for the pup's

CHEMICAL TOXINS
Scour your garage for potential puppy dangers. Remove weed killers, pesticides and antifreeze materials. Antifreeze is highly toxic and even a few drops can kill an adult dog. The sweet taste attracts the animal, who will quickly consume it from the floor or curbside.

vaccinations; the breeder will inform you of which ones the pup has already received and the vet can continue from there.

INTRODUCTION TO THE FAMILY
Everyone in the house will be excited about the puppy coming home and will want to pet him and play with him, but it is best to make the introduction low-key so as not to overwhelm the puppy. He is apprehensive already. It is the first time he has been separated from his mother and the breeder, and the ride to your home is likely to be the first time he has been in a car. The last thing you want to do is smother him, as this will only frighten him further. This is not to say that human contact is not extremely necessary at this stage, because this is the time when a connection between the pup and his human family is formed. Gentle petting and soothing words should help console him,

as well as just putting him down and letting him explore on his own (under your watchful eye, of course).

The pup may approach the family members or may busy himself with exploring for a while. Gradually, each person should spend some time with the pup, one at a time, crouching down to get as close to the pup's level as possible and letting him sniff each person's hands and

petting him gently. He definitely needs human attention and he needs to be touched—this is how to form an immediate bond. Just remember that the pup is experiencing a lot of things for the first time, at the same time. There are new people, new noises, new smells, and new things to investigate: so be gentle, be affectionate and be as comforting as you can be.

DID YOU KNOW?

Breeders rarely release puppies until they are eight to ten weeks of age. This is an acceptable age for most breeds of dog, excepting toy breeds, which are not released until around 12 weeks, given their petite sizes. If a breeder has a puppy that is 12 weeks or more, it is likely well socialised and housetrained. Be sure that it is otherwise healthy before deciding to take it home.

ARE YOU A FIT OWNER?

If the breeder from whom you are buying a puppy asks you a lot of personal questions, do not be insulted. Such a breeder wants to be sure that you will be a fit provider for his puppy.

PUP'S FIRST NIGHT HOME

You have travelled home with your new charge safely in his crate. He's been to the vet for a thorough check-up; he's been weighed, his papers examined; perhaps he's even been vaccinated and wormed as well. He's met the family, licked the whole family, including the excited children and the less-than-happy cat. He's explored his area, his new bed, the garden and anywhere else he's been permitted. He's eaten his first meal at home and relieved himself in the proper place. He's heard lots of new sounds, smelled new friends and seen more of the outside world than ever before.

That was just the first day! He's worn out and is ready for bed…or so you think!

It's puppy's first night and you are ready to say 'Good night'—keep in mind that this is puppy's first night ever to be sleeping alone. His dam and littermates are no longer at paw's length and he's a bit scared, cold and lonely. Be reassuring to your new family member. This is not the time to spoil him and give in to his inevitable whining.

Puppies whine. They whine to let others know where they are and hopefully to get company out of it. Place your pup in his new bed or crate in his room and close the door. Mercifully, he may fall asleep without a peep. When the inevitable occurs, ignore the whining: he is fine. Be strong and keep his interest in mind. Do not allow yourself to feel guilty and visit the pup. He will fall asleep eventually.

Many breeders recommend placing a piece of bedding from his former home in his new bed so that he recognises the scent of his littermates. Others still advise placing a hot water bottle in his bed for warmth. This latter may be a good idea provided the pup doesn't attempt to suckle—he'll get good and wet and may not fall asleep so fast.

Puppy's first night can be somewhat stressful for the pup and his new family. Remember

STRESS-FREE
Some experts in canine health advise that stress during a dog's early years of development can compromise and weaken his immune system and may trigger the potential for a shortened life expectancy. They emphasise the need for happy and stress-free growing-up years.

BOY OR GIRL?
An important consideration to be discussed is the sex of your puppy. For a family companion, a bitch may be the better choice, considering the female's inbred concern for all young creatures and her accompanying tolerance and patience. It is always advisable to spay a pet bitch, which may guarantee her a longer life.

that you are setting the tone of nighttime at your house. Unless you want to play with your pup every evening at 10 p.m., midnight and 2 a.m., don't initiate the habit. Your family will thank you, and so will your pup!

PREVENTING PUPPY PROBLEMS

SOCIALISATION
Now that you have done all of the preparatory work and have helped your pup get accustomed to his

MANNERS MATTER

During the socialisation process, a puppy should meet people, experience different environments and definitely be exposed to other canines. Through playing and interacting with other dogs, your puppy will learn lessons, ranging from controlling the pressure of his jaws by biting his litter mates to the inner-workings of the canine pack that he will apply to his human relationships for the rest of his life. That is why removing a puppy from its litter too early (before eight weeks) can be detrimental to the pup's development.

PROPER SOCIALISATION

The socialisation period for puppies is from age 8 to 16 weeks. This is the time when puppies need to leave their birth family and take up residence with their new owners, where they will meet many new people, other pets, etc. Failure to be adequately socialised can cause the dog to grow up fearing others and being shy and unfriendly due to a lack of self-confidence.

new home and family, it is about time for you to have some fun! Socialising your Shiba pup gives you the opportunity to show off your new friend, and your pup gets to reap the benefits of being an adorable furry creature that people will want to pet and, in general, think is absolutely precious!

Besides getting to know his new family, your puppy should be exposed to other people, animals and situations, but of course he must not come into close contact with dogs you don't know well until his course of injections is fully complete. This will help him become well adjusted as he grows up and less prone to being timid or fearful of the new things he will encounter. Your pup's sociali-sation began with the breeder but now it is your responsibility to continue it. The socialisation he receives up until the age of 12 weeks is the most critical, as this is the time when he forms his impressions of the outside world. Be especially careful during the eight-to-ten-week period, also known as the fear period. The interaction he receives during this time should be gentle and reassuring. Lack of socialisation can manifest itself in fear and aggression as the dog grows up. He needs lots of human contact, affection, handling and exposure to other animals.

Once your pup has received his necessary vaccinations, feel free to take him out and about (on his lead, of course). Walk him around the neighbourhood, take him on your daily errands, let people pet him, let him meet other dogs and pets, etc. Puppies do not have to try to make friends; there will be no shortage of

SOCIALISATION

Thorough socialisation includes not only meeting new people but also being introduced to new experiences such as riding in the car, having his coat brushed, hearing the television, walking in a crowd—the list is endless. The more your Shiba experiences as a pup, and the more positive the experiences are, the less of a shock and the less frightening it will be for him to encounter new things.

PUPPY PROBLEMS

The majority of problems that are commonly seen in young pups will disappear as your dog gets older. However, how you deal with problems when he is young will determine how he reacts to discipline as an adult dog. It is important to establish who is boss (hopefully it will be you!) right away when you are first bonding with your dog. This bond will set the tone for the rest of your life together.

people who will want to introduce themselves. Just make sure that you carefully supervise each meeting. If the neighbourhood children want to say hello, for example, that is great—children and pups most often make great companions. Sometimes an excited child can unintentionally handle a pup too roughly, or an overzealous pup can playfully nip a little too hard. You want to make socialisation experiences positive ones. What a pup learns during this very formative stage will affect his attitude toward future encounters. You want your dog to be comfortable around everyone. A pup that has a bad experience with a child may

A FORTNIGHT'S GRACE
It will take at least two weeks for your puppy to become accustomed to his new surroundings. Give him lots of love, attention, handling, frequent opportunities to relieve himself, a diet he likes to eat and a place he can call his own.

HOW VACCINES WORK
If you've just bought a puppy, you surely know the importance of having your pup vaccinated, but do you understand how vaccines work? Vaccines contain the same bacteria or viruses that cause the disease you want to prevent, but they have been chemically modified so that they don't cause any harm. Instead, the vaccine causes your dog to produce antibodies that fight the harmful bacteria. Thus, if your pup is exposed to the disease in the future, the antibodies will destroy the viruses or bacteria.

grow up to be a dog that is shy around or aggressive toward children.

CONSISTENCY IN TRAINING
Dogs, being pack animals, naturally need a leader, or else they try to establish dominance in their packs. When you welcome a dog into your family, the choice of who becomes the leader and who becomes the 'pack' is entirely up to you! Your pup's intuitive quest for dominance, coupled with the fact that it is nearly impossible to look at an adorable Shiba pup with his 'puppy-dog' eyes and not cave in, give the pup almost an unfair advantage in getting the upper hand! A pup will definitely test the waters to see what he can and cannot do. Do not give in to

those pleading eyes—stand your ground when it comes to disciplining the pup and make sure that all family members do the same. It will only confuse the pup when Mother tells him to get off the sofa when he is used to sitting up there with Father to watch the nightly news. Avoid discrepancies by having all members of the household decide on the rules before the pup even comes home...and be consistent in enforcing them! Early training shapes the dog's personality, so you cannot be unclear in what you expect.

COMMON PUPPY PROBLEMS

The best way to prevent puppy problems is to be proactive in stopping an undesirable behaviour as soon as it starts. The

TRAINING TIP
Training your dog takes much patience and can be frustrating at times, but you should see results from your efforts. If you have a puppy that seems untrainable, take him to a trainer or behaviourist. The dog may have a personality problem that requires the help of a professional, or perhaps you need help in learning how to train your dog.

THE RIDE HOME
Taking your dog from the breeder to your home in a car can be a very uncomfortable experience for both of you. The puppy will have been taken from his warm, friendly, safe environment and brought into a strange new environment. An environment that moves! Be prepared for loose bowels, urination, crying, whining and even fear biting. With proper love and encouragement when you arrive home, the stress of the trip should quickly disappear.

old saying 'You can't teach an old dog new tricks' does not necessarily hold true, but it is true that it is much easier to discourage bad behaviour in a young developing pup than to wait until the pup's bad behaviour becomes the adult dog's bad habit. There are some problems that are especially prevalent in puppies as they develop.

NIPPING

As puppies start to teethe, they feel the need to sink their teeth into anything available…unfortunately that includes your fingers, arms, hair and toes. You may find this behaviour cute for the first five seconds…until you feel just how sharp those puppy teeth are. This is something you want to discourage immediately and consistently with a firm 'No!' (or whatever number of firm 'No's' it takes for him to understand that you mean business). Then replace your finger with an appropriate chew toy. While this behaviour is merely annoying when the dog is young, it can become dangerous as your Shiba's adult teeth grow in and his jaws develop, and he continues to think it is okay to gnaw on human appendages. Your Shiba does not mean any harm with a friendly nip, but he also does not know his own strength.

CRYING/WHINING

Your pup will often cry, whine, whimper, howl or make some type of commotion when he is left alone. This is basically his way of calling out for attention to make sure that you know he is there and that you have not forgotten about him. He feels insecure when he is left alone, when you are out of the house and he is in his crate or when you are in another part of the house and he cannot see you. The noise he is making is an expression of the anxiety he feels at being alone, so he needs to be taught that being alone is okay. You are not actually training the dog to stop making noise, you are training him to feel comfortable when he is alone and thus removing the need for him to make the noise. This is where the crate with cosy bedding and a toy comes in handy. You want to know that he is safe when you are not there to supervise, and you know that he will be safe in his crate rather than roaming freely about the house. In order for the pup to stay in his crate without making a fuss, he needs to be comfortable in his crate. On that note, it is extremely important that the crate is never used as a form of punishment, or the pup will have a negative association with the crate.

Accustom the pup to the crate in short, gradually increasing time intervals in which you put him in the crate, maybe with a treat, and stay in the room with him. If he cries or makes a fuss, do not go to him, but stay in his sight. Gradually he will realise that staying in his crate is all right without your help, and it will not be so traumatic for him when you are not around. You may want to leave the radio on softly when you leave the house; the sound of human voices may be comforting to him.

DIETARY AND FEEDING CONSIDERATIONS

Today the choices of food for your Japanese Shiba are many and varied. There are simply dozens of brands of food in all sorts of flavours and textures, ranging from puppy diets to those for seniors. There are even hypoallergenic and low-calorie diets available. Because your Japanese Shiba's food has a bearing on coat, health and temperament, it is essential that the most suitable diet is selected for a Japanese Shiba of his age. It is fair to say, however, that even experienced owners can be perplexed by the enormous range of foods available. Only understanding what is best for your dog will help you reach a valued decision.

Dog foods are produced in three basic types: dried, semi-moist and tinned. Dried foods are useful for the cost-conscious for overall they tend to be less expensive than semi-moist or tinned. They also contain the least fat and the most preservatives. In general, tinned foods are made up of 60–70 percent water, while semi-moist ones often contain so much sugar that they are perhaps the least preferred by owners, even though their dogs seem to like them.

When selecting your dog's diet, three stages of development must be considered: the puppy stage, adult stage and the senior or veteran stage.

PUPPY STAGE

Puppies instinctively want to suck milk from their mother's

> **FEEDING TIP**
> You must store your dried dog food carefully. Open packages of dog food quickly lose their vitamin value, usually within 90 days of being opened. Mould spores and vermin could also contaminate the food.

TEST FOR PROPER DIET
A good test for proper diet is the colour, odour and firmness of your dog's stool. A healthy dog usually produces three semi-hard stools per day. The stools should have no unpleasant odour. They should be the same colour from excretion to excretion.

some excellent ones available, if the puppies do not feed, the breeder will have to feed them himself. For those with less experience, advice from a veterinary surgeon is important so that not only the right quantity of milk is fed but also that of correct quality, fed at suitably frequent intervals, usually every two hours during the first few days of life.

Puppies should be allowed to nurse from their mothers for about the first six weeks, although from the third or fourth week you should begin to introduce small portions of suitable solid food. Most breeders like to introduce alternate milk and meat meals initially, building up to weaning time.

By the time the puppies are seven or a maximum of eight weeks old, they should be fully weaned and fed solely on a proprietary puppy food. Selection of the most suitable, good-quality diet at this time is essential, for a puppy's fastest growth rate is during the first year of life. Veterinary surgeons are usually able to offer advice in this regard and, although the frequency of meals will have been reduced over time, only when a young dog has reached the age of about 10 to 12 months should an adult diet be fed.

Puppy and junior diets

teats and a normal puppy will exhibit this behaviour from just a few moments following birth. If puppies do not attempt to suckle within the first half-hour or so, they should be encouraged to do so by placing them on the nipples, having selected ones with plenty of milk. This early milk supply is important in providing colostrum to protect the puppies during the first eight to ten weeks of their lives. Although a mother's milk is much better than any milk formula, despite there being

should be well balanced for the needs of your dog, so that except in certain circumstances additional vitamins, minerals and proteins will not be required.

ADULT DIETS

A dog is considered an adult when it has stopped growing, so in general the diet of a Japanese Shiba can be changed to an adult one at about 10 to 12 months of age. Again you should rely upon your veterinary surgeon or dietary specialist to recommend an acceptable maintenance diet. Major dog food manufacturers specialise in this type of food, and it is merely necessary for you to select the one best suited to your dog's needs. Active dogs may have different requirements than sedate dogs.

SENIOR DIETS

As dogs get older, their metabolism changes. The older dog usually exercises less, moves more slowly and sleeps more. This change in lifestyle and physiological performance requires a change in diet. Since these changes take place slowly, they might not be recognisable. What is easily recognisable is weight gain. By continuing to feed your dog an adult-maintenance diet when it is slowing down metabolically, your dog will gain weight. Obesity in an

FOOD PREFERENCE
Selecting the best dried dog food is difficult. There is no majority consensus among veterinary scientists as to the value of nutrient analyses (protein, fat, fibre, moisture, ash, cholesterol, minerals, etc.). All agree that feeding trials are what matters, but you also have to consider the individual dog. Its weight, age, activity and what pleases its taste all must be considered. It is probably best to take the advice of your veterinary surgeon. Every dog's dietary requirements vary, even during the lifetime of a particular dog.

If your dog is fed a good dried food, it does not require supplements of meat or vegetables. Dogs do appreciate a little variety in their diets so you may choose to stay with the same brand, but vary the flavour. Alternatively, you may wish to add a little flavoured stock to give a difference to the taste.

TIPPING THE SCALES

Good nutrition is vital to your dog's health, but many people end up over-feeding or giving unnecessary supplements. Here are some common doggie diet don'ts:

• Adding milk, yoghurt and cheese to your dog's diet may seem like a good idea for coat and skin care, but dairy products are very fattening and can cause indigestion.

• Diets high in fat will not cause heart attacks in dogs but will certainly cause your dog to gain weight.

• Most importantly, don't assume your dog will simply stop eating once he doesn't need any more food. Given the chance, he will eat you out of house and home!

intestines become less efficient. These age-related factors are best handled with a change in diet and a change in feeding schedule to give smaller portions that are more easily digested.

There is no single best diet for every older dog. While many dogs do well on light or senior diets, other dogs do better on puppy diets or other special premium diets such as lamb and rice. Be sensitive to your senior Japanese Shiba's diet and this will help control other problems that may arise with your old friend.

older dog compounds the health problems that already accompany old age.

As your dog gets older, few of his organs function up to par. The kidneys slow down and the

'DOES THIS COLLAR MAKE ME LOOK FAT?'

While humans may obsess about how they look and how trim their bodies are, many people believe that extra weight on their dogs is a good thing. The truth is, pets should not be over- or under-weight, as both can lead to or signal sickness. In order to tell how fit your pet is, run your hands over his ribs. Are his ribs buried under a layer of fat or are they sticking out considerably? If your pet is within his normal weight range, you should be able to feel the ribs easily. If you stand above him, the outline of his body should resemble an hourglass. Some breeds do tend to be leaner while some are a bit stockier, but making sure your dog is the right weight for his breed will certainly contribute to his good health.

A nursing dam will have different nutritional requirements than other dogs. Discuss the diet of your Shiba with your vet as well as your breeder.

WHAT ARE YOU FEEDING YOUR DOG?

Read the label on your dog food. Many dog foods only advise what 50–55% of the contents are, leaving the other 45% in doubt.

Calcium 1.3%
Fatty Acids 1.6%
Crude Fibre 4.6%
Moisture 11%
Crude Fat 14%
Crude Protein 22%
45.5% ? ? ?

WATER

Just as your dog needs proper nutrition from his food, water is an essential 'nutrient' as well. Water keeps the dog's body properly hydrated and promotes normal function of the body's systems. During toilet training it is necessary to keep an eye on how much water your Japanese Shiba is drinking, but once he is reliably trained he should have access to clean fresh water at all times, especially if you feed dried food. Make certain that the dog's water bowl is clean, and change the water often.

FEEDING TIPS

Dog food must be at room temperature, neither too hot nor too cold. Fresh water, changed daily and served in a clean bowl, is mandatory, especially when feeding dried food.

Never feed your dog from the table while you are eating. Never feed your dog leftovers from your own meal. They usually contain too much fat and too much seasoning.

Dogs must chew their food. Hard pellets are excellent; soups and slurries are to be avoided.

Don't add left-overs or any extras to normal dog food. The normal food is usually balanced and adding something extra destroys the balance.

Except for age-related changes, dogs do not require dietary variations. They can be fed the same diet, day after day, without their becoming ill.

DO DOGS HAVE TASTE BUDS?

Watching a dog 'wolf' or gobble his food, seemingly without chewing, leads an owner to wonder whether their dogs can taste anything. Yes, dogs have taste buds, with sensory perception of sweet, salty and sour. Puppies are born with fully mature taste buds.

EXERCISE

The Shiba challenge is keeping up with this active little spitz dog! A Shiba is always ready for a walk and, in cool weather, will welcome an hour walk with his owner once or twice a day! If you are fortunate to have a sizeable garden, the Shiba will enjoy running and playing for hours each day. Shibas will play with their owners, chasing a ball, flying disk or some other favourite toy. Perhaps the best exercise for the Shiba is another Shiba! The author solved his

DRINK, DRANK, DRUNK—MAKE IT A DOUBLE

In both humans and dogs, as well as most living organisms, water forms the major part of nearly every body tissue. Naturally, we take water for granted, but without it, life as we know it would cease.

For dogs, water is needed to keep their bodies functioning biochemically. Additionally, water is needed to replace the water lost while panting. Unlike humans who are able to sweat to dissipate heat, dogs must pant to cool down, thereby losing the vital water from their bodies needed to regulate their body temperatures. Humans lose electrolyte-containing products and other body-fluid components through sweating; dogs do not lose anything except water.

Water is essential always, but especially so when the weather is hot or humid or when your dog is exercising or working vigorously.

Shiba exercise and entertainment problem by acquiring a second Shiba within six months of his first Shiba. Male and female Shibas can be best of friends and love the time they spend chasing each other and playing. Fighting over toys and fetching toys with their owners are marvellous exercise for these feisty Nipponese wonders.

For their size, Shibas require considerable exercise. They can keep up with an owner on his morning jog and can even run alongside a bicycle for a not-too-long ride on a cool day. Avoid too much exercise in hot weather. These are Nordic dogs that prefer the cooler climes. Shibas can overheat in their enthusiasm to keep up with their owner or another dog.

Not only is exercise essential

CHANGE IN DIET

As your dog's caretaker, you know the importance of keeping his diet consistent, but sometimes when you run out of food or if you're on holiday, you have to make a change quickly. Some dogs will experience digestive problems, but most will not. If you are planning on changing your dog's menu, do so gradually to ensure that your dog will not have any problems. Over a period of four to five days, slowly add some new food to your dog's old food, increasing the percentage of new food each day.

GRAIN-BASED DIETS

Some less expensive dog foods are based on grains and other plant proteins. While these products may appear to be attractively priced, many breeders prefer a diet based on animal proteins and believe that they are more conducive to your dog's health. Many grain-based diets rely on soy protein that may cause flatulence (passing gas).

There are many cases, however, when your dog might require a special diet. These special requirements should only be recommended by your veterinary surgeon.

to keep the dog's body fit, it is essential to his mental well-being. A bored Shiba will find something to do, which often manifests itself in some type of destructive behaviour. A Shiba left outside without toys or stimulation will dig holes, eat shrubs or escape! Fortunately,

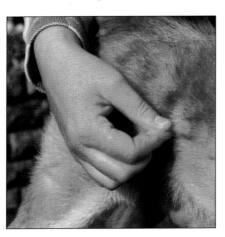

The Shiba has a double coat, consisting of a hard outer layer of hair and a soft, cottony undercoat. When a Shiba sheds twice annually, the undercoat becomes loose and requires daily grooming.

Shibas like toys and bones and can occupy themselves for hours. Do not give your Shiba opportunity to hone its creative resources. You will be sorry. Provide the Shiba with ample exercise, toys for amusement and lots of attention and he will be happy and well behaved.

THE CANINE GOURMET

Your dog does not prefer a fresh bone. Indeed, he wants it properly aged and, if given such a treat indoors, he is more likely to try to bury it in the carpet than he is to settle in for a good chew! If you have a garden, give him such delicacies outside and guide him to a place suitable for his 'bone yard.' He will carefully place the treasure in its earthy vault and seemingly forget about it. Trust me, his seeming distaste or lack of thanks for your thoughtfulness is not that at all. He will return in a few days to inspect it, perhaps to re-bury the thing, and when it is just right, he will relish it as much as you do that cooked-to-perfection steak. If he is in a concrete or bricked kennel run, he will be especially frustrated at the hopelessness of the situation. He will vacillate between ignoring it completely, giving it a few licks to speed the curing process with saliva, and trying to hide it behind the water bowl! When the bone has aged a bit, he will set to work on it.

GROOMING EQUIPMENT

How much grooming equipment you purchase will depend on how much grooming you are going to do. Here are some basics:

- Natural bristle brush
- Slicker brush
- Metal comb
- Scissors
- Blaster
- Rubber mat
- Dog shampoo
- Spray hose attachment
- Ear cleaner
- Cotton wipes
- Towels
- Nail clippers

GROOMING

BRUSHING

Shibas do not require too much grooming time of their owners, except during their bi-annual coat casting. During the shedding season, the Shiba will blow his whole undercoat, the white fluffy down coat that gives the Shiba coat its fullness. Owners will need to brush the coat twice a day for about two weeks during these periods. During the other months of the year, the Shiba can be given a quick once-over each week. A soft bristle or slicker brush is ideal as well as a wide-toothed metal comb. Brush the whole coat, including the chest,

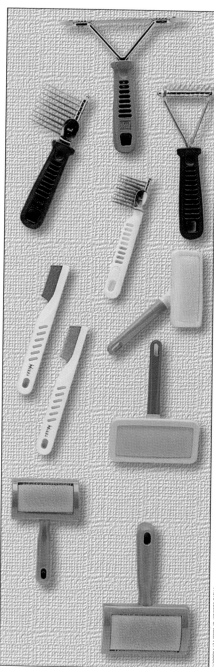

Your local pet shop will have the combs and brushes necessary for grooming your Shiba. Purchase the best quality slicker brush and rake that you can buy. These tools are ideal for the Shiba's double coat.

This lovely dam has graciously agreed to model for the grooming photos. The Shiba coat requires regular grooming to keep looking shiny and clean.

During moulting season, a slicker brush or rake works efficiently to remove the dead undercoat.

Misting the coat during grooming sessions keeps the coat moist and avoids hairs from breaking.

SOAP IT UP

The use of human soap products like shampoo, bubble bath and hand soap can be damaging to a dog's coat and skin. Human products are too strong and remove the protective oils coating the dog's hair and skin (that make him water-resistant). Use only shampoo made especially for dogs and you may like to use a medicated shampoo, which will always help to keep external parasites at bay.

underparts and tail. If introduced to brushing as a pup, most Shibas do not mind being groomed and enjoy the attention from their fawning owners.

BATHING

Brushing is one thing...but don't say the word B-A-T-H! Most Shibas do not welcome the idea of bathing! Getting wet and being a Shiba do not complement one another. You will have to introduce the Shiba to bathing early on. Most Shibas scream the first time water touches their coats. Be prepared and be the top dog. Talk your Shiba through it with gentle encouragement and a strong grip. Even though your Shiba may only weigh a stone, get a friend to help you bath the dog the first time. You will need the extra hands to keep the Shiba under control.

Fortunately, dogs do not need to be bathed as often as humans, but regular bathing is essential for healthy skin and a healthy, shiny coat. Brush your Japanese Shiba thoroughly before wetting his coat. Make certain that your dog has a good non-slip surface to stand on. Begin by wetting the dog's coat. A shower or hose attachment is necessary for thoroughly wetting and rinsing the coat. Check the water temperature to make sure that it is neither too hot nor too cold.

Next, apply shampoo to the dog's coat and work it into a good lather. You should purchase a shampoo that is made for dogs. Do not use a product made for human hair.

The Shiba's hindquarters should be attended to in order to create a proper full skirt (pantaloons on a dog!).

When trained from puppyhood, the Shiba stands still and patiently during her salon appointment.

Don't forget to brush the tail to keep it plush and free from debris or loose hairs. It is a key component in the Shiba's appearance.

BATHING BEAUTY

Once you are sure that the dog is thoroughly rinsed, squeeze the excess water out of the coat with your hand and dry him with a heavy towel. You may choose to use a blaster on his coat to ensure thorough dryness. In cold weather, never allow your dog outside with a wet coat.

There are 'dry bath' products on the market, which are sprays and powders intended for spot cleaning, that can be used between regular baths, if necessary. They are not substitutes for regular baths, but they are easy to use for touch-ups as they do not require rinsing.

Wash the head last; you do not want shampoo to drip into the dog's eyes while you are washing the rest of his body. Shibas hate water near their ears, so be especially careful. Work the shampoo all the way down to the skin. You can use this opportunity to check the skin for any bumps, bites or other abnormalities. Do not neglect any area of the body—get all of the hard-to-reach places.

Once the dog has been thoroughly shampooed, he requires an equally thorough rinsing. Shampoo left in the coat can be irritating to the skin. Protect his eyes from the shampoo by shielding them with

your hand and directing the flow of water in the opposite direction. You should also avoid getting water in the ear canal. Be prepared for your dog to shake out his coat—you might want to stand back, but make sure you have a hold on the dog to keep him from running through the house. Since this is such an ordeal for most Shibas, it pays to repeat the shampooing process before drying the dog.

Ear Cleaning

The ears should be kept clean with a cotton wipe and ear powder made especially for dogs. Be on the lookout for any signs of infection or ear mite infestation, which are too common in Shibas. If your Japanese Shiba has been shaking his head or scratching at his ears frequently, this usually indicates a problem. If his ears have an unusual odour, this is a sure sign of mite infestation or infection, and a signal to have his ears checked by the veterinary surgeon. Shibas hate having their ears touched, but cleaning the ears will prevent having to cure a mite problem later on.

Nail Clipping

Your Japanese Shiba should be accustomed to having his nails trimmed at an early age, since it will be part of your maintenance routine throughout his life. Not

Nail Maintenance

Nail Casing
Quick
Cut Line

Dark-Coloured Nails

With black or dark nails, where the quick is not easy to see, it's best to clip only the tip of the nail or to use a file.

Light-Coloured Nails

In light-coloured nails, clipping is much simpler because you can see the vein (or quick) that grows inside the casing.

PEDICURE TIP

A dog that spends a lot of time outside on a hard surface, such as cement or pavement, will have his nails naturally worn down and may not need to have them trimmed as often, except maybe in the colder months when he is not outside as much. Regardless, it is best to get your dog accustomed to this procedure at an early age so that he is used to it. Shibas are especially sensitive about having their feet touched, but if a dog has experienced it since he was young, he should not be bothered by it.

only does it look nicer, but long nails can scratch someone unintentionally. Also, a long nail has a better chance of ripping and bleeding, or causing the feet to spread. A good rule of thumb is that if you can hear your dog's nails clicking on the floor when he walks, his nails are too long. Shibas have perfect little cat-like feet but they hate to have their feet touched. You must convince your Shiba that touching his paws is a good thing, and begin this by rubbing his feet a few times a day from the first day.

Before you start cutting, make sure you can identify the 'quick' in each nail. The quick is a blood vessel that runs through the centre of each nail and grows rather close to the end. Since black and tan and red sesame Shibas' nails are jet black, the quick is very difficult to see. The quick will bleed if accidentally cut, which will be quite painful for the dog as it contains nerve endings. Keep some type of clotting agent on hand, such as a styptic pencil or styptic powder (the type used for shaving). This will stop the bleeding quickly when applied to the end of the cut nail. Do not panic if you cut the quick, just stop the bleeding and talk soothingly to your dog. Once he has calmed down, move on to the next nail. It is better to clip a little at a time with the Shiba.

Hold your pup steady as you begin trimming his nails; you do not want him to make any sudden movements or run away. Talk to him soothingly and stroke him as you clip. Holding his foot in your hand, simply take off the end of each nail in one quick clip. You can purchase nail clippers that are specially made for dogs; you can probably find them wherever you buy pet or grooming supplies.

TRAVELLING WITH YOUR DOG

CAR TRAVEL
You should accustom your Japanese Shiba to riding in a car at an early age. You may or may not take him in the car often, but at the very least he will need to go to the vet and you do not want these trips to be traumatic for the dog or troublesome for you. The safest way for a dog to ride in the car is in his crate.

Another option is a specially made safety harness for dogs, which straps the dog in much like a seat belt. Shibas will accept the harness, though they don't particularly welcome any device that's designed to confine or restrict them! Do not let the dog roam loose in the vehicle— this is very dangerous! If you should stop short, your dog can be thrown and injured. If the dog starts climbing on you and pestering you while you are driving, you will not be able to concentrate on the road. It is an unsafe situation for everyone—human and canine.

For long trips, be prepared to stop to let the dog relieve himself. Take with you whatever you need to clean up after him, including some paper kitchen towels and perhaps some old towelling for use should he have an accident in the car or suffer from travel sickness.

AIR TRAVEL

While it is possible to take a dog on a flight within Britain, this is fairly unusual and advance permission is always required. The dog will be required to travel in a fibreglass crate and you should always check in advance with the airline regarding specific requirements. To help the dog be at ease, put one of his favourite toys in the crate with him. Do not feed the dog for at least six hours before the trip to minimise his need to relieve himself. However, certain regulations specify that water must always be made available to the dog in the crate.

Make sure your dog is properly identified and that your contact information appears on his ID tags and on his crate. Animals travel in a different area of the plane than human passengers so every rule must be strictly followed so as to prevent the risk of getting separated from your dog.

The only safe way to travel with a Shiba is in her crate. Although Shibas would much rather be smelling the breeze through the window or licking the windshield, they belong safely stowed in their crates.

Your Shiba should never be without an identification tag attached to a light collar.

BOARDING

So you want to take a family holiday—and you want to include all members of the family. You would probably make arrangements for accommodation ahead of time anyway, but this is especially important when travelling with a dog. You do not want to make an overnight stop at the only place around for miles and find out that they do not allow dogs.

TRAVEL TIP

Never leave your dog alone in the car. In hot weather your dog can die from the high temperature inside a closed vehicle; even a car parked in the shade can heat up very quickly. Leaving the window open is dangerous as well since the dog can hurt himself trying to get out.

Also, you do not want to reserve a place for your family without confirming that you are travelling with a dog because if it is against their policy you may not have a place to stay.

Alternatively, if you are travelling and choose not to bring your Japanese Shiba, you will have to make arrangements for him while you are away. Some options are to take him to a neighbour's house to stay while you are gone, to have a trusted neighbour pop in often or stay at your house, or to bring your dog to a reputable boarding kennel. If you choose to board him at a kennel, you should visit in advance to see the facilities provided, how clean they are and where the dogs are kept. Talk to some of the employees and see how they treat the dogs—do they spend time with the dogs, play with them, exercise them, etc.? Also find out the kennel's policy on vaccinations and what they require. This is for all of the dogs' safety, since when dogs are kept together, there is a greater risk of diseases being passed from dog to dog.

IDENTIFICATION

Your Japanese Shiba is your valued companion and friend who likes to run away! That is why you always keep two very close eyes on him at all times and why you have made sure that he cannot escape from the garden or wriggle out of his collar and run away from you. However, when it comes to Shibas, escape is a part of life and accidents can happen. If this unfortunate event should occur, the first thing on your mind will be finding him. Proper identification, including an ID tag, a tattoo and possibly a microchip, will increase the chances of his being returned to you safely and quickly. This is not an option for Shiba owners—it is a 'must'. It pays to be prepared. Your neighbours are key in helping you keep your Shiba alive and safe. Since the breed is so appealing and eye-catching, your neighbours will likely recognise the little tyke as yours. It pays to be considerate and friendly to all your neighbours as they can be part of your regular Shiba search crew.

IDENTIFICATION OPTIONS

As puppies become more and more expensive, especially those puppies of high quality for showing and/or breeding, they have a greater chance of being stolen. The usual collar dog tag is, of course, easily removed. But there are two techniques that have become widely used for identification.

The puppy microchip implantation involves the injection of a small microchip, about the size of a corn kernel, under the skin of the dog. If your dog shows up at a clinic or shelter, or is offered for resale under less than savoury circumstances, it can be positively identified by the microchip. The microchip is scanned and a registry quickly identifies you as the owner. This is not only protection against theft, but should the dog run away or go chasing a squirrel and get lost, you have a fair chance of getting it back.

Tattooing is done on various parts of the dog, from its belly to its cheeks. The number tattooed can be your telephone number or any other number which you can easily memorise. When professional dog thieves see a tattooed dog, they usually lose interest in it. Both microchipping and tattooing can be done at your local veterinary clinic. For the safety of our dogs, no laboratory facility or dog broker will accept a tattooed dog as stock.

PARENTAL GUIDANCE

Training a dog is a life experience. Many parents admit that much of what they know about raising children they learned from caring for their dogs. Dogs respond to love, fairness and guidance, just as children do. Become a good dog owner and you may become an even better parent.

Living with an untrained Shiba is a lot like owning a lovely Yamaha spinet piano that you do not know how to play—it is a nice object to look at but it does not do much more than that to bring you pleasure. Now try taking piano lessons and suddenly the piano comes alive and brings forth magical sounds and rhythms that set your heart singing and your body swaying.

The same is true with your Japanese Shiba. Any dog is a big responsibility and if not trained sensibly may develop unacceptable behaviour that annoys you or could even cause family friction. An untrained Shiba brings no joy to a home, but a trained Shiba offers his owner a lifetime of wondrous affection and amusement.

To train your Japanese Shiba, you may like to enrol in an obedience class. Teach him good manners as you learn how and why he behaves the way he does. Find out how to communicate with your dog and how to recognise and understand his communications with you. Suddenly the dog takes on a new role in your life—he is clever, interesting, well-behaved and fun to be with. He demonstrates his bond of devotion to you daily. Your Japanese Shiba will look up to you for guidance, and it is indeed a boast to your ego to know that such a perfect little creature thinks the world of you!

Those involved with teaching dog obedience and counselling owners about their dogs' behaviour have discovered some interesting facts about dog ownership. For example, training dogs when they are puppies results in the highest rate of success in developing well-mannered and well-adjusted adult dogs. Training an older dog, from six months to six years of age, can produce almost equal results providing that the owner accepts the dog's slower rate of learning capability and is willing to work patiently to help the dog succeed at developing to his fullest potential. Unfortunately, many owners of untrained adult dogs lack the patience factor, so they do not persist until their dogs are successful at learning particular behaviours.

Training a puppy aged 10 to 16 weeks (20 weeks at the most) is like working with a dry sponge in a pool of water. The pup soaks up whatever you show him and constantly looks for more things to do and learn. At this early age, his body is not yet producing hormones, and therein lies the reason for such a high rate of

REAP THE REWARDS

If you start with a normal, healthy dog and give him time, patience and some carefully executed lessons, you will reap the rewards of that training for the life of the dog. And what a life it will be! The two of you will find immeasurable pleasure in the companionship you have built together with love, respect and understanding.

Young puppies, before they reach the age of puberty, are the most impressionable and therefore easier to train. Once the pup begins to rely upon his new owner, instead of his dam, for guidance, he is ready to learn about the world around him.

success. Without hormones, he is focused on his owners and not particularly interested in investigating other places, dogs, people, etc. You are his leader: his provider of food, water, shelter and security. He latches onto you and wants to stay close. He will usually follow you from room to room, will not let you out of his sight when you are outdoors with him and will respond in like manner to the people and animals you encounter. If you greet a friend warmly, he will be happy to greet the person as well. If, however, you are hesitant, even anxious, about the approach of a stranger, he will respond accordingly.

Once the puppy begins to produce hormones, his natural curiosity emerges and he begins to investigate the world around him. It is at this time when you may notice that the untrained dog begins to wander away from you and even ignore your commands to stay close. When this behaviour becomes a problem, the owner has two choices: get rid of the dog or train him. It is strongly urged that you choose the latter option.

There are usually classes within a reasonable distance from the owner's home, but you can also do a lot to train your dog yourself. Sometimes there are classes available but the tuition is too costly. Whatever the circumstances, the solution to the

THE GOLDEN RULE

The golden rule of dog training is simple. For each 'question' (command), there is only one correct answer (reaction). One command = one reaction. Keep practising the command until the dog reacts correctly without hesitating. Be repetitive but not monotonous. Dogs get bored just as people do!

problem of lack of lesson availability lies within the pages of this book.

This chapter is devoted to helping you train your Japanese Shiba at home. If the recommended procedures are followed faithfully, you may expect positive results that will prove rewarding both to you and your dog. The key to training a Shiba is consistency—you must commit to the time, set up a schedule and follow it faithfully. Shibas need structure and welcome the regularity of a routine. They do not like monotonous repetition, even for the tastiest treats, and will not repeat a behaviour *ad nauseum*, as would a retriever or shepherd.

Whether your new charge is a puppy or a mature adult, the methods of teaching and the techniques we use in training basic behaviours are the same. After all, no dog, whether puppy or adult, likes harsh or inhumane methods. All creatures, however, respond favourably to gentle motivational methods and sincere praise and encouragement. Now let us get started.

TOILET TRAINING

You can train a puppy to relieve itself wherever you choose, but this must be somewhere suitable. You should bear in mind from the outset that when your puppy is

FAMILY TIES

If you have other pets in the home and/or interact often with the pets of friends and other family members, your dog will respond to those pets in much the same manner as you do. It is only when you show fear of or resentment toward another animal that he will act fearful or unfriendly.

More motivated by food than a burning desire to please their owners, Shibas will respond to basic bribes without any injury to their considerable pride. This Shiba doesn't mind the down position as long as she gets to nibble something tasty!

old enough to go out in public places, any canine deposits must be removed at once. You will always have to carry with you a small plastic bag or 'poop-scoop.'

Outdoor training includes such surfaces as grass, soil and cement. Indoor training usually means training your dog to newspaper.

When deciding on the surface and location that you will want your Japanese Shiba to use, be sure it is going to be permanent. Training your dog to grass and then changing your mind two months later is extremely difficult for both dog and owner.

Next, choose the command you will use each and every time you want your puppy to void. 'Hurry up' and 'Toilet' are examples of commands commonly used by dog owners.

Get in the habit of giving the puppy your chosen relief

command before you take him out. That way, when he becomes an adult, you will be able to determine if he wants to go out when you ask him. A confirmation will be signs of interest, wagging his tail, watching you intently, going to the door, etc.

CANINE DEVELOPMENT SCHEDULE

It is important to understand how and at what age a puppy develops into adulthood. If you are a puppy owner, consult the following Canine Development Schedule to determine the stage of development your puppy is currently experiencing. This knowledge will help you as you work with the puppy in the weeks and months ahead.

Period	Age	Characteristics
FIRST TO THIRD	**BIRTH TO SEVEN WEEKS**	Puppy needs food, sleep and warmth, and responds to simple and gentle touching. Needs mother for security and disciplining. Needs littermates for learning and interacting with other dogs. Pup learns to function within a pack and learns pack order of dominance. Begin socialising with adults and children for short periods. Begins to become aware of its environment.
FOURTH	**EIGHT TO TWELVE WEEKS**	Brain is fully developed. Needs socialising with outside world. Remove from mother and littermates. Needs to change from canine pack to human pack. Human dominance necessary. Fear period occurs between 8 and 12 weeks. Avoid fright and pain.
FIFTH	**THIRTEEN TO SIXTEEN WEEKS**	Training and formal obedience should begin. Less association with other dogs, more with people, places, situations. Period will pass easily if you remember this is pup's change-to-adolescence time. Be firm and fair. Flight instinct prominent. Permissiveness and over-disciplining can do permanent damage. Praise for good behaviour.
JUVENILE	**FOUR TO EIGHT MONTHS**	Another fear period about 7 to 8 months of age. It passes quickly, but be cautious of fright and pain. Sexual maturity reached. Dominant traits established. Dog should understand sit, down, come and stay by now.

NOTE: THESE ARE APPROXIMATE TIME FRAMES. ALLOW FOR INDIVIDUAL DIFFERENCES IN PUPPIES.

TAKE THE LEAD
Do not carry your dog to his toilet area. Lead him there on a leash or, better yet, encourage him to follow you to the spot. If you start carrying him to his spot, you might end up doing this routine forever and your dog will have the satisfaction of having trained YOU.

for example, and always immediately after sleeping and eating. The older the puppy, the less often he will need to relieve himself. Finally, as a mature healthy adult, he will require only three to five relief trips per day.

TOILETING TIP
Most of all, be consistent. Always take your dog to the same location, always use the same command, and always have him on lead when he is in his relief area, unless a fenced-in garden is available.

By following the Success Method, your puppy will be completely housetrained by the time his muscle and brain development reach maturity. Keep in mind that small breeds usually mature faster than large breeds, but all puppies should be trained by six months of age.

Get in the habit of walking your Shiba daily, even if you have a fenced garden. For house-training purposes, a daily walk ensures that the owner knows if and when his dog is relieving himself.

PUPPY'S NEEDS

Puppy needs to relieve himself after play periods, after each meal, after he has been sleeping and at any time he indicates that he is looking for a place to urinate or defecate.

The urinary and intestinal tract muscles of very young puppies are not fully developed. Therefore, like human babies, puppies need to relieve themselves frequently.

Take your puppy out often—every hour for an eight-week-old,

> **ATTENTION!**
> Your dog is actually training you at the same time you are training him. Dogs do things to get attention. They usually repeat whatever succeeds in getting your attention.

HOUSING

Since the types of housing and control you provide for your puppy have a direct relationship on the success of housetraining, we consider the various aspects of both before we begin training.

Taking a new puppy home and turning him loose in your house can be compared to turning a child loose in a sports arena and telling the child that the place is all his! The sheer enormity of the place would be too much for him to handle.

Instead, offer the puppy clearly defined areas where he can play, sleep, eat and live. A room of the house where the family gathers is the most obvious choice. Puppies are social animals and need to feel a part of the pack right from the start. Hearing your voice, watching you while you are doing things and smelling you nearby are all positive reinforcers that he is now a member of your pack. Usually a family room, the kitchen or a nearby adjoining breakfast area is ideal for providing safety and security for both puppy and owner.

Within that room there should be a smaller area that the puppy can call his own. An alcove, a wire dog crate or a fenced (not boarded!) corner from which he can view the activities of his new family will be fine. The size of the area or crate is the key factor here. The crate or area must be large enough for the puppy to lie down and stretch out as well as stand up without rubbing his head on the top, yet small enough so that he cannot relieve himself at one end and sleep at the other without coming into contact with his droppings until fully trained to relieve himself outside.

Dogs are, by nature, clean animals and will not remain close to their relief areas unless forced to do so. In those cases, they then become dirty dogs and usually remain that way for life.

The designated area should

Establish house rules with your Japanese Shiba puppy from the very beginning. This pup has the full run of the house, including sitting on the family sofa. Shibas respond to structure, so make your intentions clear.

Activity naturally triggers the dog's need to relieve himself. After a run around the garden, which in Shiba language we call 'the crazies,' your dog will need to find a place to relieve himself.

contain clean bedding and a toy. Water must always be available, in a non-spill container.

CONTROL

By control, we mean helping the puppy to create a lifestyle pattern that will be compatible to that of his human pack (YOU!). Just as we guide little children to learn our way of life, we must show the puppy when it is time to play, eat, sleep, exercise and even entertain himself.

Your puppy should always sleep in his crate. He should also learn that, during times of household confusion and excessive human activity such as at breakfast when family members are preparing for the day, he can play by himself in relative safety and comfort in his designated area. Each time you leave the puppy alone, he should understand exactly where he is to stay. Puppies are chewers. They cannot tell the difference between lamp cords, television wires, shoes, table legs, etc. Chewing into a television wire, for example, can be fatal to the puppy while a shorted wire can start a fire in the house.

If the puppy chews on the arm of the chair when he is alone, you will probably discipline him angrily when you get home. Thus, he makes the association that your coming home means he is going to be punished. (He will not remember chewing the chair and is incapable of making the association of the discipline with his naughty deed.)

Other times of excitement, such as family parties, etc., can be fun for the puppy providing he can view the activities from the security of his designated area. He is not underfoot and he is not being fed all sorts of titbits that will probably cause him stomach distress, yet he still feels a part of the fun.

SCHEDULE

A puppy should be taken to his relief area each time he is released from his designated area, after meals, after a play session and when he first awakens in the morning (at age eight weeks, this

HOW MANY TIMES A DAY?

AGE	RELIEF TRIPS
To 14 weeks	10
14–22 weeks	8
22–32 weeks	6
Adulthood	4
(dog stops growing)	

These are estimates, of course, but they are a guide to the MINIMUM opportunities a dog should have each day to relieve itself.

can mean 5 a.m.!). The puppy will indicate that he's ready 'to go' by circling or sniffing busily—do not misinterpret these signs. For a puppy less than ten weeks of age, a routine of taking him out every hour is necessary. As the puppy grows, he will be able to wait for longer periods of time.

Keep trips to his relief area short. Stay no more than five or six minutes and then return to the house. If he goes during that time, praise him lavishly and take him indoors immediately. If he does not, but he has an accident when you go back indoors, pick him up immediately, say 'No! No!' and return to his relief area. Wait a few minutes, then return to the house again. Never hit a puppy or rub his face in urine or excrement when he has had an accident! Shibas have long memories and do not respond to physical correction. You will injure your Shiba's

trust, a most precious gift from any noble animal.

Once indoors, put the puppy in his crate until you have had time to clean up his accident. Then release him to the family area and watch him more closely than before. Chances are, his accident was a result of your not picking up his signal or waiting too long before offering him the opportunity to relieve himself. Never hold a grudge against the puppy for accidents.

Let the puppy learn that going outdoors means it is time to relieve himself, not play. Once trained, he will be able to play indoors and out and still differentiate between the times for play versus the times for relief.

Help him develop regular hours for naps, being alone, playing by himself and just

A dog that is trained to relieve herself on grass will always seek out that surface. Adult dogs need to be given access to the relief area about four times a day.

resting, all in his crate. Encourage him to entertain himself while you are busy with your activities. Let him learn that having you near is comforting, but it is not your main purpose in life to provide him with undivided attention.

Each time you put a puppy in his own area, use the same command, whatever suits best.

Soon he will run to his crate or special area when he hears you say those words.

THE SUCCESS METHOD

Success that comes by luck is usually short lived. Success that comes by well-thought-out proven methods is often more easily achieved and permanent. This is the Success Method. It is designed to give you, the puppy owner, a simple yet proven way to help your puppy develop clean living habits and a feeling of security in his new environment.

THE SUCCESS METHOD

1 Tell the puppy 'Crate time!' and place him in the crate with a small treat (a piece of cheese or half of a biscuit). Let him stay in the crate for five minutes while you are in the same room. Then release him and praise lavishly. Never release him when he is fussing. Wait until he is quiet before you let him out.

2 Repeat Step 1 several times a day.

3 The next day, place the puppy in the crate as before. Let him stay there for ten minutes. Do this several times.

4 Continue building time in five-minute increments until the puppy stays in his crate for 30 minutes with you in the room. Always take him to his relief area after prolonged periods in his crate.

5 Now go back to Step 1 and let the puppy stay in his crate for five minutes, this time while you are out of the room.

6 Once again, build crate time in five-minute increments with you out of the room. When the puppy will stay willingly in his crate (he may even fall asleep!) for 30 minutes with you out of the room, he will be ready to stay in it for several hours at a time.

6 Steps to Successful Crate Training

Crate training provides safety for you, the puppy and the home. It also provides the puppy with a feeling of security, and that helps the puppy achieve self-confidence and clean habits.

Remember that one of the primary ingredients in housetraining your puppy is control. Regardless of your lifestyle, there will always be occasions when you will need to have a place where your dog can stay and be happy and safe. Crate training is the answer for now and in the future.

In conclusion, a few key elements are really all you need for a successful housetraining method—consistency, frequency, praise, control and supervision. By following these procedures

Always clean up after your Shiba, whether you are in a public place or your own garden.

with a normal, healthy puppy, you and the puppy will soon be past the stage of 'accidents' and ready to move on to a full and rewarding life together.

TRAINING EQUIPMENT

COLLAR AND LEAD

For a Japanese Shiba, the collar and lead that you use for training must be one with which you are easily able to work, not too heavy for the dog and perfectly safe. Be sure that the collar is sturdy and fits properly, as Shibas are good at wriggling their way out of their collars. Check the tightness of the collar daily. Young Shibas grow fast: the collar should be snug, but not tight.

THE CLEAN LIFE

By providing sleeping and resting quarters that fit the dog, and offering frequent opportunities to relieve himself outside his quarters, the puppy quickly learns that the outdoors (or the newspaper if you are training him to paper) is the place to go when he needs to urinate or defecate. It also reinforces his innate desire to keep his sleeping quarters clean. This, in turn, helps develop the muscle control that will eventually produce a dog with clean living habits.

An open crate is fine for inside your home. For puppies, however, never put the water bowl inside the crate.

to beg at the table—the only way to teach a dog to beg at the table is to give him food from the table. In training, rewarding the dog with a food treat will help him associate praise and the treats with learning new behaviours that obviously please his owner.

TRAINING BEGINS: ASK THE DOG A QUESTION

In order to teach your dog anything, you must first get his attention. After all, he cannot learn anything if he is looking away from you with his mind on something else.

To get his attention, ask him, 'School?' and immediately walk over to him and give him a treat as you tell him 'Good dog.' Wait a minute or two and repeat the routine, this time with a treat in your hand as you approach within a foot of the dog. Do not go directly to him, but stop about a foot short of him and hold out the treat as you ask, 'School?' He will see you approaching with a treat in your hand and most likely begin walking toward you. As you meet, give him the treat and praise again.

The third time, ask the question, have a treat in your hand and walk only a short distance toward the dog so that he must walk almost all the way to you. As he reaches you, give him the treat and praise again.

By this time, the dog will

A training collar is effective for the Shiba, though make sure you understand how to use the collar before putting it on your dog.

TREATS

Most Shibas are easily bribed! Food holds a special place in the heart of every Shiba. Have a bag of treats on hand. Something nutritious and easy to swallow works best. Use a soft treat, a chunk of cheese or a piece of cooked chicken rather than a dry biscuit. By the time the dog has finished chewing a dry treat, he will forget why he is being rewarded in the first place! Using food rewards will not teach a dog

probably be getting the idea that if he pays attention to you, especially when you ask that question, it will pay off in treats and enjoyable activities for him. In other words, he learns that 'school' means doing great things with you that are fun and result in positive attention for him.

Remember that the dog does not understand your verbal language; he only recognises sounds. Your question translates to a series of sounds for him, and those sounds become the signal to go to you and pay attention; if he does, he will get to interact with you plus receive treats and praise.

THE BASIC COMMANDS

TEACHING SIT

Now that you have the dog's attention, attach his lead and hold it in your left hand and a food treat in your right. Place your food hand at the dog's nose and let him lick the treat but not take it from you. Say 'Sit' and slowly raise your food hand from in front of the dog's nose up over his head so that he is looking at the ceiling.

> **OPEN MINDS**
> Dogs are as different from each other as people are. What works for one dog may not work for another. Have an open mind. If one method of training is unsuccessful, try another.

As he bends his head upward, he will have to bend his knees to maintain his balance. As he bends his knees, he will assume a sit position. At that point, release the food treat and praise lavishly with comments such as 'Good dog! Good sit!,' etc. Remember to always praise enthusiastically, because dogs relish verbal praise from their owners and feel so proud of themselves whenever they accomplish a behaviour.

You will not use food forever in getting the dog to obey your commands. Food is only used to teach new behaviours, and once the dog knows what you want when you give a specific command, you will wean him off the food treats but still maintain

When teaching the Shiba to sit, a little pressure on the stubborn end of the dog may give her the idea of what is expected. You can probably teach your Shiba to sit in one or two lessons.

appreciate being placed in a subordinate position. These are naturally dominant dogs that exude an air of superiority. Shibas feel superior to other dogs and wish to be perceived by their owners as equals. It takes a very crafty owner to convince a Shiba to 'down,' but it is indeed possible. Consistency and respect lead the way.

Have the dog sit close alongside your left leg, facing in the same direction as you are. Hold the lead in your left hand and a food treat in your right. Now place your left hand lightly on the top of the dog's shoulders where they meet above the spinal cord. Do not push down on the dog's shoulders; simply rest your left hand there so you can guide the dog to lie down close to your left leg rather than to swing away from your side when he drops. Many Shibas resent handling and owners must earn such 'familiarity.'

Now place the food hand at the dog's nose, say 'Down' very softly (almost a whisper), and slowly lower the food hand to the dog's front feet. When the food hand reaches the floor, begin moving it forward along the floor in front of the dog. Keep talking softly to the dog, saying things like, 'Do you want this treat? You can do this, good dog.' Your reassuring tone of voice will help calm the dog as he tries to follow

Practise the sit exercise with your Shiba a few times. Do not torture your Shiba with endless repetitions, or she'll bore of your routine.

the verbal praise. After all, you will always have your voice with you, and there will be many times when you have no food rewards but expect the dog to obey.

TEACHING DOWN

Teaching the down exercise is easy when you understand how the dog perceives the down position, and it is very difficult when you do not. Dogs perceive the down position as a submissive one, therefore teaching the down exercise using a forceful method can sometimes make the dog develop such a fear of the down that he either runs away when you say 'Down' or he attempts to snap at the person who tries to force him down. Japanese dogs in particular do not

the food hand in order to get the treat.

When the dog's elbows touch the floor, release the food and praise softly. Try to get the dog to maintain that down position for several seconds before you let him sit up again. The goal here is to get the dog to settle down and not feel threatened in the down position.

TEACHING STAY

It is easy to teach the dog to stay in either a sit or a down position. Again, we use food and praise during the teaching process as we help the dog to understand exactly what it is that we are expecting him to do.

To teach the sit/stay, start with the dog sitting on your left side as before and hold the lead in your left hand. Have a food treat in your right hand and place your food hand at the dog's nose. Say 'Stay' and step out on your right foot to stand directly in front of the dog, toe to toe, as he licks and nibbles the treat. Be sure to keep his head facing upward to maintain the sit position. Count to five and then swing around to stand next to the dog again with him on your left. As soon as you get back to the original position, release the food and praise lavishly.

To teach the down/stay, do the down as previously described. As soon as the dog lies down, say

FEAR AGGRESSION

Pups who are subjected to physical abuse during training commonly end up with behavioural problems as adults. One common result of abuse is fear aggression, in which a dog will lash out, bare his teeth, snarl and finally bite someone by whom he feels threatened. For example, your daughter may be playing with the dog one afternoon. As they play hide-and-seek, she backs the dog into a corner, and as she attempts to tease him playfully, he bites her hand. Examine the cause of this behaviour. Did your daughter ever hit the dog? Did someone who resembles your daughter hit or scream at the dog? Fortunately, fear aggression is relatively easy to correct. Have your daughter engage in only positive activities with the dog, such as feeding, petting and walking. She should not give any corrections or negative feedback. If the dog still growls or cowers away from her, allow someone else to accompany them. After approximately one week, the dog should feel that he can rely on her for many positive things, and he will also be prevented from reacting fearfully towards anyone who might resemble her.

'Stay' and step out on your right foot just as you did in the sit/stay. Count to five and then return to stand beside the dog with him on your left side. Release the treat and praise as always.

Within a week or ten days, you can begin to add a bit of distance between you and your dog when you leave him. When you do, use your left hand open

Once you have accomplished the down command, the down-stay requires little more than the right tone of voice and your Shiba's indulgence.

with the palm facing the dog as a stay signal, much the same as the hand signal a constable uses to stop traffic at an intersection. Hold the food treat in your right hand as before, but this time the food is not touching the dog's nose. He will watch the food hand and quickly learn that he is going to get that treat as soon as you return to his side.

When you can stand 1 metre away from your dog for 30 seconds, you can then begin building time and distance in both stays. Eventually, the dog

DOUBLE JEOPARDY

A dog in jeopardy never lies down. He stays alert on his feet because instinct tells him that he may have to run away or fight for his survival. Therefore, if a dog feels threatened or anxious, he will not lie down. Consequently, it is important to have the dog calm and relaxed as he learns the down exercise.

can be expected to remain in the stay position for prolonged periods of time until you return to him or call him to you. Always praise lavishly when he stays.

TEACHING COME

If you make teaching 'come' an exciting experience, you should

'NO' MEANS 'NO!'

Dogs do not understand our language. They can be trained to react to a certain sound, at a certain volume. If you say 'No, Oliver' in a very soft pleasant voice it will not have the same meaning as 'No, Oliver!!' when you shout it as loud as you can. You should never use the dog's name during a reprimand, just the command NO!! Since dogs don't understand words, comics often use dogs trained with opposite meanings. Thus, when the comic commands his dog to SIT the dog will stand up, and vice versa.

PRACTICE MAKES PERFECT!

- Have training lessons with your dog every day in several short segments—three to five times a day for a few minutes at a time is ideal.
- Do not have long practice sessions. The dog will become easily bored.
- Never practise when you are tired, ill, worried or in an otherwise negative mood. This will transmit to the dog and may have an adverse effect on its performance.

Think fun, short and above all POSITIVE! End each session on a high note, rather than a failed exercise, and make sure to give a lot of praise. Enjoy the training and help your dog enjoy it, too.

CONSISTENCY PAYS OFF

Dogs need consistency in their feeding schedule, exercise and toilet breaks and in the verbal commands you use. If you use 'Stay' on Monday and 'Stay here, please' on Tuesday, you will confuse your dog. Don't demand perfect behaviour during training classes and then let him have the run of the house the rest of the day. Above all, lavish praise on your pet consistently every time he does something right. The more he feels he is pleasing you, the more willing he will be to learn.

never have a 'student' that does not love the game or that fails to come when called. The secret, it seems, is never to teach the word 'come.' Since Shibas seem to never hear the word 'come,' it pays to find other ways of coercing them to return to you!

At times when an owner most wants his dog to come when called, the owner is likely to be upset or anxious and he allows these feelings to come through in the tone of his voice when he calls his dog. Hearing that desperation in his owner's voice, the dog fears the results of going to him and therefore either disobeys outright or runs in the opposite direction. The secret, therefore, is to teach the dog a game and,

when you want him to come to you, simply play the game. It is practically a no-fail solution!

To begin, have several members of your family take a few food treats and each go into a different room in the house. Take turns calling the dog, and each person should celebrate the dog's finding him with a treat and lots of happy praise. When a person calls the dog, he is actually

'WHERE ARE YOU?'
When calling the dog, do not say 'Come.' Say things like, 'Rover, where are you? See if you can find me! I have a biscuit for you!' Keep up a constant line of chatter with coaxing sounds and frequent questions such as, 'Where are you?' The dog will learn to follow the sound of your voice to locate you and receive his reward.

inviting the dog to find him and get a treat as a reward for 'winning.'

A few turns of the 'Where are you?' game and the dog will understand that everyone is playing the game and that each person has a big celebration awaiting his success at locating them. Once he learns to love the game, simply calling out 'Where are you?' will bring him running from wherever he is when he hears that all-important question.

The come command is recognised as one of the most important things to teach a dog, but there are trainers who work with thousands of dogs and never teach the actual word 'Come.' Yet these dogs will race to respond to a person who uses the dog's name followed by 'Where are you?' For example, a woman has a 12-year-old companion dog who went blind, but who never fails to locate her owner when asked, 'Where are you?'

Children, in particular, love to play this game with their dogs. Children can hide in smaller places like a shower or bath, behind a bed or under a table. The dog needs to work a little bit harder to find these hiding places, but when he does he loves to celebrate with a treat and a tussle with a favourite youngster.

For your Shiba's safety, the 'come' command deserves special effort on the owner's part. Given the breed's propensity to flee at every opportunity, having a Shiba that actually responds to an owner's cries of 'Where are you?' or any other phrase is a true lifesaver. When your Shiba comes running back to you, it is cause of true celebration—you might even consider hosting a parade in his honour!

TEACHING HEEL

Heeling means that the dog walks beside the owner without pulling. It takes time and patience on the owner's part to succeed at teaching the dog that he (the owner) will not proceed unless the dog is walking calmly beside him. Pulling out ahead on the lead is definitely not acceptable.

Begin by holding the lead in your left hand as the dog sits beside your left leg. Move the loop end of the lead to your right hand but keep your left hand short on the lead so it keeps the dog in close next to you.

Say 'Heel' and step forward on your left foot. Keep the dog close to you and take three steps. Stop and have the dog sit next to you in what we now call the 'heel position.' Praise verbally, but do not touch the dog. Hesitate a moment and begin again with 'Heel,' taking three steps and stopping, at which point the dog is told to sit again.

Your goal here is to have the dog walk those three steps

'COME' . . . BACK
Never call your dog to come to you for a correction or scold him when he reaches you. That is the quickest way to turn a 'Come' command into 'Go away fast!' Dogs think only in the present tense, and your dog will connect the scolding with coming to you, not with the misbehaviour of a few moments earlier.

without pulling on the lead. Once he will walk calmly beside you for three steps without pulling, increase the number of steps you take to five. When he will walk politely beside you while you take five steps, you can increase the length of your walk to ten steps. Keep increasing the length of your stroll until the dog will walk quietly beside you without pulling as long as you want him to heel. When you stop heeling, indicate to the dog that the exercise is over by verbally praising as you pet him and say

---

TUG OF WALK?
If you begin teaching the heel by taking long walks and letting the dog pull you along, he misinterprets this action as an acceptable form of taking a walk. When you pull back on the lead to counteract his pulling, he reads that tug as a signal to pull even harder!

'OK, good dog.' The 'OK' is used as a release word meaning that the exercise is finished and the dog is free to relax.

If you are dealing with a dog who insists on pulling you around, simply 'put on your brakes' and stand your ground until the dog realises that the two of you are not going anywhere until he is beside you and moving at your pace, not his. It may take some time just standing there to convince the dog that you are the leader and you will be the one to decide on the direction and speed of your travel.

Each time the dog looks up at you or slows down to give a slack lead between the two of you, quietly praise him and say, 'Good heel. Good dog.' Eventually, the dog will begin to respond and within a few days he will be walking politely beside you without pulling on the lead. At first, the training sessions should be kept short and very positive; soon the dog will be able to walk nicely with you for increasingly longer distances. Remember also to give the dog free time and the opportunity to run and play when you have finished heel practice.

WEANING OFF FOOD IN TRAINING
Food is used in training new behaviours. Once the dog understands what behaviour goes with a specific command, it is time to start weaning him off the

food treats. At first, give a treat after each exercise. Then, start to give a treat only after every other exercise. Mix up the times when you offer a food reward and the times when you only offer praise so that the dog will never know when he is going to receive both food and praise and when he is going to receive only praise. This is called a variable ratio reward system and it proves successful because there is always the chance that the owner will produce a treat, so the dog never stops trying for that reward. No matter what, ALWAYS give verbal praise.

OBEDIENCE CLASSES

It is a good idea to enrol in an obedience class if one is available in your area. If yours is a show dog, ringcraft classes would be more appropriate. Many areas have dog clubs that offer basic obedience training as well as preparatory classes for obedience competition. There are also local dog trainers who offer similar classes.

At working trials, dogs can earn titles at various levels of competition. The beginning levels of competition include basic behaviours such as sit, down, heel, etc. The more advanced levels of competition include jumping, retrieving, scent discrimination and signal work. The advanced levels require a dog and owner to put a lot of time and effort into their training and the titles that can be earned at these levels of competition are very prestigious.

HOW TO WEAN THE 'TREAT HOG'

If you have trained your dog by rewarding him with a treat each time he performs a command, he may soon decide that without the treat, he won't sit, stay or come. The best way to fix this problem is to start asking your dog to do certain commands twice before being rewarded. Slowly increase the number of commands given and then vary the number: three sits and a treat one day, five sits for a biscuit the next day. Your dog will soon realise that there is no set number of sits before he gets his reward, and he'll likely do it the first time you ask in the hope of being rewarded sooner rather than later.

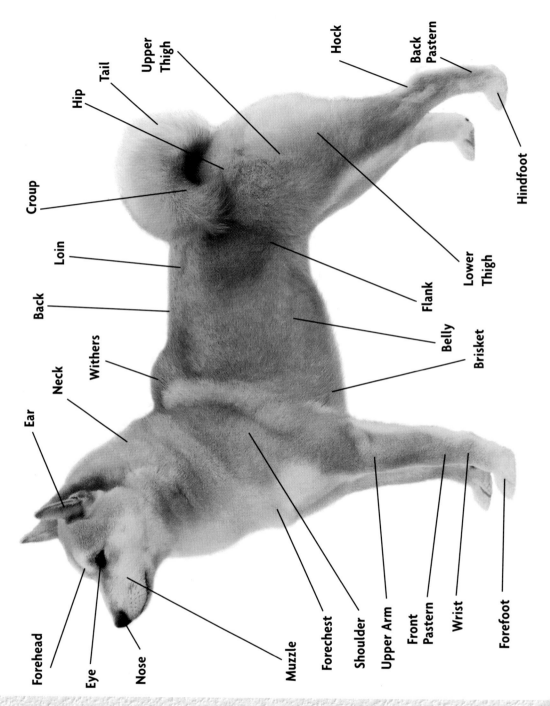

PHYSICAL STRUCTURE OF THE JAPANESE SHIBA

Health Care of Your

JAPANESE SHIBA

Your choice of the Shiba Inu offers you many rewards, not the least of which is the breed's hardiness and longevity. There is nothing physically exaggerated about the Shiba, a natural breed that exhibits a near wolf-like form, complete with pointed muzzle, weather-proof plumage and erect, hooded ears. It's not too often a wolf needs a vet, and most Shibas rarely see the vet. The author's veterinary surgeon claims that if all his clients owned Shiba-Inus, he would be out of business!

With proper care and veterinary assistance, the Shiba-Inu can live to be an active and healthy teenager. The average lifespan of the Shiba is about 15 years, though some lucky Shibas have lived to 17 with consistent good health.

Nonetheless, an owner must be aware of the possible problems that can arise with any dog, even a dog as resilient as the Shiba. It must be pointed out, though, that some Shibas are worriers and, as a result, suffer from recurrent problems. Among the most common of these are ear infections, hot spots (acute moist dermatitis) and inhalant allergies, usually associated with summer

grasses and pollen. The well-versed owner is always ready to combat these nuisance problems, which can usually be handled at home.

SELECTING A VETERINARY SURGEON
Your selection of a veterinary surgeon should not be based upon personality (as most are) but upon their convenience to your home. You want a vet who is close because you might have emergencies or need to make multiple visits for treatments. You want a vet who has services that you might require such as tattooing and grooming, as well as sophisticated pet supplies and a good reputation for ability and responsiveness. There is nothing more frustrating than having to wait a day or more to get a response from your veterinary surgeon.

All veterinary surgeons are licensed and their diplomas and/or certificates should be displayed in their waiting rooms. There are, however, many veterinary specialities that usually require further studies and internships. There are specialists in heart problems (veterinary cardiologists), skin problems (veterinary dermatologists), teeth

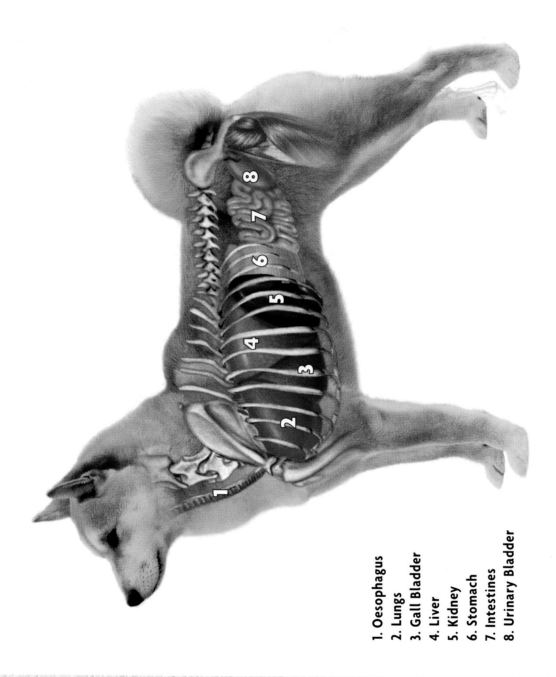

1. Oesophagus
2. Lungs
3. Gall Bladder
4. Liver
5. Kidney
6. Stomach
7. Intestines
8. Urinary Bladder

INTERNAL ORGANS OF THE JAPANESE SHIBA

Breakdown of Veterinary Income by Category

%	Category
2%	Dentistry
4%	Radiology
12%	Surgery
15%	Vaccinations
19%	Laboratory
23%	Examinations
25%	Medicines

and gum problems (veterinary dentists), eye problems (veterinary ophthalmologists) and x-rays (veterinary radiologists), as well as vets who have specialities in bones, muscles or other organs. Most veterinary surgeons do routine surgery such as neutering, stitching up wounds and docking tails for those breeds in which such is required for show purposes. When the problem affecting your dog is serious, it is not unusual or impudent to get another medical opinion, although in Britain you are obliged to advise the vets concerned about this. You might

also want to compare costs among several veterinary surgeons. Sophisticated health care and veterinary services can be very costly. It is not infrequent that important decisions are based upon financial considerations.

PREVENTATIVE MEDICINE
It is much easier, less costly and more effective to practise preventative medicine than to fight bouts of illness and disease. Properly bred puppies come from parents who were selected based upon their genetic disease profile. Their mothers should have been vaccinated, free of all internal and external parasites and properly nourished. The dam can pass on disease resistance to her puppies, which can last for eight to ten weeks. She can also pass on parasites and many infections. That's why you should visit the veterinary surgeon who cared for the dam.

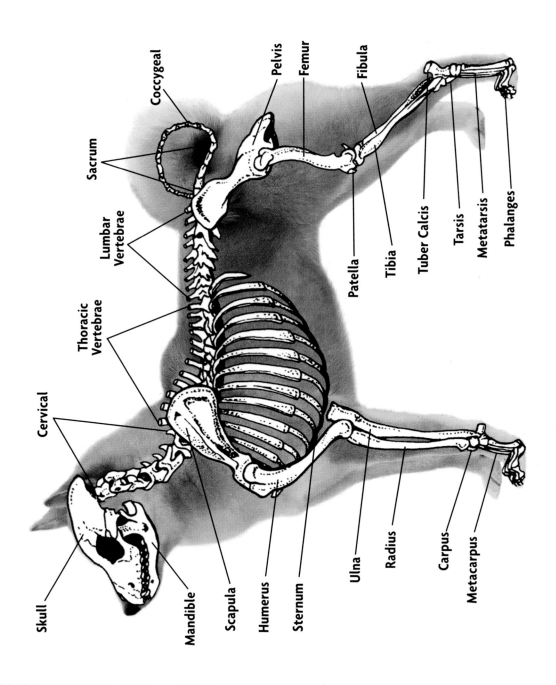

Coccygeal

Pelvis

Femur

Fibula

Sacrum

Lumbar Vertebrae

Patella

Tibia

Tuber Calcis

Tarsis

Metatarsis

Phalanges

Thoracic Vertebrae

Cervical

Skull

Mandible

Scapula

Humerus

Sternum

Ulna

Radius

Carpus

Metacarpus

SKELETAL STRUCTURE OF THE JAPANESE SHIBA

> **'P' STANDS FOR PROBLEM**
> Urinary tract disease is a serious condition that requires immediate medical attention. Symptoms include urinating in inappropriate places or the need to urinate frequently in small amounts. Urinary tract disease is most effectively treated with antibiotics. To help promote good urinary tract health, owners must always be sure that a constant supply of fresh water is available to their pets.

VACCINATION SCHEDULING

Most vaccinations are given by injection and should only be done by a veterinary surgeon. Both he and you should keep a record of the date of the injection, the identification of the vaccine and the amount given. Some vets give a first vaccination at eight weeks, but most dog breeders prefer the course not to commence until about ten weeks because of negating any antibodies passed on by the dam. The vaccination scheduling is usually based on a 15-day cycle. You must take your vet's advice regarding when to vaccinate as this may differ according to the vaccine used. Most vaccinations immunize your puppy against viruses.

The usual vaccines contain immunizing doses of several different viruses such as distemper, parvovirus, parainfluenza and hepatitis although some veterinary surgeons recommend separate vaccines for each disease. There are other vaccines available when the puppy is at risk. You should rely upon professional advice. This is especially true for the booster-shot programme. Most vaccination programmes require a booster when the puppy is a year old and once a year thereafter. In some cases, circumstances may require more or less frequent immunizations. Kennel cough, more formally known as tracheobronchitis, is treated with a vaccine that is sprayed into the dog's nostrils. Kennel cough is usually included in routine vaccination, but this is often not so effective as for other major diseases.

> **PARVO FOR THE COURSE**
> Canine parvovirus is a highly contagious disease that attacks puppies and older dogs. Spread through contact with infected faeces, parvovirus causes bloody diarrhoea, vomiting, heart damage, dehydration, shock and death. To prevent this tragedy, have your puppy begin his series of vaccinations at six to eight weeks. Be aware that the virus is easily spread and is carried on a dog's hair and feet, water bowls and other objects, as well as people's shoes and clothing.

HEALTH AND VACCINATION SCHEDULE

Age in Weeks:	6th	8th	10th	12th	14th	16th	20-24th	1 yr
Worm Control	✔	✔	✔	✔	✔	✔	✔	
Neutering								✔
Heartworm*		✔		✔		✔	✔	
Parvovirus	✔		✔		✔		✔	✔
Distemper		✔		✔		✔		✔
Hepatitis		✔		✔		✔		✔
Leptospirosis								✔
Parainfluenza	✔		✔		✔			
Dental Examination		✔					✔	✔
Complete Physical		✔					✔	✔
Coronavirus				✔			✔	✔
Kennel Cough	✔							
Hip Dysplasia								✔
Rabies*							✔	

Vaccinations are not instantly effective. It takes about two weeks for the dog's immune system to develop antibodies. Most vaccinations require annual booster shots. Your veterinary surgeon should guide you in this regard.
*Not applicable in the United Kingdom

WEANING TO FIVE MONTHS OLD
Puppies should be weaned by the time they are about two months old. A puppy that remains for at least eight weeks with its mother and littermates usually adapts better to other dogs and people later in its life.

Some new owners have their puppy examined by a veterinary surgeon immediately, which is a good idea. Vaccination programmes usually begin when the puppy is very young.

The puppy will have its teeth examined and have its skeletal conformation and general health checked prior to certification by the veterinary surgeon. Puppies may have problems with their kneecaps, cataracts and other eye problems, heart murmurs and undescended testicles. They may also have personality problems and your veterinary surgeon might have training in temperament evaluation.

FIVE TO TWELVE MONTHS OF AGE
Unless you intend to breed or show your dog, neutering the puppy at six months of age is

recommended. Discuss this with your veterinary surgeon. Neutering has proven to be extremely beneficial to both male and female puppies. Besides eliminating the possibility of pregnancy, it inhibits (but does not prevent) breast cancer in bitches and prostate cancer in male dogs. Under no circum-stances should a bitch be spayed prior to her first season.

Your veterinary surgeon should provide your puppy with a thorough dental evaluation at six

months of age, ascertaining whether all the permanent teeth have erupted properly. A home dental care regimen should be initiated at six months, including brushing weekly and providing good dental devices (such as nylon bones). Regular dental care promotes healthy teeth, fresh breath and a longer life.

ONE TO SEVEN YEARS
Once a year, your grown dog should visit the vet for an examination and vaccination

DISEASE REFERENCE CHART

	What is it?	What causes it?	Symptoms
Leptospirosis	Severe disease that affects the internal organs; can be spread to people.	A bacterium, which is often carried by rodents, that enters through mucous membranes and spreads quickly throughout the body.	Range from fever, vomiting and loss of appetite in less severe cases to shock, irreversible kidney damage and possibly death in most severe cases.
Rabies	Potentially deadly virus that infects warm-blooded mammals. Not seen in United Kingdom.	Bite from a carrier of the virus, mainly wild animals.	1st stage: dog exhibits change in behaviour, fear. 2nd stage: dog's behaviour becomes more aggressive. 3rd stage: loss of coordination, trouble with bodily functions.
Parvovirus	Highly contagious virus, potentially deadly.	Ingestion of the virus, which is usually spread through the faeces of infected dogs.	Most common: severe diarrhoea. Also vomiting, fatigue, lack of appetite.
Kennel cough	Contagious respiratory infection.	Combination of types of bacteria and virus. Most common: *Bordetella bronchiseptica* bacteria and parainfluenza virus.	Chronic cough.
Distemper	Disease primarily affecting respiratory and nervous system.	Virus that is related to the human measles virus.	Mild symptoms such as fever, lack of appetite and mucous secretion progress to evidence of brain damage, 'hard pad.'
Hepatitis	Virus primarily affecting the liver.	Canine adenovirus type I (CAV-1). Enters system when dog breathes in particles.	Lesser symptoms include listlessness, diarrhoea, vomiting. More severe symptoms include 'blue-eye' (clumps of virus in eye).
Coronavirus	Virus resulting in digestive problems.	Virus is spread through infected dog's faeces.	Stomach upset evidenced by lack of appetite, vomiting, diarrhoea.

Normal hairs of a dog enlarged 200 times original size. The cuticle (outer covering) is clean and healthy. Unlike human hair that grows from the base, a dog's hair also grows from the end, as shown in the inset. Scanning electron micrographs by Dr Dennis Kunkel, University of Hawaii.

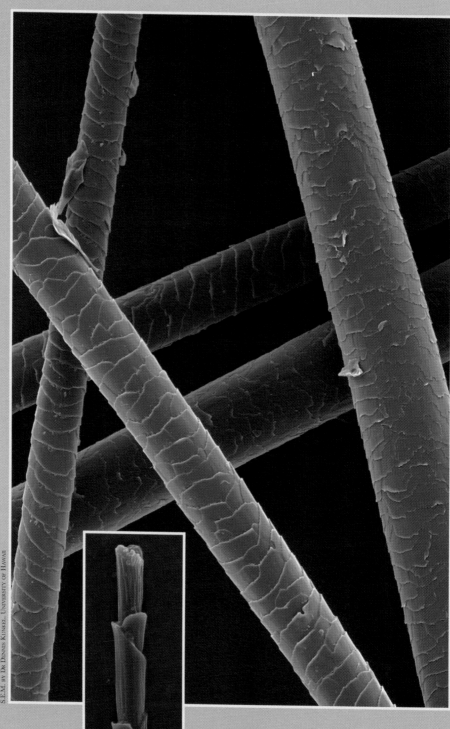

boosters, if needed. Some vets recommend blood tests, thyroid level check and dental evaluation to accompany these annual visits. A thorough clinical evaluation by the vet can provide critical background information for your dog. Blood tests are often performed at one year of age, and dental examinations around the third or fourth birthday. In the

PUPPY VACCINATIONS

Your veterinary surgeon will probably recommend that your puppy be vaccinated before you take him outside. There are airborne diseases, parasite eggs in the grass and unexpected visits from other dogs that might be dangerous to your puppy's health.

The Eyes Have It!

Eye disease is more prevalent amongst dogs than most people think, ranging from slight infections that are easily treated to serious complications that can lead to permanent sight loss. Eye diseases need veterinary attention in their early stages to prevent irreparable damage. This list provides descriptions of some common eye diseases:

Cataracts: Symptoms are white or grey discoloration of the eye lens and pupil, which causes fuzzy or completely obscured vision. Surgical treatment is required to remove the damaged lens and replace it with an artificial one.

Conjunctivitis: An inflammation of the mucous membrane that lines the eye socket, leaving the eyes red and puffy with excessive discharge. This condition is easily treated with antibiotics.

Corneal damage: The cornea is the transparent covering of the iris and pupil. Injuries are difficult to detect, but manifest themselves in surface abnormality, redness, pain and discharge. Most infections of the cornea are treated with antibiotics and require immediate medical attention.

Dry eye: This condition is caused by deficient production of tears that lubricate and protect the eye surface. A telltale sign is yellow-green discharge. Left undiagnosed, your dog will experience considerable pain, infections and possibly blindness. Dry eye is commonly treated with antibiotics, although more advanced cases may require surgery.

Glaucoma: This is caused by excessive fluid pressure in the eye. Symptoms are red eyes, grey or blue discoloration, pain, enlarged eyeballs and loss of vision. Antibiotics sometimes help, but surgery may be needed.

long run, quality preventative care for your pet can save money, teeth and lives.

SKIN PROBLEMS IN SHIBAS

Veterinary surgeons are consulted by dog owners for skin problems more than any other group of diseases or maladies. Dogs' skin is almost as sensitive as human skin and both suffer from almost the same ailments (though the occurrence of acne in dogs is rare!). For this reason, veterinary dermatology has developed into a speciality practised by many veterinary surgeons.

Since many skin problems have visual symptoms that are almost identical, it requires the skill of an experienced veterinary dermatologist to identify and cure many of the more severe skin disorders. Pet shops sell many treatments for skin problems but most of the treatments are directed at symptoms and not the underlying problem(s). If your dog is suffering from a skin disorder, you should seek professional assistance as quickly as possible. As with all diseases, the earlier a problem is identified and treated, the more successful is the cure.

PARASITE BITES

Many of us are allergic to insect bites. The bites itch, erupt and may even become infected. Dogs have the same reaction to fleas, ticks and/or mites. When an insect lands on you, you have the chance to whisk it away with your hand. Unfortunately, when your dog is bitten by a flea, tick or mite, it can only scratch it away or bite it. By the time the dog has been bitten, the parasite has done some of its damage. It may also

reactions to an outside stimulus. Auto-immune diseases cause serious damage to the tissues that are involved.

The best known auto-immune disease is lupus, which affects people as well as dogs. The symptoms are variable and may affect the kidneys, bones, blood chemistry and skin. It can be fatal to both dogs and humans, though it is not thought to be transmissible. It is usually successfully treated with cortisone, prednisone or a similar corticosteroid, but extensive use of these drugs can have harmful side effects.

HOT SPOTS

Shibas, like other double-coated breeds, have a tendency to suffer from hot spots, also known as acute moist dermatitis or pyotraumatic dermatitis. These nuisances usually occur on the dog's side, near his tail or on the tail itself. The dog tends to scratch, lick and

Your breeder should have begun the puppies' vaccination schedule at about six weeks of age. Discuss vaccinations, allergies and skin problems with your breeder to learn his perspective on these concerns for Shibas.

have laid eggs to cause further problems in the near future. The itching from parasite bites is probably due to the saliva injected into the site when the parasite sucks the dog's blood.

AUTO-IMMUNE SKIN CONDITIONS

Auto-immune skin conditions are commonly referred to as being allergic to yourself, while allergies are usually inflammatory

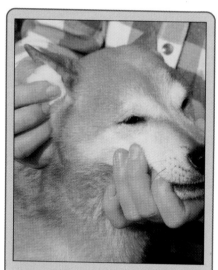

MANY KINDS OF EARS
Not every dog's ears are the same. Ears that are open to the air are healthier than ears with poor air circulation. Sometimes a dog can have two differently shaped ears. You should not probe inside your dog's ears. Only clean that which is accessible with a soft cotton wipe.

bite at a small spot on the coat, which eventually becomes a large, open wound. Hot spots frequently accompany flea infestation. It is also possible to develop a hot spot on the cheek or ear, due to an ear infection. Left untreated, a hot spot can become ulcerated, so owners must tend to them without delay. Your vet is best to handle this so that the hot spot doesn't become worse over time. It usually requires an injection with a corticosteroid as well as cleaning and shaving the surrounding area. An antibacterial ointment may be applied until the hot spot heals.

In addition to coat problems and ear infections, hot spots can also develop as a result of allergies, including inhalant allergies as well as food or flea allergies. Some breeders believe that hot spots can also be linked to leaving the Shiba's coat wet after a bath. Be sure to dry the dog's coat thoroughly, especially in the rump region and under the tail.

INHALANT ALLERGIES
Shibas can be susceptible to inhalant allergies, which in the past have been called grass allergies, though this is misleading. Dogs can be affected by breathing in various pollens and moulds (as well as everyday dust around the house). This leads to itching, which may be year-round (for mould spores and household dust) or seasonal (for weeds, pollen and grasses).

Humans have hay fever, rose fever and other fevers from which they suffer during the pollinating season. Many dogs suffer the same allergies. When the pollen count is high, your dog might suffer but don't expect him to sneeze and have a runny nose like humans. Dogs react to pollen allergies the same way they react to fleas—they scratch and bite themselves. Signs of inhalant allergies present themselves around one to three years of age, sometimes as early as six months of age. Scratching can lead to traumatised skin and hot spots. The allergy can be managed with antihistamines and cortisone-based preparations as well as medicated soothing baths.

FOOD PROBLEMS

FOOD ALLERGIES

Dogs are allergic to many foods that are best-sellers and highly

BE CAREFUL WHERE YOU WALK YOUR DOG

Dogs who have been exposed to lawns sprayed with herbicides have double and triple the rate of malignant lymphoma. Town dogs are especially at risk, as they are exposed to tailored lawns and gardens. Dogs perspire and absorb through their footpads. Be careful where your dog walks and always avoid any area that appears yellowed from chemical overspray.

DENTAL HEALTH

A dental examination is in order when the dog is between six months and one year of age so any permanent teeth that have erupted incorrectly can be corrected. It is important to begin a brushing routine, preferably using a two-sided brushing technique, whereby both sides of the tooth are brushed at the same time. Durable nylon and safe edible chews should be a part of your puppy's arsenal for good health, good teeth and pleasant breath. The vast majority of dogs three to four years old and older have diseases of the gums from lack of dental attention. Using the various types of dental chews can be very effective in controlling dental plaque.

Most Shiba pups are as resilient and healthy as the tiny bear cubs they resemble.

recommended by breeders and veterinary surgeons. Changing the brand of food that you buy may not eliminate the problem if the element to which the dog is allergic is contained in the new brand.

Recognising a food allergy is difficult. Humans vomit or have rashes when they eat a food to which they are allergic. Dogs neither vomit nor (usually) develop a rash. They react in the same manner as they do to an airborne or flea allergy; they itch, scratch and bite, thus making the diagnosis extremely difficult. While pollen allergies and parasite bites are usually seasonal, food allergies are year-round problems.

FOOD INTOLERANCE

Food intolerance is the inability of the dog to completely digest certain foods. Puppies that may have done very well on their mother's milk may not do well on cow's milk. The result of this food intolerance may be loose bowels, passing gas and stomach pains. These are the only obvious

Vitamins Recommended for Dogs

Some breeders and vets recommend the supplementation of vitamins to a dog's diet—others do not. Before embarking on a vitamin programme, consult your vet.

Vitamin / Dosage	Food source	Benefits
A / 10,000 IU/week	Eggs, butter, yoghurt, meat	Skin, eyes, hind legs, haircoat
B / Varies	Organs, cottage cheese, sardines	Appetite, fleas, heart, skin and coat
C / 2000 mg+	Fruit, legumes, leafy green vegetables	Healing, arthritis, kidneys
D / Varies	Cod liver, cheese, organs, eggs	Bones, teeth, endocrine system
E / 250 IU daily	Leafy green vegetables, meat, wheat germ oil	Skin, muscles, nerves, healing, digestion
F / Varies	Fish oils, raw meat	Heart, skin, coat, fleas
K / Varies	Naturally in body, not through food	Blood clotting

Fatty Risks

Any dog of any breed can suffer from obesity. Studies show that nearly 30 percent of our dogs are overweight, primarily from high caloric intake and low energy expenditure. The hound and gundog breeds are the most likely affected, and females are at a greater risk of obesity than males. Pet dogs that are neutered are twice as prone to obesity as intact, whole dogs.

Regardless of breed, your dog should have a visible 'waist' behind his rib cage and in front of the hind legs. There should be no fatty deposits on his hips or over his rump, and his abdomen should not be extended.

Veterinary specialists link obesity with respiratory problems, cardiac disease and liver dysfunction as well as low sperm count and abnormal oestrous cycles in breeding animals. Other complications include musculoskeletal disease (including arthritis), decreased immune competence, diabetes mellitus, hypothyroidism, pancreatitis and dermatosis. Other studies have indicated that excess fat leads to heat stress, as obese dogs cannot regulate their body temperatures as well as normal-weight dogs.

Don't be discouraged if you discover that your dog has a heart problem or a complicated neurological condition requiring special attention. It is possible to tend to his special medical needs. Veterinary specialists focus on areas such as cardiology, neurology and oncology. Veterinary medical associations require rigorous training and experience before granting certification in a speciality. Consulting a specialist may offer you greater peace of mind when seeking treatment for your dog.

symptoms of food intolerance and that makes diagnosis difficult.

TREATING FOOD PROBLEMS

It is possible to handle food allergies and food intolerance yourself. Put your dog on a diet that it has never had. Obviously if it has never eaten this new food it can't have been allergic or intolerant of it. Start with a single ingredient that is not in the dog's diet at the present time. Ingredients like chopped beef or fish are common in dogs' diets, so try something more exotic like rabbit, pheasant or even just vegetables. Keep the dog on this diet (with no additives) for a month. If the symptoms of food allergy or intolerance disappear, chances are your dog has a food allergy.

Don't think that the single ingredient cured the problem. You

THE SAME ALLERGIES
Chances are that you and your dog will have the same allergies. Your allergies are readily recognisable and usually easily treated. Your dog's allergies may be masked.

still must find a suitable diet and ascertain which ingredient in the old diet was objectionable. This is most easily done by adding ingredients to the new diet one at a time. Let the dog stay on the modified diet for a month before you add another ingredient. Eventually, you will determine the ingredient that caused the adverse reaction.

An alternative method is to carefully study the ingredients in the diet to which your dog is allergic or intolerant. Identify the main ingredient in this diet and eliminate the main ingredient by buying a different food that does not have that ingredient. Keep experimenting until the symptoms disappear after one month on the new diet.

CARETAKER OF TEETH
You are your dog's caretaker and his dentist. Vets warn that plaque and tartar buildup on the teeth will damage the gums and allow bacteria to enter the dog's bloodstream, causing serious damage to the animal's vital organs. Studies show that over 50 percent of dogs have some form of gum disease before age three. Daily or weekly tooth cleaning (with a brush or soft gauze pad wipes) can add to your dog's life.

DID YOU KNOW?
Your dog's protein needs are changeable. High activity level, stress, climate and other physical factors may require your dog to have more protein in his diet. Check with your veterinary surgeon.

A SKUNKY PROBLEM

Have you noticed your dog dragging his rump along the floor? If so, it is likely that his anal sacs are impacted or possibly infected. The anal sacs are small pouches located on both sides of the anus under the skin and muscles. They are about the size and shape of a grape and contain a foul-smelling liquid. Their contents are usually emptied when the dog has a bowel movement, but if they are not emptied completely, they will impact, which will cause your dog a lot of pain. Fortunately, your veterinary surgeon can tend to this problem easily by draining the sacs for the dog. Be aware that your dog might also empty his anal sacs in cases of extreme fright.

Owners must take precautions with fertilisers and pesticides when treating flowers in their garden. The curious Shiba will taste-test almost everything in her path.

Don't Eat the Daisies!

Many plants and flowers are beautiful to look at, but can be highly toxic if ingested by your dog. Reactions range from abdominal pain and vomiting to convulsions and death. If the following plants are in your home, remove them. If they are outside your house or in your garden, avoid accidents by making sure your dog is never left unsupervised in those locations.

Azalea	Dumb cane	Mescal bean
Belladonna	Dutchman's breeches	Mushrooms
Bird of paradise	Elephant's ear	Nightshade
Bulbs	Hydrangea	Philodendron
Calla lily	Jack-in-the-pulpit	Poinsettia
Cardinal flower	Jasmine	Prunus species
Castor bean	Jimsonweed	Tobacco
Chinaberry tree	Larkspur	Yellow jasmine
Daphne	Laurel	Yews, *Taxus* species
	Lily of the valley	

EXTERNAL PARASITES

FLEAS

Of all the problems to which dogs are prone, none is more well known and frustrating than fleas. Flea infestation is relatively simple to cure but difficult to prevent. Parasites that are harboured inside the body are a bit more difficult to eradicate but they are easier to control.

To control flea infestation, you have to understand the flea's life cycle. Fleas are often thought of as a summertime problem, but centrally heated homes have changed the patterns and fleas can be found at any time of the year. The most effective method of flea control is a two-stage approach: one stage to kill the adult fleas, and the other to control the development of pre-adult fleas. Unfortunately, no single active ingredient is effective against all stages of the life cycle.

LIFE CYCLE STAGES

During its life, a flea will pass through four life stages: egg, larva, pupa and adult. The adult stage is the most visible and irritating stage of the flea life cycle, and this is why the majority of flea-control products concentrate on this stage.

A scanning electron micrograph (S. E. M.) of a dog flea, *Ctenocephalides canis*.

S. E. M. BY DR DENNIS KUNKEL, UNIVERSITY OF HAWAII

Magnified head of a dog flea, *Ctenocephalides canis*.

S. E. M. BY DR DENNIS KUNKEL, UNIVERSITY OF HAWAII

A Look at Fleas

Fleas have been around for millions of years and have adapted to changing host animals. They are able to go through a complete life cycle in less than one month or they can extend their lives to almost two years by remaining as pupae or cocoons. They do not need blood or any other food for up to 20 months.

They have been measured as being able to jump 300,000 times and can jump 150 times their length in any direction including straight up. Those are just a few of the reasons why they are so successful in infesting a dog!

The fact is that adult fleas account for only 1% of the total flea population, and the other 99% exist in pre-adult stages, i.e. eggs, larvae and pupae. The pre-adult stages are barely visible to the naked eye.

THE LIFE CYCLE OF THE FLEA

Eggs are laid on the dog, usually in quantities of about 20 or 30, several times a day. The female adult flea must have a blood meal before each egg-laying session. When first laid, the eggs will cling to the dog's fur, as the eggs are still moist. However, they will quickly dry out and fall from the dog, especially if the dog moves around or scratches. Many eggs will fall off in the dog's favourite area or an area in which he spends a lot of time, such as his bed.

Once the eggs fall from the dog onto the carpet or furniture, they will hatch into larvae. This takes from one to ten days. Larvae are not particularly mobile, and will usually travel only a few inches from where they hatch. However, they do have a tendency to move away from light and heavy traffic—under furniture and behind doors are common places to find high quantities of flea larvae.

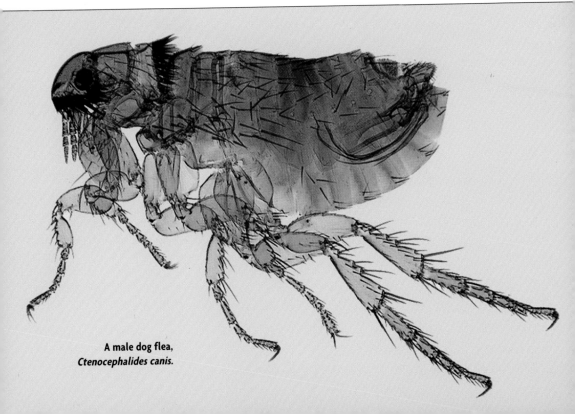

A male dog flea,
Ctenocephalides canis.

The flea larvae feed on dead organic matter, including adult flea faeces, until they are ready to change into adult fleas. Fleas will usually remain as larvae for around seven days. After this period, the larvae will pupate into protective pupae. While inside the pupae, the larvae will undergo metamorphosis and change into adult fleas. This can take as little time as a few days, but the adult fleas can remain inside the pupae waiting to hatch for up to two years. The pupae are signalled to hatch by certain stimuli, such as physical pressure—the pupae's being stepped on, heat from an animal lying on the pupae or increased carbon dioxide levels and vibrations—indicating that a suitable host is available.

Once hatched, the adult flea must feed within a few days. Once the adult flea finds a host, it will not leave voluntarily. It only becomes dislodged by grooming or the host animal's scratching. The adult flea will remain on the host for the duration of its life unless forcibly removed.

> **DID YOU KNOW?**
> Never mix flea control products without first consulting your veterinary surgeon. Some products can become toxic when combined with others and can cause serious or fatal consequences.

> **DID YOU KNOW?**
> Flea-killers are poisonous. You should not spray these toxic chemicals on areas of a dog's body that he licks, on his genitals or on his face. Flea killers taken internally are a better answer, but check with your vet in case internal therapy is not advised for your dog.

TREATING THE ENVIRONMENT AND THE DOG
Treating fleas should be a two-pronged attack. First, the environment needs to be treated; this includes carpets and furniture, especially the dog's bedding and areas underneath furniture. The environment should be treated with a household spray containing an Insect Growth Regulator (IGR) and an insecticide to kill the adult fleas. Most IGRs are effective against eggs and larvae; they actually mimic the fleas' own hormones and stop the eggs and larvae from developing into adult fleas. There are currently no treatments available to attack the pupa stage of the life cycle, so the adult insecticide is used to kill the newly hatched adult fleas before they find a host. Most IGRs are active for many months, whilst adult insecticides are only active for a few days.

When treating with a household spray, it is a good idea to vacuum before applying the product. This stimulates as many

Opposite page: A scanning electron micrograph of a dog or cat flea, *Ctenocephalides*, magnified more than 100x. This image has been colorized for effect.

The Life Cycle of the Flea

Eggs

Larva

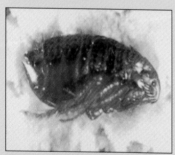

Pupa

Adult

Photos courtesy of Fleabusters® Rx for fleas.

Flea Control

IGR (INSECT GROWTH REGULATOR)

Two types of products should be used when treating fleas—a product to treat the pet and a product to treat the home. Adult fleas represent less than 1% of the flea population. The pre-adult fleas (eggs, larvae and pupae) represent more than 99% of the flea population and are found in the environment; it is in the case of pre-adult fleas that products containing an Insect Growth Regulator (IGR) should be used in the home.

IGRs are a new class of compounds used to prevent the development of insects. They do not kill the insect outright, but instead use the insect's biology against it to stop it from completing its growth. Products that contain methoprene are the world's first and leading IGRs. Used to control fleas and other insects, this type of IGR will stop flea larvae from developing and protect the house for up to seven months.

EN GARDE:
CATCHING FLEAS OFF GUARD!

Consider the following ways to arm yourself against fleas:

• Add a small amount of pennyroyal or eucalyptus oil to your dog's bath. These natural remedies repel fleas.

• Supplement your dog's food with fresh garlic (minced or grated) and a hearty amount of brewer's yeast, both of which ward off fleas.

• Use a flea comb on your dog daily. Submerge fleas in a cup of bleach to kill them quickly.

• Confine the dog to only a few rooms to limit the spread of fleas in the home.

• Vacuum daily...and get all of the crevices! Dispose of the bag every few days until the problem is under control.

• Wash your dog's bedding daily. Cover cushions where your dog sleeps with towels, and wash the towels often.

pupae as possible to hatch into adult fleas. The vacuum cleaner should also be treated with a flea treatment to prevent the eggs and larvae that have been hoovered into the vacuum bag from hatching.

The second stage of treatment is to apply an adult insecticide to the dog. Traditionally, this would be in the form of a collar or a spray, but more recent innovations include digestible insecticides that poison the fleas when they ingest the dog's blood. Alternatively, there are drops that, when placed on the back of the animal's neck, spread throughout the fur and skin to kill adult fleas.

PHOTO BY DWIGHT R KUHN

Dwight R Kuhn's magnificent action photo showing a flea jumping from a dog's back.

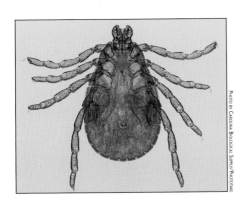

PHOTO BY CAROLINA BIOLOGICAL SUPPLY/PHOTOTAKE

PHOTO BY DR DENNIS KUNKEL, UNIVERSITY OF HAWAII

TICKS AND MITES

Though not as common as fleas, ticks and mites are found all over the tropical and temperate world. They don't bite, like fleas; they harpoon. They dig their sharp proboscis (nose) into the dog's skin and drink the blood. Their only food and drink is dog's blood. Dogs can get Lyme disease, Rocky Mountain spotted fever (normally found in the US only), paralysis and many other diseases from ticks and mites. They may live where fleas are found and they like to hide in cracks or seams in walls wherever dogs live. They are controlled the same way fleas

A brown dog tick, *Rhipicephalus sanguineus*, is an uncommon but annoying tick found on dogs.

The head of a dog tick, *Dermacentor variabilis*, enlarged and coloured for effect.

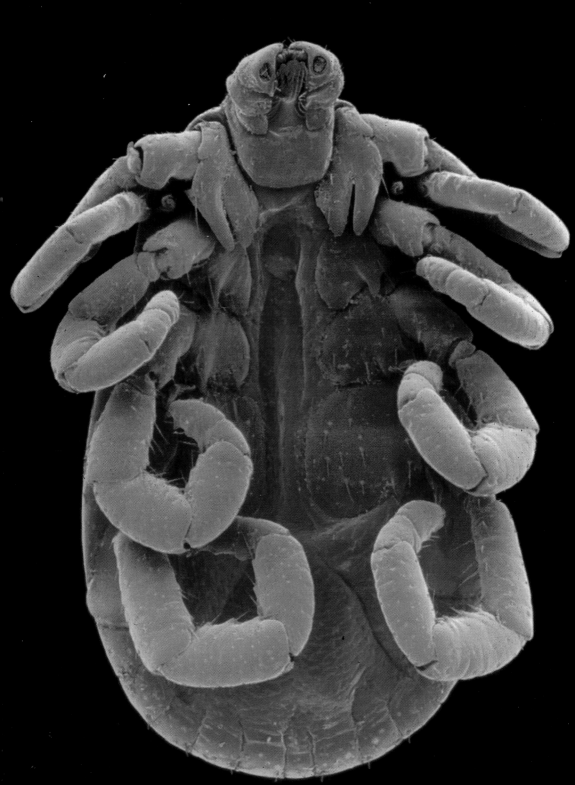

are controlled.

The dog tick, *Dermacentor variabilis*, may well be the most common dog tick in many geographical areas, especially those areas where the climate is hot and humid.

Most dog ticks have life expectancies of a week to six months, depending upon climatic conditions. They can neither jump nor fly, but they can crawl slowly and can range up to 5 metres (16 feet) to reach a sleeping or unsuspecting dog.

BEWARE THE DEER TICK

The great outdoors may be fun for your dog, but it also is a home to dangerous ticks. Deer ticks carry a bacterium known as *Borrelia burgdorferi* and are most active in the autumn and spring. When infections are caught early, penicillin and tetracycline are effective antibiotics, but if left untreated the bacteria may cause neurological, kidney and cardiac problems as well as long-term trouble with walking and painful joints.

Opposite page: The dog tick, *Dermacentor variabilis*, is probably the most common tick found on dogs. Look at the strength in its eight legs! No wonder it's hard to detach them.

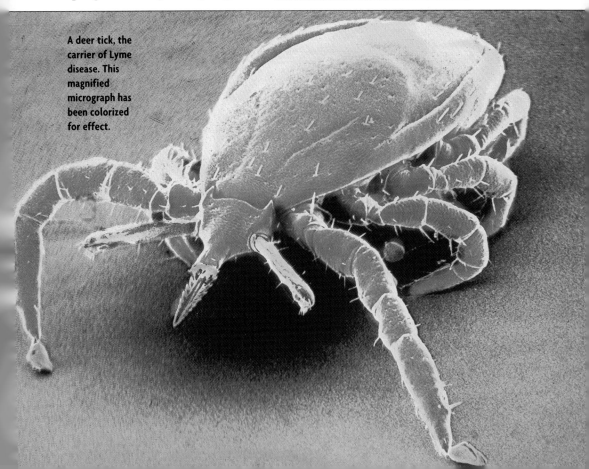

A deer tick, the carrier of Lyme disease. This magnified micrograph has been colorized for effect.

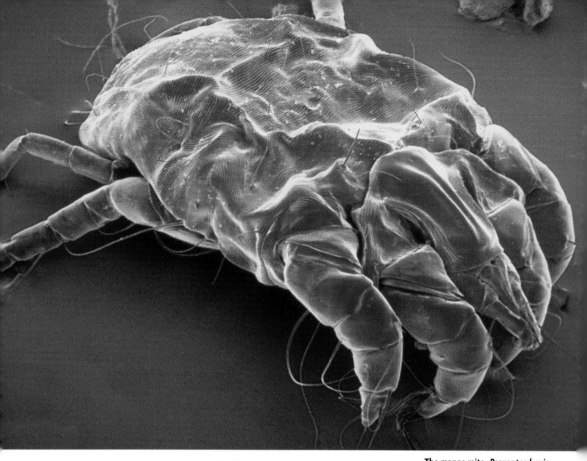

PHOTO BY DWIGHT R KUHN

The mange mite, *Psoroptes bovis.*

Human lice look like dog lice; the two are closely related.

MANGE

Mites cause a skin irritation called mange. Some are contagious, like *Cheyletiella*, ear mites, scabies and chiggers. Mites that cause ear-mite infestations are usually controlled with Lindane, which can only be administered by a vet, followed by Tresaderm at home.

It is essential that your dog be treated for mange as quickly as possible because some forms of mange are transmissible to people.

INTERNAL PARASITES

Most animals—fishes, birds and mammals, including dogs and humans—have worms and other parasites that live inside their bodies. According to Dr Herbert R Axelrod, the fish pathologist, there are two kinds of parasites: dumb and smart. The smart parasites live in peaceful cooperation with their hosts (symbiosis), while the dumb parasites kill their hosts. Most of the worm infections are relatively easy to control. If they are not controlled, they weaken the host dog to the point that other medical problems occur, but they are not dumb parasites.

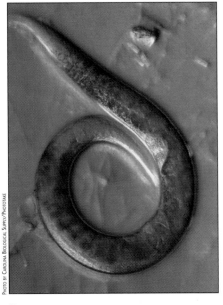

The roundworm, *Rhabditis*. The roundworm can infect both dogs and humans.

PHOTO BY CAROLINA BIOLOGICAL SUPPLY/PHOTOTAKE

ROUNDWORM

Average size dogs can pass 1,360,000 roundworm eggs every day.

For example, if there were only 1 million dogs in the world, the world would be saturated with 1,300 metric tonnes of dog faeces. These faeces would contain 15,000,000,000 roundworm eggs.

It's known that 7–31% of home gardens and children's play boxes in the US contain roundworm eggs.

Flushing dog's faeces down the toilet is not a safe practice because the usual sewage treatments do not destroy roundworm eggs.

Infected puppies start shedding roundworm eggs at 3 weeks of age. They can be infected by their mother's milk.

ROUNDWORMS

The roundworms that infect dogs are scientifically known as *Toxocara canis*. They live in the dog's intestines. The worms shed eggs continually. It has been estimated that a dog produces about 150 grammes of faeces every day. Each gramme of faeces averages 10,000–12,000 eggs of roundworms. There are no known areas in which dogs roam that do not contain roundworm eggs. The greatest danger of roundworms is that they infect people too! It is wise to have your dog tested regularly for roundworms.

Pigs also have roundworm infections that can be passed to humans and dogs. The typical roundworm parasite is called *Ascaris lumbricoides*.

DEWORMING

Ridding your puppy of worms is VERY IMPORTANT because certain worms that puppies carry, such as tapeworms and roundworms, can infect humans.

Breeders initiate a deworming programme at or about four weeks of age. The routine is repeated every two or three weeks until the puppy is three months old. The breeder from whom you obtained your puppy should provide you with the complete details of the deworming programme.

Your veterinary surgeon can prescribe and monitor the programme of deworming for you. The usual programme is treating the puppy every 15–20 days until the puppy is positively worm-free.

It is advised that you only treat your puppy with drugs that are recommended professionally.

HOOKWORMS

The worm *Ancylostoma caninum* is commonly called the dog hookworm. It is also dangerous to humans and cats. It has teeth by which it attaches itself to the intestines of the dog. It changes the site of its attachment about six times a day and the dog loses blood from each detachment, possibly causing iron-deficiency anaemia. Hookworms are easily purged from the dog with many medications. Milbemycin oxime, which also serves as a heartworm preventative in Collies, can be used for this purpose.

In Britain the 'temperate climate' hookworm (*Uncinaria stenocephala*) is rarely found in pet or show dogs, but can occur in hunting packs, racing Greyhounds and sheepdogs because the worms can be prevalent wherever dogs are exercised regularly on grassland.

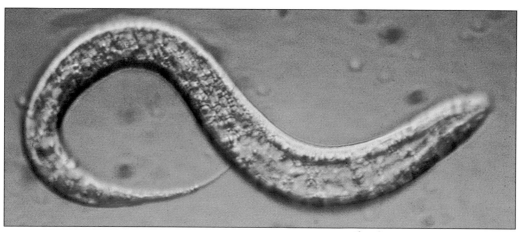

The infective stage of the hookworm larva.

PHOTO BY DWIGHT R. KUHN

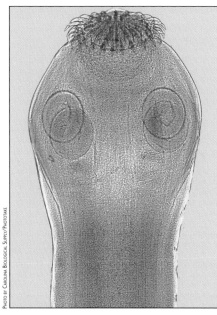

PHOTO BY CAROLINA BIOLOGICAL SUPPLY/PHOTOTAKE

Left:
Male and female hookworms, *Ancylostoma caninum*, are uncommonly found in pet or show dogs in Britain. Hookworms may infect other dogs that have exposure to grasslands.

Right:
The head and rostellum (the round prominence on the scolex) of a tapeworm, which infects dogs and humans.

TAPEWORM

Humans, rats, squirrels, foxes, coyotes, wolves, mixed breeds of dogs and purebred dogs are all susceptible to tapeworm infection. Except in humans, tapeworm is usually not a fatal infection.

Infected individuals can harbour a thousand parasitic worms.

Tapeworms have two sexes—male and female (many other worms have only one sex—male and female in the same worm).

If dogs eat infected rats or mice, they get the tapeworm disease.

One month after attaching to a dog's intestine, the worm starts shedding eggs. These eggs are infective immediately.

Infective eggs can live for a few months without a host animal.

TAPEWORMS

There are many species of tapeworm. They are carried by fleas! The dog eats the flea and starts the tapeworm cycle. Humans can also be infected with tapeworms, so don't eat fleas! Fleas are so small that your dog could pass them onto your hands, your plate or your food and thus make it possible for you to ingest a flea that is carrying tapeworm eggs.

While tapeworm infection is not life-threatening in dogs (smart parasite!), it can be the cause of a very serious liver disease for humans. About 50 percent of the humans infected with *Echinococcus multilocularis*, a type of tapeworm that causes alveolar hydatis, perish.

HEARTWORMS

Heartworms are thin, extended worms up to 30 cms (12 ins) long, which live in a dog's heart and the major blood vessels surrounding it. Dogs may have up to 200 worms. Symptoms may be loss of energy, loss of appetite, coughing, the development of a pot belly and anaemia.

Heartworms are transmitted by mosquitoes. The mosquito drinks the blood of an infected dog and takes in larvae with the blood. The larvae, called microfilaria, develop within the body of the mosquito and are passed on to the next dog bitten after the larvae mature. It takes two to three weeks for the larvae to develop to the infective stage within the body of the mosquito. Dogs should be treated at about six weeks of age, and maintained on a prophylactic dose given monthly.

Blood testing for heartworms is not necessarily indicative of how seriously your dog is infected. This is a dangerous disease. Although heartworm is a problem for dogs in America, Australia, Asia and Central Europe, dogs in the United Kingdom are not currently affected by heartworm.

The heart of a dog infected with canine heartworm, *Dirofilaria immitis*.

First Aid at a Glance

Burns
Place the affected area under cool water; use ice if only a small area is burnt.

Bee/Insect bites
Apply ice to relieve swelling; antihistamine dosed properly.

Animal bites
Clean any bleeding area; apply pressure until bleeding subsides; go to the vet.

Spider bites
Use cold compress and a pressurised pack to inhibit venom's spreading.

Antifreeze poisoning
Induce vomiting with hydrogen peroxide. Seek *immediate* veterinary help!

Fish hooks
Removal best handled by vet; hook must be cut in order to remove.

Snake bites
Pack ice around bite; contact vet quickly; identify snake for proper antivenin.

Car accident
Move dog from roadway with blanket; seek veterinary aid.

Shock
Calm the dog, keep him warm; seek immediate veterinary help.

Nosebleed
Apply cold compress to the nose; apply pressure to any visible abrasion.

Bleeding
Apply pressure above the area; treat wound by applying a cotton pack.

Heat stroke
Submerge dog in cold bath; cool down with fresh air and water; go to the vet.

Frostbite/Hypothermia
Warm the dog with a warm bath, electric blankets or hot water bottles.

Abrasions
Clean the wound and wash out thoroughly with fresh water; apply antiseptic.

 Remember: an injured dog may attempt to bite a helping hand from fear and confusion. Always muzzle the dog before trying to offer assistance.

When you purchase your Shiba you should make it clear to the breeder whether you want one just as a loveable companion and pet, or if you hope to be buying a Shiba with show prospects. No reputable breeder will sell you a young puppy saying that it is definitely of show quality, for so much can go wrong during the early months of a puppy's development. If you plan to show, what you will hopefully have acquired is a puppy with 'show potential.'

To the novice, exhibiting a Shiba in the show ring may look easy but it takes a lot of hard work and devotion to do top winning at a show such as the prestigious Crufts, not to mention a little luck too!

The first concept that the canine novice learns when watching a dog show is that each dog first competes against members of its own breed. Once the judge has selected the best member of each breed, provided that the show is judged on a Group system, that chosen dog will compete with other dogs in its group. Finally the best of each group will compete for Best in Show and Reserve Best in Show.

The second concept that you must understand is that the dogs are not actually compared against one another. The judge compares each dog against the breed standard, which is a written description of the ideal specimen of the breed. While some early breed standards were indeed based on specific dogs that were famous or popular, many dedicated enthusiasts say that a perfect specimen, described in the standard, has never walked into a show ring, has never been bred and, to the woe of dog breeders around the globe, does not exist.

Breeders attempt to get as close to this ideal as possible, with every litter, but theoretically the 'perfect' dog is so elusive that it is impossible. (And if the 'perfect' dog were born, breeders and judges would never agree that it was indeed 'perfect.')

If you are interested in exploring dog shows, your best bet is to join your local breed club. These clubs often host both Championship and Open Shows, and sometimes Match meetings and special events, all of which could be of interest, even if you are only an onlooker. Clubs also send out newsletters and some organise training days and seminars in order that people may learn more about their chosen breed. To locate the breed club closest to you, contact The Kennel Club, the ruling body for the British dog world. The Kennel Club governs not only conformation shows but also working trials, agility trials and field trials. The Kennel Club furnishes the rules and regulations for all these events plus general dog registration and other basic requirements of dog ownership. Its annual show, called the Crufts Dog Show, held in Birmingham, is the largest benched show in England. Every year over 20,000 of the UK's best dogs qualify to participate in this marvellous show which lasts four days.

The Kennel Club governs many different kinds of shows in Great Britain, Australia, South Africa and beyond. At the most competitive and prestigious of these shows, the Championship Shows, a dog can earn Challenge Certificates, and thereby become a Show Champion or a Champion. A dog must earn three Challenge Certificates under three different judges to earn the prefix of 'Sh

WINNING THE TICKET
Earning a championship at Kennel Club shows is the most difficult in the world. Compared to the United States and Canada where it is relatively not 'challenging,' collecting three green tickets not only requires much time and effort, it can be very expensive! Challenge Certificates, as the tickets are properly known, are the building blocks of champions—good breeding, good handling, good training and good luck!

Ch' or 'Ch.' Note that some breeds must also qualify in a field trial in order to gain the title of full champion, though this rule does not apply to the Japanese Shiba.are awarded to a very small percentage of the dogs competing, and dogs that are already Champions compete with others for these coveted CCs. The number of Challenge Certificates awarded in any one year is based upon the total number of dogs in each breed entered for competition.

There are three types of Championship Shows: an all-breed General Championship Show for all Kennel-Club-recognised breeds; a Group Championship Show that is limited to breeds within one of the groups; and a Breed Show that is usually confined to a single breed. The Kennel Club determines which breeds at which Championship Shows will have the opportunity to earn Challenge Certificates (or tickets). Serious exhibitors often will opt not to participate if the tickets are withheld at a particular show. This

This handsome Japanese Shiba has placed in his class at a show in the UK. Red-coloured dogs are by far the most popular in the show ring in Britain and the US.

policy makes earning championships even more difficult to accomplish.

Open Shows are generally less competitive and are frequently used as 'practice shows' for young dogs. There are hundreds of Open Shows each year that can be delightful social events and are great first show experiences for the novice. Even if you're considering just watching a show to wet your paws, an Open Show is a great choice.

While Championship and Open Shows are most important for the beginner to understand, there are other types of shows in which the interested dog owner can participate. Training clubs sponsor Matches that can be entered on the day of the show for a nominal fee. In these introductory-level exhibitions, two dogs are pulled out of a hat and 'matched,' the winner of that match goes on to the next round, and eventually only one dog is left undefeated.

Exemption Shows are much more light-hearted affairs with usually only four pedigree classes and several 'fun' classes, all of which can be entered on that day. Exemption Shows are sometimes held in conjunction with small agricultural shows and the proceeds must be given to a charity. Limited Shows are also available in small number, but entry is restricted to members of the club which hosts the show, although one can usually join the club when making an entry.

Before you actually step into the ring, you would be well advised to sit back and observe the judge's ring procedure. If it is your first time in the ring, do not be over-anxious and run to the front of the line. It is much better to stand back and study how the exhibitor in front of you is performing. The judge asks each handler to 'stand' the dog, hopefully showing the dog off to his best advantage. The judge will observe the dog from a distance and from different angles, approach the dog, check his teeth, overall structure, alertness and muscle tone, as well as consider how well the dog 'conforms' to the standard. Most importantly, the judge will have the exhibitor move the dog around the ring in some pattern that he or she should specify (another advantage to not going first, but always listen since some judges change their directions, and the judge is always right!). Finally the judge will give the dog one last look before moving on to the next exhibitor.

If you are not in the top three at your first show, do not be discouraged. Be patient and consistent and you may eventually find yourself in the winning line-up. Remember that the winners were once in your shoes and have devoted many hours and much money to earn the placement. If you find that your dog is losing

TIDINESS COUNTS
Surely you've spent hours grooming your dog to perfection for the show ring, but don't forget about yourself! While the dog should be the centre of attention, it is important that you also appear clean and tidy. Wear smart, appropriate clothes and comfortable shoes in a colour that contrasts with your dog's coat. Look and act like a professional.

every time and never getting a nod, it may be time to consider a different dog sport or just enjoy your Shiba as a pet.

As a Shiba owner, you have selected your dog so that you and your loved ones can have a companion, a watchdog, a friend and a four-legged family member. You invest time, money and effort to care for and train the family's new charge. Of course, this chosen canine behaves perfectly! Well, perfectly like a dog.

THINK LIKE A DOG

Dogs do not think like humans, nor do humans think like dogs, though we try. Unfortunately, a dog is incapable of comprehending how humans think, so the responsibility falls on the owner to adopt a proper canine mindset. Dogs cannot rationalise, and dogs exist in the present moment. Many dog owners make the mistake in training of thinking that they can reprimand their dog for something he did a while ago. Basically, you cannot even reprimand a dog for something he did 20 seconds ago! Either catch him in the act or forget it! It is a waste of your and your dog's time—in his mind, you are reprimanding him for whatever he is doing at that moment. Shibas do not take kindly to being harshly scolded. Remember this is an intelligent, sensitive animal who *expects* respect and consideration. Shibas act rather like 12-year-old children: smart enough to know better but always trying to get away with murder, testing your limits, patience and mental acumen.

The following behavioural problems represent those which owners most commonly encounter. Every dog is unique and every situation is unique. No author could purport to solve your Shiba's problems simply by reading a script. Here we outline some basic 'dogspeak' so that owners' chances of solving behavioural problems are increased. Discuss bad habits with your veterinary surgeon and he/she can recommend a behavioural specialist to consult in appropriate cases. Since behavioural abnormalities are the main reason owners abandon their pets, we hope that you will make a valiant effort to solve your Shiba's problems. Patience and understanding are virtues that must dwell in every pet-loving household.

SEPARATION ANXIETY

Recognised by behaviourists as the most common form of stress for

SMILE!

Dogs and humans may be the only animals that smile. Dogs imitate the smile on their owner's face when he greets a friend. The dog only smiles at its human friends. It never smiles at another dog or cat. Usually it rolls up its lips and shows its teeth in a clenched mouth while it rolls over onto its back begging for a soft scratch.

dogs, separation anxiety can also lead to destructive behaviours in your dog. It's more than your Shiba's howling his displeasure at your leaving the house and his being left alone. This is a normal reaction, no different from the child who cries as his mother leaves him on the first day at school. In fact, if you are constantly with your dog, he will come to expect you with him all of the time, making it even more traumatic for him when you are not there. Obviously, you enjoy spending time with your dog, and he thrives on your love and attention. However, it should not become a dependent relationship in which he is heartbroken without you. This broken heart can also bring on destructive behaviour as well as loss of appetite, depression and lack of interest in play and interaction. Canine behaviourists have been spending much energy

in helping owners better understand the importance of this stressful condition.

AGGRESSION

This is a problem that concerns all responsible dog owners. Aggression can be a very big problem in dogs, but more so in a dominant, intelligent dog like the Shiba. In most cases of Shiba aggression, it is a bitch-bitch situation. The females are quite dog-aggressive and dominant. You can only keep one bitch in a household, as the bitches will always challenge one another. Male dogs tend to be more docile, though 'disagreements' between males do happen but not as regularly as with the bitches.

Aggression, when not controlled, always becomes dangerous. An aggressive dog, no matter the size, may lunge at, bite

Decoding the Shiba mind is akin to curing the common cold: a riddle that cannot be solved. Looking into the eyes of a Shiba certainly assures us humans that this is a very intelligent breed of dog.

or even attack a person or another dog. Aggressive behaviour is not to be tolerated. It is more than just inappropriate behaviour; it is painful for a family to watch their dog become unpredictable in his behaviour to the point where they are afraid of him. While not all aggressive behaviour is dangerous, growling, baring teeth, etc., can be frightening. It is important to ascertain why the dog is acting in this manner. Aggression is a display of dominance, and the dog should not have the dominant role in its pack, which is, in this case, your family.

It is important not to challenge an aggressive dog as this could provoke an attack. Observe your Shiba's body language. Does he make direct eye contact and stare? Does he try to make himself as large as possible: ears pricked, chest out, tail flared? Height and size signify authority in a dog pack—being taller or 'above' another dog literally means that he is 'above' in social status. These body signals tell you that your Shiba thinks he is in charge, a problem that needs to be addressed. An aggressive dog is unpredictable; you never know when he is going to strike and what he is going to do. You cannot understand why a dog that is playful one minute is growling the next.

The best solution is to consult a behavioural specialist, one who has experience with the Shiba if possible. Together, perhaps you can pinpoint the cause of your dog's aggression and do something about it. An aggressive dog cannot be trusted, and a dog that cannot be trusted is not safe to have as a family pet. If, very unusually, you find that your pet has become untrustworthy and you feel it necessary to seek a new home with a more suitable family and environment, explain fully to the new owners all your reasons for rehoming the dog to be fair to all concerned.

SEXUAL BEHAVIOUR

Dogs exhibit certain sexual behaviours that may have influenced your choice of male or female when you first purchased your Shiba. To a certain extent, spaying/neutering will eliminate these behaviours, but if you are purchasing a dog that you wish to breed from, you should be aware of what you will have to deal with throughout the dog's life.

Female dogs usually have two oestruses per year with each season lasting about three weeks. These are the only times in which a female dog will mate, and she usually will not allow this until the second week of the cycle, but this does vary from bitch to bitch. If not bred during the heat cycle, it is not uncommon for a bitch to experience a false pregnancy, in which her mammary glands swell and she

X MARKS THE SPOT

As a pack animal, your dog marks his territory as a way of letting any possible intruders know that this is his space and that he will defend his territory if necessary. Your dog marks by urinating because urine contains pheromones that allow other canines to identify him. While this behaviour seems like a nuisance, it speaks litres about your dog's mental health. Stable, well-trained dogs living in quiet, less populated areas may mark less frequently than less confident dogs inhabiting busy urban areas that attract many possible invaders. If your dog only marks in certain areas in your home, your bed or just the front door, these are the areas he feels obligated to defend. If your dog marks frequently, see your veterinary surgeon or an animal behaviourist.

indoors on furniture legs, curtains and the sofa. Such behaviour can be very frustrating for the owner and early training is strongly urged before the 'urge' strikes your dog. Neutering the male at an appropriate early age can solve this problem before it becomes a habit.

Other problems associated with males are wandering and mounting. Both of these habits, of course, belong to the unneutered dog, whose sexual drive leads him away from home in search of the bitch in heat. Males will mount females in heat, as well as any other dog, male or female, who happens to catch their fancy. Other possible mounting partners include his owner, the furniture, guests to the home and strangers on the street. Discourage such behaviour early on. Owners must further recognise that mounting is not merely a sexual expression but also one of dominance, exhibited by males and females alike. Be consistent and persistent and you will find that you can 'move mounters.'

exhibits maternal tendencies toward toys or other objects.

With male dogs, owners must be aware that whole dogs (dogs who are not neutered) have the natural inclination to mark their territory. Males mark their territory by spraying small amounts of urine as they lift their legs in a macho ritual. Marking can occur both outdoors in the garden and around the neighbourhood as well as

Puppies will chew anything...until they are scolded. Be firm and fair when reprimanding your misbehaving Shiba puppy and you will gain his respect.

CHEWING

The national canine pastime is chewing! Every dog loves to sink his 'canines' into a tasty bone, but sometimes that bone is a part of his owner's hand! Dogs need to chew, to massage their gums, to make their new teeth feel better and to exercise their jaws. This is a natural behaviour deeply embedded in all things canine. Our role as owners is not to stop the dog's chewing, but to redirect it to positive, chew-worthy objects. Be an informed owner and purchase proper chew toys like strong nylon bones that will not splinter. Be sure that the objects are safe and durable, since your dog's safety is at risk. Again, the owner is responsible for ensuring a dog-proof environment. The best answer is prevention, that is, put your shoes, handbags and other tasty objects in their proper places (out of the reach of the growing canine mouth). Direct puppies to their toys whenever you see them tasting the furniture legs or the leg of your trousers. Make a loud noise to attract the pup's attention and immediately escort him to his chew toy and engage him with the toy for at least four minutes, praising and encouraging him all the while.

Some trainers recommend deterrents, such as hot pepper, a bitter spice or a product designed for this purpose, to discourage the dog from chewing unwanted objects. Test these products yourself before investing in large quantities.

JUMPING UP

Jumping up is a dog's friendly way of saying hello! Some dog owners do not mind when their dog jumps up. The problem arises when guests come to the house and the dog greets them in the same manner—whether they like it or not! However friendly the greeting may be, the chances are that your visitors may not appreciate your dog's enthusiasm. The dog will not be able to distinguish upon whom he can jump and whom he cannot. Therefore, it is probably best to discourage this behaviour entirely.

Pick a command such as 'Off' (avoid using 'Down' since you will use that for the dog to lie down), and tell him 'Off' when he jumps up. Place him on the ground on all fours and have him sit, praising him the whole time. Always lavish him with praise and petting when he is in the sit position. In this way you can give him a warm affectionate greeting, let him know that you are as excited to see him as he is to see you and instil good manners at the same time!

DIGGING

Digging, which is seen as a destructive behaviour to humans, is actually quite a natural behaviour in dogs. Although terriers (the 'earth dogs') are most associated with the digging, any dog's desire to dig can be irrepressible and most frustrating to his owners. When digging occurs in your garden, it is actually a normal behaviour redirected into something the dog can do in his everyday life. In the wild, a dog would be actively seeking food, making his own shelter, etc. He would be using his paws in a purposeful manner for his survival. Since you provide him with food and shelter, he has no need to use his paws for these purposes, and so the energy that he would be using may manifest itself in the form of little holes all over your garden and flower beds.

In Shibas, digging may have less to do with nature than it has to do with escape! Most Shibas practise their digging—conveniently—next to a fence. A persistent Shiba can easily dig a hole deep enough to get under a fence to run away. When your Shiba shows signs of digging to escape, it's time for an owner to take real precautions to prevent the dog's disappearance.

Sometimes, however, your dog is digging random holes out of boredom—it is somewhat similar to someone eating a whole bag of crisps in front of the TV—because they are there and there is nothing better to do! Basically, the answer is to provide the dog with adequate play and exercise so that his mind and paws are occupied, and so that he feels as if he is doing something useful.

Of course, digging is easiest to control if it is stopped as soon as possible, but it is often hard to catch a dog in the act. If your dog is a compulsive digger and is not easily distracted by other activities, you can designate an area on your property where he is allowed to dig. If you catch him digging in an off-limits area of the garden, immediately bring him to the approved area and praise him for digging there. Keep a close eye on him so that you can catch him in the act—that is the only way to make him understand what is permitted and what is not. If you take him to a hole he dug an hour ago and tell him 'No,' he will understand that you are not fond of holes, or dirt, or flowers. If you catch him while he is stifle-deep in your tulips, that is when he will get your message.

BARKING
Dogs cannot talk—oh, what they would say if they could! Instead, barking is a dog's way of 'talking.' It can be somewhat frustrating because it is not always easy to tell what a dog means by his bark—is he excited, happy, frightened or angry? Whatever it is that the dog is trying to say, he should not be punished for barking. It is only when the barking becomes excessive, and when the excessive barking becomes a bad habit, that the behaviour needs to be modified.

Fortunately, Shibas in general and quiet dogs and rarely use their voices. Certainly they will bark to warn you of an intrusion or something wrong, but hardly ever for the mere sake of vocalising.

FOOD STEALING

Is your dog devising ways of stealing food from your coffee table? If so, you must answer the following questions: Is your Shiba hungry, or is he 'constantly famished' like many dogs seem to be? Face it, some dogs are more food-motivated than others. They are totally obsessed by the smell of food and can only think of their next meal. Food stealing is terrific fun and always yields a great reward—FOOD, glorious food.

The owner's goal, therefore, is to be sensible about where food is placed in the home, and to reprimand your dog whenever he

Human food is much more tasty than dried dog food, so Shibas are poised and professional beggars. To prevent your dog from begging at the table, never feed him from the table (even once!).

is caught in the act of stealing. But remember, only reprimand your dog if you actually see him stealing, not later when the crime is discovered for that will be of no use at all and will only serve to confuse him.

The author's Shibas have proven remarkably inventive in their plots to steal food. As you know, Shibas love to eat and are always ready for a taste of human food. Stealing food from the rubbish bin is an age-old penchant of the Shiba, and one which the breed does with professional ease. On occasion my Shibas have actually opened the fridge while I was not at home and helped themselves to a belly-bursting meal. One time the two Shibas actually dragged an entire turkey from the top shelf of the fridge and left a very sad carcass in the middle of the kitchen floor. Reprimanding them did no good whatsoever, as they seemingly didn't recognise the ravaged bird and were too tired to become concerned. Another time, the dynamic duo broke into the ice box to steal three pounds of baked livers, which I had prepared for bait for the following day's dog show. The iron-enriched Shibas had absolutely no interest in a liver treat the next day at the show and kept looking away from me as if to say, 'Stop it please, it's nauseating me!'

BEGGING

Just like food stealing, begging is a favourite pastime of hungry puppies! It achieves that same lovely result—FOOD! Dogs quickly learn that their owners keep the 'good food' for themselves, and that we humans do not dine on dried food alone. Begging is a conditioned response related to a specific stimulus, time and place. The sounds of the kitchen, cans and bottles opening, crinkling bags, the smell of food in preparation, etc., will excite the dog and soon the paws are in the air!

Here is the solution to stopping this behaviour: Never give in to a beggar! You are rewarding the dog for sitting pretty, jumping up, whining and rubbing his nose into you by giving him food. By ignoring the dog, you will (eventually) force the behaviour into extinction. Note that the behaviour is likely to get worse before it disappears, so be sure there are not any 'softies' in the family who will give in to little 'Oliver' every time he whimpers, 'More, please.'

COPROPHAGIA

Faeces eating is, to humans, one of the most disgusting behaviours that their dog could engage in, yet to the dog it is perfectly normal. It is hard for us to understand why a dog would want to eat its own faeces. He could be seeking certain nutrients that are missing from his diet; he could be just plain hungry; or he could be attracted by the pleasing (to a dog) scent. While coprophagia most often refers to the dog's eating his own faeces, a dog may just as likely eat that of another animal as well if he comes across it, especially if the dog has access to the family cat's litter tray. Vets have found that diets with a low digestibility, containing relatively low levels of fibre and high levels of starch, increase coprophagia. Therefore, high-fibre diets may decrease the likelihood of dogs' eating faeces. Once the dog develops diarrhoea from faeces eating, it will likely stop this distasteful habit.

Speed, timing and careful planning are required to steal food from the rubbish bin. Kabuki has been perfecting her techniques since puppyhood.

The allure of the litterbox! If your Shiba acquires the taste for feline faeces, keep the litterbox out of the dog's reach. There may be no better solution.

INDEX

*Page numbers in **boldface** indicate illustrations.*

My Japanese Shiba

PUT YOUR PUPPY'S FIRST PICTURE HERE

Dog's Name _____

Date _____ Photographer _____

ACKNOWLEDGMENTS

This magazine has been published by Wharncliffe History Magazines in association with Pen and Sword Military Books Limited, with the purpose of creating an awareness and an interest in the subject of military history.

For over twenty years Pen and Sword has published numerous military, naval and aviation books covering various conflicts throughout history. A vast number of military titles have been published over the past few years, covering the personal accounts of soldiers who have taken part in many conflicts, stretching from the First World War through to the Falklands War. The book featured in this magazine is one of many titles covering the subject of the The Great War.

This publication would not have been possible if it had not been for the skill and dedication of the author, Richard van Emden who has painstakingly researched and written about these conflicts in order to bring them to light.

Only extracts have been taken from this title, *Britain's Last Tommies* to produce this magazine and much more information can be gleaned by reading the book. Pen and Sword have included more colour illustrations and images to the text in order to add further interest for the reader, making this a special commerative publication.

Pen and Sword Books would like to thank Richard van Emden, whose work appears in this magazine BRITAIN'S LAST TOMMIES – *Final Memories from Soldiers of the 1914 – 18 War*.

Wharncliffe

HISTORY MAGAZINES

in association with

PEN & SWORD MILITARY BOOKS LTD.

If you would like to place an advertisement in any of our publications please contact;

CAROLYN MILLS

SALES MANAGER

TELEPHONE: 01226 734704

FAX: 01226 734703

E-mail: carolynm@whmagazines.co.uk

THE DRILL HALL • EASTGATE • BARNSLEY
• SOUTH YORKSHIRE • S70 2EU

VISIT OUR UPDATED WEBSITE TODAY!

www.pen-and-sword.co.uk

Visit now for:

• Up to the minute latest releases •

• Full back catalogue •

• Search engine •

• Exclusive web discount •

• Keep up to date with our monthly newsletter •

...and much more.

Wharncliffe
HISTORY MAGAZINES

In association with;

Pen & Sword Military Books.

First published in Great Britain in 2009 by
Wharncliffe History Magazines
47 Church Street
Barnsley
South Yorkshire
S70 2AS

Copyright © Wharncliffe Publishing, 2009

Edited by Roni Wilkinson

Design, layout & photograph colouring:
Jon Wilkinson, David Hemingway
& Dominic Allen

ISBN: 978 184884 257 1

Printed and bound in the United Kingdom

For a complete list of Pen & Sword titles please
contact
PEN & SWORD BOOKS LIMITED
47 Church Street, Barnsley, South Yorkshire,
S70 2AS, England
E-mail: enquiries@pen-and-sword.co.uk
Website: www.pen-and-sword.co.uk

CONTENTS

'I had lost three good mates. My reaction was terrible, it was like losing a part of my life. When one day they sound the last post for me, I'm sure I'll be meeting my friends again.'

HARRY PATCH AGED 107.

FRONT COVER PHOTOGRAPH OF HARRY PATCH & ABOVE IMAGE: RODERICK FIELD

INTRODUCTION

The final Roll Call of the Great War is complete. There is now no Briton left alive who served in any capacity on the Western Front, nor in any other theatre of war on land. There are no Frenchmen or Belgians, no Russians or Anzacs, no former enemies from Germany, Austria, or Turkey; the war that came to epitomize both the worst of human cruelty and brutality and the best of human endeavour and courage, has finally passed in to history.

The final Roll Call of the Great War is complete. There is now no Briton left alive who served in any capacity on the Western Front, nor in any other theatre of war on land. There are no Frenchmen or Belgians, no Russians or Anzacs, no former enemies from Germany, Austria, or Turkey; the war that came to epitomize both the worst of human cruelty and brutality and the best of human endeavour and courage, has finally passed in to history.

In July this year, Harry Patch, the last fighting Tommy, died peacefully at the residential home where he had lived for the last thirteen years. The previous day he had rallied; he had looked at photos in his autobiography and had been conscious and aware of the visits of close friends. Nevertheless, he was very frail and above all utterly weary, and at 111, and as Britain's and Europe's oldest man, he was ready to slip away.

Harry was fully aware that he was the last man to serve in the trenches; the last veteran to be wounded in action; the last man to go over the top, perhaps the defining public image of the Great War. He may also have been aware that he had taken Henry Allingham's mantle of being Britain's oldest man.

Henry had died exactly a week before. He too was simply worn out by the exertions of 113 years of life. With the loss of both these men, the Great War that has had such a profound influence on world history, was no more.

There was a curious hiatus between the deaths of these two men and those of the other veterans who had recently passed away. In 2005 nine of the 11 surviving veterans who had seen action in France or Flanders all died: Cecil Withers, Smiler Marshall, Alfred Anderson, Harold Lawton, William Elder, Alfred Finnigan, Charles Lloyd, George Rice, Charles Watson. For three and a half years, Harry and Henry carried on. Harry revisited the battlefields around Ypres to further his calls for peace and reconciliation between nations, and Henry travelled around the United Kingdom talking to school children, revisiting the horrors of his war while encouraging those same children to make the best of their talents and their lives.

It could so easily have been the case that the last veterans were bed-ridden and senile; instead, both men

were extraordinarily bright and, in their own different ways, eloquent and persuasive; Harry kept his keen eyesight until the end.

The final reunion of these two old soldiers was last November (2008) when they met at the Cenotaph with a naval veteran, Bill Stone. Three men each representing one of the armed forces, each man laying the a wreath to the dead; Henry, determined to stand, brought proceedings to a halt as he fought to get upright. Finally he had to concede that infirmity would keep him in his chair. It was a poignant reminder that these men who shared 330 years between them were a last tantalising link with the past. Bill died in January.

Recollections from Henry and Harry appear in this special commemorative magazine as do those of a large number of other former soldiers and airmen. Many of them returned to the Western Font on a number of occasions, others refused to revisit the nightmare land of their youth. Harry refused to go for over eighty years until he reluctantly went again in 2002. After his first heart-rending visit he returned again and again, confronting and coming to terms with his own personal demons until, last September, he visited Ypres and unveiled a memorial to his comrades on the very spot where he had gone over the top in 1917; it was the first time those who were with him saw a man at ease both with himself and the battlefield on which he had once fought. He wished to go again this year but faced with the reality of his own frailty, asked for his passport to be placed in his top pocket. His spirit would go back even if his body could not. He died two weeks later.

This magazine pays special homage to the 1914-1918 generation by bringing together the memories of dozens of Great War veterans, the vast majority of whom reached 100 years of age. It was my great privilege to meet them and interview them over 25 years. Men like Henry and Harry, and Cecil and Charles and Alfred and the rest; ordinary men with their gripes and grumbles, prone sometimes to stubbornness like everybody else; ordinary men who lived, nevertheless, through extraordinary times. As a nation we will remember them, and we will miss them.

Richard van Emden, August 2009.
Author, *The Last Fighting Tommy*

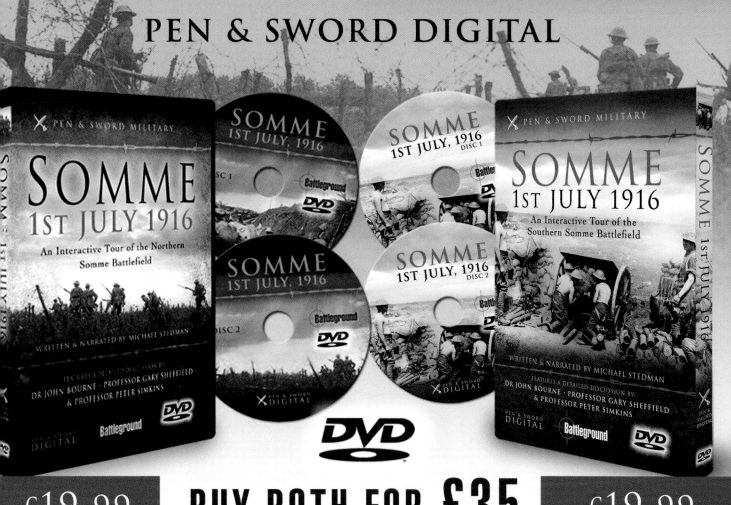

It was a popular notion, not least amongst the tens of thousands of young boys who clamoured to leave boring, poorly paid jobs in order to enlist. If their parents disapproved, they would say that they would be home before the turkey or goose hit the oven, and the chances were that they would never see active service.

OUTBREAK OF HOSTILITIES – SUMMER 1914

The war, widely expected by the general public for a decade or more, had finally arrived, and when news filtered through, any private fears, any attempts at public demonstrations against it, were lost amid the Union Jacks and the carefree singing and dancing.

By Richard van Emden

Extracted from *Britain's Last Tommies* and reproduced by permission of Pen & Sword Books Ltd.

In one or two places the mood turned ugly, and Germans and German businesses were attacked but, for the most part, news of the arrival of war was taken in good part. The reality of the situation, the massive German conscript army that was marching towards France through poor defenceless Belgium, was forgotten; the professional British Army would go to the continent to deliver a bloody nose to the Germans, and return home triumphant. The war, it was widely assumed, would be over by Christmas. It was a popular notion, not least amongst the tens of thousands of young boys who clamoured to leave boring, poorly paid jobs in order to enlist. If their parents disapproved, they would say that they would be home before the turkey or goose hit the oven, and the chances were that they would never see active service. A few months in the countryside, breathing fresh air and being paid for it, was reason enough to allow a son to go to war; parents would be spoilsports to stop it, and downright unpatriotic into the bargain.

When the Archduke Ferdinand, heir to the Austro-Hungarian throne, and his wife were assassinated in Sarajevo by a young Serbian nationalist, Gavrilo Princip, few people even gave the murders a thought, let alone believed it to be of any great consequence. Why should they? In the summer months of July and August, as workers sweltered in their factories and a lucky few took their annual week's holiday, a handful of gunshots hundreds of miles away could not be important.

Unknown to most British people, however, there was a pre-war system of alliances, which would spell the end of peace as they knew it. After the assassination, Austria, backed by its more powerful ally Germany, used the opportunity to give Serbia an ultimatum that would effectively subjugate the small Balkan power to her

German soldiers of the 47th Infantry Regiemnt advance through eastern France, August 1914.

neighbour. Serbia, in turn, appealed to her old ally Russia for support, and it was given. Russia had an agreement with France dating back to 1892 that, if Russia should enter a European war, France would come to her aid. Since 1904, this system of alliances had been extended to Britain. Her 'splendid isolation' had been broken first when she agreed a treaty with Japan in 1902, and two years later, France and Britain had signed an entente cordiale, including an understanding that in a general conflict with Germany, Britain would side with her neighbour. It was an understanding, but not a guaranteed commitment.

In the desire to avoid war on two fronts, the Germans struck out at France by sending three armies through Belgium, a country whose neutrality was guaranteed by Britain, as well as other nations, including Germany. The pressure to become involved was too great. Britain issued an ultimatum to Germany to withdraw and when, at on 11o'clock on the evening of 4 August, the ultimatum expired, Britain became involved in her first conflict on mainland Europe for almost a century.

As the regular army mobilized and set sail for France, the new Secretary of State for War, Lord Kitchener, made his now famous appeal for volunteers. The public might be under the misapprehension that the war would be short, but the iconic Field Marshal was not. He knew, as did other senior commanders, that the war would last beyond Christmas, and probably beyond one or two Christmases after that. Kitchener appealed for an initial 100,000 recruits who would be trained to take the field later in the war. In the meantime the regular army and the territorials would hold the line. This new civilian army was not expected to be fully ready for action until 1917, but losses at the front ensured its deployment long before that date.

Kitchener's recruitment poster.

Kitchener's public standing was immense, at a time when military men figured large in the popular consciousness. Britain's standing in the world was largely due to, and depended on, courageous and patriotic soldiers who upheld the nation's honour and

A Scottish regiment in full marching order arrives at a railway station en-route for the Continent.

prestige around the globe. Kitchener had won his public spurs in crucial victories at the tail end of the nineteenth century at the Battle of Omdurman, and Khartoum and his name had become synonymous with steadfastness and courage. His appeal met with a resounding response from the men of Britain, who flocked in large numbers to recruiting stations across the country. However, it was only with the news of the first setback of the war, the Battle of Mons and the subsequent retreat almost to the gates of Paris, that there was the largest flood of recruits. Men who had held back from enlisting on a wait-and-see basis now found that their country really did need them, and urgently.

The summer months of 1914 had seen the army on manoeuvres, both the regular army and the territorials training at camps across Britain. The ranks of the territorials were filled with young lads keen to have a two-week break from work, and the summer camp was a chance to see friends and have a good time. In Scotland, Alfred Anderson had just finished his annual

stay at Monzie Camp near Crieff. He had been looking forward to his two weeks of freedom from work at his father's joinery in Newtyle. Alfred, one of six children, had joined the territorials in 1912 with other local lads and was eighteen when war broke out. Another such lad was George Rice, from Birmingham. He was enjoying his break in Wales with the Durham Light Infantry when news came of war.

The regular army had set sail for France, sending an Expeditionary Force of six divisions, numbering 80,000 men. The first units began to arrive on the continent within ten days of mobilization, a remarkable feat in itself, and these were moved cautiously northeast until they reached the small Belgian town of Mons. Cavalry were then sent forward, scouring the countryside in an attempt to make contact with the enemy. The first skirmishes took place on the morning of 22 August but it was not until the following day that the fighting began in earnest, as the Germans attacked British infantry deployed along the bank of the Mons-Condé Canal. In

fierce exchanges, the Germans suffered grievous losses, but their numbers were overwhelming and the British were forced to withdraw for fear of being enveloped by enemy troops crossing further down the Canal. A retreat from Mons began that would not be halted for two weeks, by which time the BEF had been forced to march over 200 miles to the southeast of Paris. The

Much of the fighting at Mons took place in built up areas from which much of the civilian population had not had time to flee.

Human degris; German corpses after an attack.

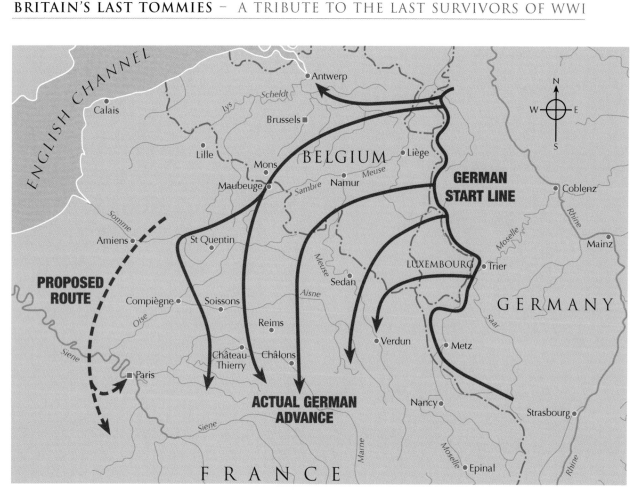

The German advance through Belgium.

Germans followed closely behind, but in doing so committed a gross tactical error. The pre-war blueprint for an invasion of France, known as the Schlieffen Plan, had included the encirclement and capture of Paris, in order to knock France out of the conflict. By failing to seize the capital and following the BEF instead, the Germans swung their forces east in an attempt to rout the British, overstretching their own supply lines, and forcing their equally exhausted troops to carry on the chase all the way to the River Marne. This opened up the German army to an assault from the flank. The French Sixth Army, which had been withdrawn to defend Paris, was now ordered east to attack the Germans, taking the enemy by complete surprise. The Germans were forced to retire to the first defensible position, a ridge known as the Chemin des Dames. As the Germans fell back, the Allies advanced again, but were incapable of shifting the Germans from the ridge. Both sides dug in on the Aisne. It was the beginning of trench warfare.

Unwilling to accede to a static war, both sides began to try to outflank each other, moving northwest in a

Tented military training camps sprung up all over England in the Summer of 1914.

struggle to envelop each other's forces. As both sides moved diagonally across northern France, they passed over the rolling countryside of the Somme, which was to play such a major role in the war two years later. The inevitable result of any outflanking manoeuvre was effectively a race to the sea, and at Nieuport on the Belgium coast, both sides settled with nowhere else to go. Behind them were hundreds of miles of front that would now be dug and fortified in a line of trenches, which would eventually run from the Belgian coast through to the Swiss Alps.

The Germans might have been dealt a formidable blow on the Marne but their numerical advantage was

still an impressive weapon even if many of their best troops had been killed or wounded. Their firepower was also pre-eminent and in chaotic fighting near the Belgium town of Ypres, the BEF fought to hold the line as the Germans pressed for a breakthrough in the late autumn and early winter of 1914. The British regular army, supported by rapidly deployed units of the territorial army, hung on, although at times it was touch and go. By December, the Germans called a halt to their offensives and dug in for winter.

At home, recruits for Kitchener's new army shivered with cold and slept in makeshift camps hastily constructed in the aftermath of the huge civilian response to the call to arms. Nearly one million men had enlisted by the end of the year, four times the number of the old regular army, which had relied on having half of its men abroad and in foreign billets at any time. Recruitment had been over-successful: men had been drawn from right across the social spectrum, many leaving jobs vital to the British war economy in order to enlist. They now sat in tents and huts waiting for equipment. For months, these eager recruits were

marched around, sporting not much more than the civilian clothes they had joined up in and using broomsticks for rifles. Morale was good at first, but in the autumn of 1914 it began to slip, as men saw little immediate prospect of service other than to flounder in the mud that inevitably surrounded camps when thousands of pairs of feet ground green fields into soup. To be serving with your friends was a good enough jape for younger recruits, but for older soldiers with families to support at home, the excitement of going to war was beginning to wear off. Separation allowances to loved ones back home were being indifferently paid as the authorities worked to set up payment schemes; dissatisfaction and resentment would grow unless conditions improved rapidly.

As the war became bogged down in the winter mud, it was evident that it would not be over quickly; instead, it was hoped that 1915 would bring victory. A Christmas gift from Princess Mary to the soldiers at the front, came with various gifts in an embossed brass tin accompanied by a photograph of the princess, and a message wishing the men a merry Christmas and a victorious New Year.

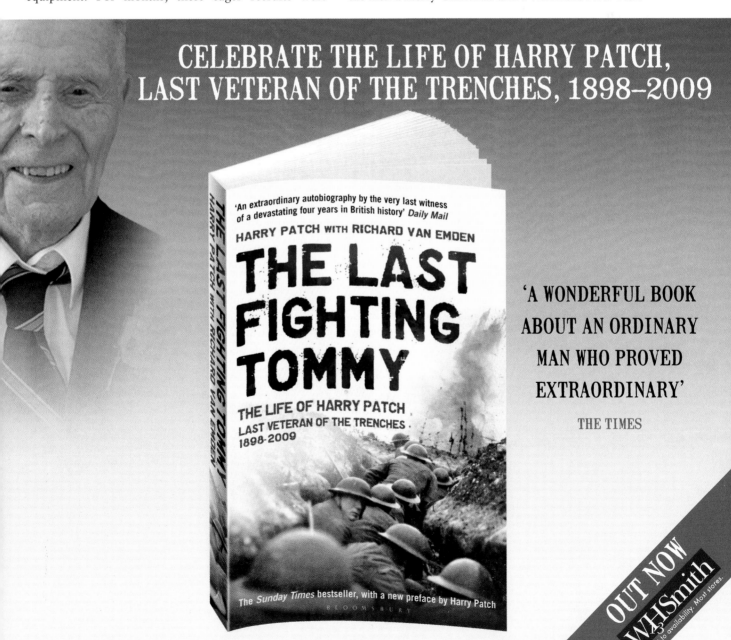

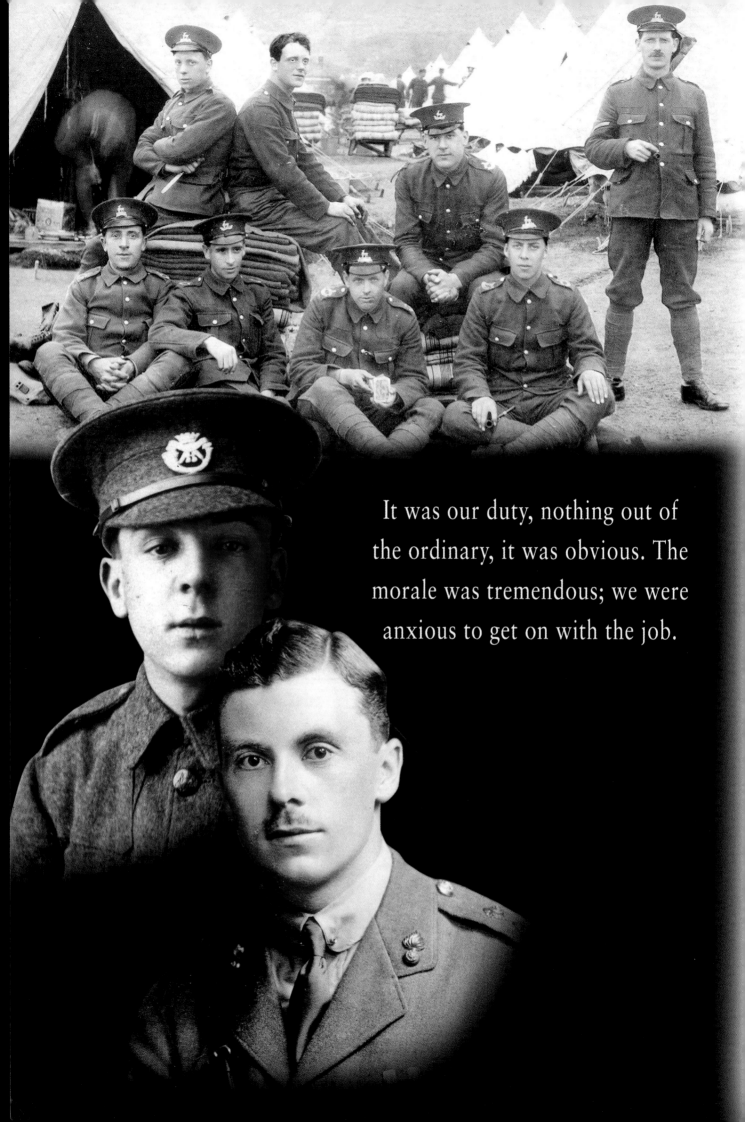

It was our duty, nothing out of the ordinary, it was obvious. The morale was tremendous; we were anxious to get on with the job.

THE FINAL WITNESSES:
EXPECTATIONS – ENLISTMENT
TRAINING – EMBARCATION

By Richard Van Emden

Extracted from *Britain's Last Tommies* and reproduced by permission of Pen & Sword Books Ltd.

PRIVATE PERCY VICTOR JOHNSON, NO39931, 21ST LONDON REGIMENT, 1 MARCH 1899-MAY 2002

When I was a youngster, I was helping a greengrocer to get food out on a stall when who should come down the Oxford Road on horseback but King George. And who should be with him but the Kaiser, stuck up there wearing a great big cape and a helmet and wonderful medals on his chest. Well, our own King George, he looked absolutely way out of his depth. When I got home I told my father and he said, "Oh, there's going to be a war, and not so very long either. That bloke's not over here for nothing." This was in about 1913. A year later, my father went off to fight in the Great War with his three brothers and in time I followed him.

LANCE CORPORAL VICTOR THOMAS COLE, NO1308, 7TH QUEEN'S OWN (ROYAL WEST KENT REGIMENT), 2 JANUARY 1897-20 NOVEMBER 1995

About this time [1913] in the grounds of the Crystal Palace there was a terrific open air floodlight display. "The Invasion", as it was called, featured a life-size English village complete with church and pub. Village folk walked slowly from the former and others drank beer outside the latter. Into this peaceful rural scene suddenly a German plane swooped (it ran down a wire) and dropped some bombs which exploded with appropriate noise and a great deal of smoke. When the air cleared it was seen that German soldiers occupied the village. All ended happily when the Territorials arrived and routed the enemy.

PRIVATE ARTHUR JAMES BURGE, NO202813, 1ST EAST SURREY REGIMENT, 19 JUNE 1895-17 AUGUST 1999

My housemaster at Malvern, the geography teacher, always started the beginning of term very patriotically. He'd got a map that showed in red all the possessions of the Empire, and where we kept order in the world. He would give us a talk that always finished with: "Now,

Percy Victor Johnson witnessed the the crowned heads of England and Germany riding down the Oxford Road, London.

boys, if your country is ever in danger you should be willing to give up your life for her." He said that every term and I never forgot it.

SAPPER ARTHUR HALESTRAP, NO316620, 138 BRIGADE, 46TH DIVISION ROYAL ENGINEERS, 8 SEPTEMBER 1898-2 APRIL 2004

History was well taught, and we knew all about the Crimea and Florence Nightingale and all the notable figures of those days. Living in Southampton, seafaring was particularly in our blood and the might of the British Navy was always in our mind. Every year there was a big review of the Navy at Spit Head, and we were taken round the fleet in a paddle steamer to see what it

Arthur Halestrap recalled: "Every year there was a big review of the Navy at Spit Head, and we were taken round the fleet in a paddle steamer."

was like. There seemed to be hundreds of ships of all sizes from little pinnaces rushing about right up to giant battleships.

A distant relative of my mother's was related to Nelson's Captain on the *Victory*, and we had to go and visit her and kneel and she would bless us. As the Royal family used to dress their children in sailor suits, so we would all follow the tradition. I had a blouse with a big collar with three white stripes on it and short trousers. That was the sort of thing that happened when I was a boy.

My father was in the volunteers and his brothers were in the South African war. I remember, at the age of three, the excitement when letters came from the front. Whilst we were at school, we were told all the current events,

and they were full of war. We knew that a conflict was being prepared and was inevitable. The only thing that we were troubled about was who would be our allies.

[Ed. Many men in Southampton worked in maritime industries. Arthur's father worked for the White Star shipping line, as did his neighbour. As a young lad, Arthur had the run of the White Star ships that docked in the port, including HMS Titanic, which Arthur was allowed to visit and walk round. Shortly afterwards, the ship sank, taking with it Arthur's neighbour who served as an engineer.]

PRIVATE CECIL CLARENCE WITHERS, NO16230, 7TH EAST SURREY REGIMENT, 9 JUNE 1898-17 APRIL 2005

I was in the scout camp at St Mary Cray near Orpington, the night war was declared, 4 August 1914, and our scoutmaster told us the news. The boys, oh, they did put their hands together, "Hooray", you know. "England is at war with Germany," he said, and we clapped hands because we knew we would be fighting for the right things. After that, they dissolved the scouts, and our scoutmaster, who was in the territorials, went away to France and was killed. He was a very nice chap.

Cecil Clarence Withers was camping when war was declared, 'The boys, oh, they did put their hands together, "Hooray".'

PRIVATE ARTHUR BURGE, 1ST EAST SURREY REGIMENT, 1895-1999

I was staying with a German family over the summer when, on 1 August 1914, my father sent a telegram, "Return home immediately." Herr Professor Dr Berne banged on my room door, and said I had half an hour to get packed to catch the train from Metz. I grabbed everything, I never had time to wash, or have a cup of tea. He walked me to the station and off I went to London.

I had my suspicions that war was breaking out; there had been so much talk. On the way to the station, the professor asked me if I could lend him two sovereigns, which I did. I didn't know why he asked. After the war, when we made claims against the Germans for reparation, I claimed the two sovereigns and got them back through the offices of Rothschilds.

PRIVATE GEORGE FRANCIS RICE, NO238217, 1/5TH DUKE OF WELLINGTON'S REGIMENT, 18 JUNE 1897-17 SEPTEMBER 2005

I was away on our annual summer camp when the war broke out. I was a member of what was known as the Special Reserve and we were on a fifteen-day exercise. The weather was gorgeous, and the scenery beautiful. There were stories in the newspapers of trouble abroad but we didn't take much notice. It was good at camp, and we were quite happy there. I found it exciting; it was like a holiday.

I went up a hill for a walk to have a good view of where we were and, as I went, a bugle sounded and I saw a lot of people running about down below. I thought, "I wonder what that is?" and went down to see. Well, blow me down, the war had started – and I was in it whether I wanted it or not."

PRIVATE ALFRED ANDERSON, NO1643, A COMPANY, 1/5TH BLACK WATCH, 25 JUNE 1896-21 NOVEMBER 2005

As members of the territorials, we had our annual camp when we were able to get away from work and enjoy some time with good friends. July 1914 was my third summer training, this time at Monzie Camp near Crieff. The weather was hot and on route marches, we wore short sleeves. One evening, just before our summer camp finished, a group of us were talking one night when we heard loud cheering from the officers' marquee, and we wondered what it was. We were told war had been declared and were advised that we would get call-up papers.

I told my parents, and my father took the news very, very badly. The first thing he said was, "You're only a laddie apprentice, you can't go to war." I said, "I'm not going to war. I'm just going to Dundee drill hall." Mum didn't say much; she was too upset.

CORPORAL GEORGE BRUMWELL JAMESON, NO242 A SQUADRON, 1/1ST NORTHUMBERLAND YEOMANRY, 19 DECEMBER 1892-2 MARCH 1999

We wanted to go to war. It was something one felt one had to do, it was a duty we owed to the country. Just as my forebears had fought in the Boer War, so I was going to go to this one. You didn't question what you were doing. There was no animosity against the Germans, not as far as we were concerned. We used to say at the time that the German soldier had to do his duty just as we had to do ours. But the Germans had no justification for attacking France by coming through Belgium. We thought that Belgium was sacrosanct, so to speak, but they were egged on by the Kaiser's self-aggrandisement and that led them to do what they did. We thought we had a better army altogether and once we got down to business, we would wipe them out.

ABLE SEAMAN ALFRED GEORGE BASTIN, L8/2717, D COMPANY, HAWKE BATTALION, ROYAL NAVAL VOLUNTEER RESERVE (RNVR), 30 JULY 1896- FEBRUARY 1997

I enlisted in the Royal Naval Volunteer Reserve as a drummer boy in July 1912, shortly before my sixteenth birthday. I was one of four children and we lived near Waterloo Station where my father worked printing tickets for the railway. My elder brother joined the East Surreys and was sent to India and my younger brother went to France. At one point all three of my father's sons were in uniform and serving during a time of war, a fact of which my father was very proud.

On 3 August 1914, I'd been out in Hyde Park to listen to the band, which I used to do every Sunday. I got home about half past nine and as I opened the door, on the floor were two envelopes. I thought, "What on earth is this, on a Sunday night?" One was from the naval volunteers mobilizing me, telling me to report to headquarters, and the other was from the Custom House appointing me to a job somewhere on the east coast. I got into my uniform and went down to headquarters, and people kept drifting in asking me who I was, and my rank. "I'm a drummer boy in the bugle band." "All

> We wanted to go to war. It was something one felt one had to do, it was a duty we owed to the country. You didn't question what you were doing. There was no animosity against the Germans, not as far as we were concerned.

right, stand on the gate and announce the new arrivals as they come in." I stood at the gate until midnight before they let me go home, telling me to report back in the morning.

A few days later, Lord Kitchener made his appeal for men and quite a number of them were miners from Yorkshire who came down to London. Well, the following month, when they were forming the 1st Naval Division, as we became known, they found that we weren't completely up to strength, and these poor blokes who only been in the army for three or four weeks and had only just been taught how to handle a bloody rifle, were given to us, with no training at all. We were gradually being fitted out, but half these men had khaki trousers and blue jackets and they had to go out to Belgium like that.

CORPORAL ERNEST ALBERT DORAN, NO2152, 2ND LONDON REGIMENT (ROYAL FUSILIERS), 25 FEBRUARY 1893-MAY 1996

I never had the slightest intention of going to fight for King and Country. It is true I joined up in August 1914, but that was only because we thought the war would be over by Christmas. We thought that by going to Malta we would have a nice holiday in the Mediterranean for a few months, then we'd come back, the war would be over, and we could get back to work.

This is how it happened. I went to work on the Monday morning as usual, and a group of us were having a cup of coffee in Lyons. Anyway, this chap came over to us and said, "How would you fellows like to go to Malta?" So we all said, "Oh, yes we'd all like to go," so the whole office enlisted, eight or nine of us. This man worked with us but he was also a member of a territorial battalion in the London Regiment, and so he took us off to Vincent Square near Victoria to enlist. I went back into the office until 4pm that afternoon to clear up any loose ends – that was on the Monday – and four days after I joined, we sailed. The authorities needed to transfer regular battalions from Malta and we were shipped out there to take their place.

PRIVATE FRANCIS 'FRANK' EDWARD SUMPTER, NO5345, A COMPANY 1ST RIFLE BRIGADE, 13 OCTOBER 1897-31 JULY 1999

I was ordered with a few men to go to Parkstone Quay, Harwich, as guard of honour to Prince Lichnowsky, the German ambassador to London, because although the BEF had set off for France, he hadn't left the country then. We went to Harwich, and the sergeant major came along, and lined up the troops to present arms. Then he looked at me and said, "Not you, you're too young, get back," so I dropped out. Instead, I had a bird's eye view of proceedings and saw the embassy staff with all their baggage and prams, quite a retinue of them, leaving the country.

LANCE CORPORAL JOSEPH ARMSTRONG, NO2123, B COY, 1ST LOYAL NORTH LANCASHIRE REGIMENT, SPECIAL RESERVE, 12 APRIL 1895-JULY 1997

I was called up on 6 August and arrived at Fulwood Barracks in Preston on the 8 August, before I was sent south to Felixstowe. As soon as I got there, they put me in the Military Police. I was walking along the promenade one morning when I was told the Company Officer wanted to see me. I'd heard that the first draft was going out to France and I thought, "Oh good, I'm going to be on the first draft," and I was quite pleased about that. When I got there, a Colour Sergeant and an officer greeted me and said, "Armstrong, you're a first class shot, they want a musketry instructor at Fulwood Barracks. You'll be given another stripe and when you get there you'll be made a Staff Sergeant." Then the officer looked at me. "Armstrong, you don't look too pleased. What's the matter?"

"I thought you were going to tell me I was on the first draft, Sir."

"What draft? Which draft?"

"Sir, I understand the first draft is to go out."

"Armstrong, you mean to tell me that you'd rather go across there amongst all that blood and shit?"

He must have thought I was crackers, but he could see

Frank Edward Sumpter witnessed the departure of the German Ambassador, Prince Lichnowsky and his wife.

"How would you fellows like to go to Malta?" was the invitation to join the great adventure Albert Doran jumped at in August 1914. A packed troopship crowded with cheerful Tommies enters the Mediterranean.

that I was determined to go, so he said, "Put him on the draft, Colour Sergeant." The next day we were marched down to Felixstowe Station as the band played "Let auld acquaintance be forgot," and were put on a train to Southampton to set sail for St Nazaire.

PRIVATE ALFRED ANDERSON, 1/5TH BLACK WATCH, 1896-2005

The quartermaster sergeant called out the roll. He was sitting at a table in the middle of the hall and he just took us as we were in the roll book, so I was about the first to volunteer because my name is A. Anderson. I didn't sign anything. You had to declare your willingness to go abroad in front of the others. That was enough. Only one or two said they couldn't volunteer for home reasons, parents to support and things like that, but very few refused to go. We did have talks amongst ourselves about it and the main thing I remember was that we would stick together. We had drilled together, been at camps with the same fellows, what else could you do? You couldn't say "I'm not staying with the battalion."

One of the lads who volunteered was Fred Geekie, who was aged only sixteen. I knew him well as we grew up in the same town of Newtyle, before his family moved to the high street in Forfar. Everybody was aware of his age, but nobody said anything. Several of us told him privately that he was too young to go, but he said, "I want to keep with the boys." It was natural, of course, I mean we had been brought up with each other. The Sergeants didn't want to know and so Geekie went out with the battalion. He was killed towards the end of the war.

SAPPER ARTHUR HALESTRAP, 46TH DIVISION ROYAL ENGINEERS, 1898-2004

The troops used to come through Southampton to embark at the docks, and it was tremendously exciting to watch the men march through the town, and to see the remounts going through, one man leading three horses. Of course we were always excited if one broke away and ran off. The Scottish regiments were the most impressive. To hear the pipes and to see all these huge lines of troops in their kilts all going the same direction, it was wonderful. Everyone would turn out and cheer

them on their way, giving them chocolate, fruit and tins of milk.

TROOPER BENJAMIN GEORGE CLOUTING, NO8292, 4TH TROOP, C SQUADRON, 4TH (ROYAL IRISH) DRAGOON GUARDS, 15 SEPTEMBER 1897-13 AUGUST 1990

It was dark below deck, for with the threat of submarine attack, all lights had been dimmed, and portholes closed and firmly screwed shut. Up on deck, there was a strict order banning all smoking, but the crossing was calm, and the night warm enough so that many troopers seemed content to just sleep where they liked up on deck.

It was light when we pulled into Boulogne, and we excitedly crowded along the ship's railing to get some early impressions. Walking along the quay were French soldiers wearing their blue jackets, red trousers, and

The British Expeditionary Force lands at Bolougne to a joyous welcome from the French people.

Refugees stream towards the port of Antwerp.

Marines of the Naval Division marching through Ostend.

Right: First Lord of the Admiralty, Winston Churchill, with General Seeley. Alfred Bastin witnessed their presence in Belgium as he approached the town of Antwerp.

peak caps. "Blimey," said one man, "even the postmen have got bayonets."

PRIVATE ALFRED ANDERSON, 1/5TH BLACK WATCH, 1896-2005

We were told mid-afternoon that we were getting a few hours off to go home and say goodbye to our parents. We went to where the transport was, a lorry and two horses and a driver, Dundee to Newtyle. It took about two hours to get there; it's a nice flat road, you see, and we trotted all the way. I saw some of my relatives and I said my goodbyes and mother gave me a bible; then it was back on the transport.

The battalion left at 7am. On the train south, the officers sat in the first class compartments with corridors whereas we had empty guards' vans. We didn't worry about the toilets when we were travelling through the country, we just slid the doors back and urinated straight out the side of the wagon.

There were only two stops and one was at York. When we got there, the platform was practically lined with people, and we thought they were a reception and that we were going to be given some refreshments. They were in fact the station staff and were there to keep us on the train. We were for getting out, but they held up their hands, and said, "Don't come out, you can't come

out," and we found out why. The engine needed water and we had to reverse to the pumps. Next time we came to the station, we went right through.

ABLE SEAMAN ALFRED BASTIN, HAWKE BATTALION, ROYAL NAVAL VOLUNTEER RESERVE, 1896-1997

We left Kingsdown Camp on the afternoon of 4 October, and went along to Dover to embark for Dunkirk. At Dover, all the kit bags were placed on the foredeck of the troop ship. The men were in a holiday mood. We were mostly reservists, Saturday night sailors, they called us, part of the London Division, but I for one wasn't worried at all. I was eighteen years old and thought the whole thing a great adventure.

We landed in Belgium and boarded trains that moved us up towards Antwerp from where refugees were pouring away, an incredible sight, with their belongings on their backs. We marched up towards the trenches, which had been prepared for us to defend the town, when suddenly we were given orders to step aside. A motor car came along at a fair pace and who should be in it but General Seeley and Winston Churchill no less, the First Lord of the Admiralty!

Repeat after me 'I swear to serve His Majesty the King, His heirs and successors, And the generals and officers set over me, so help me God." Some new recruits, holding Bibles, are sworn in at a recruiting office.

RECRUITING A NEW ARMY

[Ed. Some men wanted to volunteer straightaway; others were more circumspect, and waited to see what would happen. After the retreat from Mons, recruitment soared, in a mixture of enthusiasm and patriotism. Amongst those recruited in early September were Vic Cole and Jack Davis.

Vic Cole was a seventeen-year-old lad undertaking an apprenticeship at the Clapham School of Telegraphy. On the evening of 4 August, he had walked up the Mall and stood outside the gates of Buckingham Palace as war was declared. A month later, he enlisted in the 7th Queen's Own (Royal West Kent Regiment).

Jack Davis, a nineteen-year-old boy from London, was working at the National Liberal Club in Whitehall. He, like Vic, responded to Kitchener's call, enlisting with his friends en masse at New Scotland Yard. Vic lived to 98 years old, Jack 108, briefly holding the title of Britain's oldest man.]

2ND LIEUTENANT RICHARD MAURICE HAWKINS, 16 PLATOON, D COMPANY, 11TH ROYAL FUSILIERS, 8 MARCH 1895-26 NOVEMBER 1994

The war broke out and as a young man it was my duty to enlist. I was apprentice to Hoffmanns, a ball-bearing company, and I went into the office one day and said that like all young men I must join up. The boss called me a number of rather unpleasant things, saying that I was an ungrateful so and so. I didn't have much of a vocabulary but I told him what I thought of him and left.

Kitchener had no trouble in finding the first hundred thousand volunteers. Damn it, you couldn't get into the ruddy army, there was such a rush to get in and defeat the enemy, and prevent him from taking over this country. I went to London many times to get into the army and couldn't. The crowds were too big.

In school we'd been in the cadet corps, and we knew how to behave; we knew what we'd got to do. It was our

Richard Maurice Hawkins.

duty, nothing out of the ordinary, it was obvious. The morale was tremendous; we were anxious to get on with the job. After all, if you see somebody breaking into your home you've got to give him a clout, haven't you, get rid of him, and that's what the Germans were trying to do. It was only natural that we wanted to go to France and stop this nonsense.

PRIVATE EDWARD 'TED' FRANCIS NO1114, 1 PLATOON, A COMPANY, 16TH ROYAL WARWICKSHIRE REGIMENT, 30 JUNE 1896-24 MARCH 1996

Birmingham people were excited, laughing, joking. Young people, like myself, were saying, "We'll show those Germans, we'll push them back home, how dare they walk over little Belgium." We were anxious to get to France and have a go at them. I worked at a small factory making envelopes and stationery, but it was a boring kind of job and so I didn't want much pushing. The girls, they said, "Oh Ted, you can't stop here now," and they practically ushered me out of the factory. The talk then was that it would all be over by Christmas, so we were quite impatient to get into the army. It may have been obvious to the senior officers that it was going to be a long war, but not to us.

LANCE CORPORAL VIC COLE, 7TH QUEEN'S OWN (ROYAL WEST KENT REGIMENT), 1897-1995

I got home and met George Pulley, who was a bit of a lad, and he said, "Yes, I'm going to join the army." They were having a recruitment meeting at the top of Anerley Hill by the south tower of the Crystal Palace, and the speaker was going on about this Kaiser and keeping the Germans off the green fields of old England, and telling us how beautiful it was to be in the army. So George said, "Come on, then, let's join up." There was an old touring car there and a chap saying, "Come on, young fellows, join the army", so we climbed into the car and it took us along the Crystal Place Parade and down the hill to Bromley Drill Hall. We were driven to a nearby pub, and shown to an upstairs room with several long tables, where we signed on for the duration of the war.

PRIVATE JOHN 'JACK' DAVIS, NO12482, D COMPANY, 6TH DUKE OF CORNWALL'S LIGHT INFANTRY, 1 MARCH 1895-20 JULY 2003

I was in the Boys' Brigade and was a member of an athletics club too, so I both accepted discipline and had an organised life. The call of the army quite naturally attracted me. I enlisted in New Scotland Yard with thirty of my colleagues, en masse, because our manager at the Liberal Club was a patriotic Frenchman and so we had no difficulty in joining up and letting the women take over our jobs. Then we had a night out, the group of us, for once you accepted the traditional king's shilling, you're in. So, it being our last night of freedom, we made the best of it with the boys.

PRIVATE TED FRANCIS, 16TH ROYAL WARWICKSHIRE REGIMENT, 1896-1996

When I went to enlist, I was amazed to see a long queue of young men about the same age as myself, all laughing and joking, and I thought it was more like a queue for a music-hall than to be a soldier.

I passed easily into the army. You see, my brother and I used to practise weightlifting. Every Sunday morning we used to lift astonishing weights from the floor to above our heads, in the region of a hundredweight with single right hand lifts, first to the shoulder and then up and down. When I enlisted at the Town Hall in Birmingham, the doctor told me to strip. He just had one look at me and said, "Huh, wish they was all like that, my job would be easy, put your clothes on."

When I came home, my mother and father were waiting for me. I'd been spotted queuing by a customer who drank in Dad's pub. Oh, they tore me off a strip - my father wasn't as angry because he understood my feelings, but my mother, she said, "You little fool, don't you understand there's only thieves and vagabonds join the army – you go back and tell them that you've changed your mind and you're not going to join their army." I said, "Mother, I can't do that. I've made an oath to defend the King and Country and accepted the King's shilling and that's that. I can't go back on it, and I don't want to." "Well," mother said, "I suppose you'll be off

New recruits for the 3rd Birmingham Pals, 16th Royal Warwickshire Regiment, Edward 'Ted' Francis No1114, 1 Platoon, A Company, could well be in this parade in front of Moseley College, Birmingham.

to France in a day or two and I shan't see you again." I said, "Oh no, mother, we've got to be trained, we'll be at least five or six months in England yet."

She was very inquisitive to know more. Where would we train? But the upshot was that she was much more amenable to me being a soldier. "That's all right, the outing will do you good. I know you'll be home for Christmas because they all say it will be over by then, and to have you here at Christmas, that's all I want." I little realized that that was the last time I should see my mother, because in less than no time I had to go back for her funeral. She died of heart failure.

PRIVATE JOSEPH HENRY YARWOOD, NO68405, 94TH FIELD AMBULANCE, ROYAL ARMY MEDICAL CORPS (RAMC), 9 MAY1896-4 AUGUST 1995

It was common to invite a well-known sportsman to come to a particular town, and they'd organize this meeting – of course it was a recruiting meeting – and they would talk about how they were going to have their own local regiment. The man would say, "Now, boys, we're all going to become part of one regiment, the Swansea volunteers, or whatever, and you're invited to join," and that was very successful. Of course it was nice to go and join up with your pals, because you'd got somebody you knew with you, somebody you could rely on, a much happier feeling than if you were going into a strange crowd.

[Ed. The raw recruits had to be trained before they went to France, a process that was expected to take the best part of a year. For many, it was rather like the Scout camps of their youth, an enjoyable opportunity to be with others of a similar age and background. Those who were to undertake initial training of this eager rabble were in many cases old regular soldiers, some well into their seventieth year. Their first impressions must have proved sobering.]

PRIVATE ROBERT BURNS, NO14141, 16TH PLATOON, D COMPANY, 7TH CAMERON HIGHLANDERS, 12 NOVEMBER 1895-29 OCTOBER 2000

We thought the war would be over before we went out to France. We thought, six months at most, and we had to be trained first and how long that would take we had no idea. We were young, and we thought little more than that we would get in some fun before we had to go back to work. At 18 or 19 one is not very clever, nor very learned, I didn't know anything about world affairs or politics. We listened to what other people were doing and thought, "Why can't we do that?" We had absolutely no idea as to what was going to happen. Later, when we were in France, we'd joke, "So when's this six months up then?"

We were all in it together, pals. "Where do you come from?" "What do you do?" "Where did you work?"

"Any cigarettes? Got a light?" "Are you married? No? Any girls?" "Oh yes, half a dozen!"

The training was good fun, shoulder arms, stand easy, nothing to it, it was most enjoyable, as long as one was physically fit. I'll let you into a little secret, too. My pal told me, "If you fail your rifle practice, know what they say? You go back the next day. If you pass your rifle practice you're on a five mile run." So I made it my duty to fail my rifle practice, miss the target. So I went back to the ranges, while those who passed had to go for a long run.

There were three of us who stuck together. One of them was a farmer's son, he didn't have much of an education but he was a real friend, he knew all about life, animal life and human life. He called me Palindrome Burns because my regimental number was 14141.

2ND LIEUTENANT NORMAN MARGRAVE DILLON, 14TH NORTHUMBERLAND FUSILIERS, 27 JULY 1896-17 OCTOBER 1997

I was studying to be a mining engineer, but I was glad to get out of the mines when the Secretary of State for War made his appeal for volunteers. I was 18 and one month when I received my commission from the War Office and, after acquiring a uniform, received instructions to report to the 14th Battalion at Berkhamstead. Everyone

was in billets, but nobody knew where anything was, so I was told simply to turn up on a local football field at 8 the next morning. There I found 200 men drawn up in squares. They were nearly all miners from the Morpeth area, and had been told to go in their old clothes because uniforms would be issued to them. As I wondered what to do, an old soldier with Boer War ribbons on his chest approached and gravely saluted me, asking, "Are you our new officer?" I told him I didn't know. "I think you are, Sir, as we haven't got any." He asked for instructions but I was completely ignorant of military procedure and, not knowing what to do, I suggested the men should sit down, and then, seeing other companies dispersing, I told him to "Carry on, Sergeant Major," – he was in fact a corporal – and told him to end the parade, not knowing how to do it myself.

After breakfast, I slipped away from my billet and the first thing I did was to go to the railway station, to Smith's bookstall, and there I found various books of a military nature and picked up a War Office manual called "Infantry Training". Set out quite clearly was the whole procedure of falling-in a company and how to manoeuvre it around the parade ground. I spent a lot of time with this manual, drilling imaginary troops represented by matchsticks, until I was fairly proficient. I learnt a new movement each day and then tried it out

Private Ted Francis (top left) training with the 16th Warwickshire Regiment.

on the men. We got along famously. They hadn't a clue I was pulling the wool over their eyes, and that I was always just one step ahead of them.

LANCE CORPORAL VIC COLE, 7TH QUEEN'S OWN (ROYAL WEST KENT REGIMENT), 1897-1995

We had some old timers with the 7th Battalion. The first Major we had, I believe, had Crimean War medals on, and if they weren't Crimean, then they were from the Afghan wars of the 1870s. Major Whittaker was his name and he was at least seventy-five years old. From just a mob wandering round, we were sorted out into sections and platoons. He came out and said, "Attention! Shoulder arms!" and another officer, one of the younger ones, said quietly, "Sir, Sir, it's slope arms." 'Shoulder arms' was the order he used to give way back in the last century. We had wooden guns, cut out into shape, just to learn rifle drill; it was a long time before we got our real rifles.

2ND LIEUTENANT RICHARD HAWKINS, 11TH ROYAL FUSILIERS, 1895-1994

I was on parade with my company one morning, and Major Walters came in, nothing to do but he'd come back to serve his country. I said, "Um, excuse me, Sir, what medals are represented by those little ribbons that you're wearing?" "Well," he said, "one is the King's South African Medal and the other's the Queen's. I'm not quite sure which is which. All I can tell you is that my life was never in danger for one moment. I'm not sure I ever heard a shot fired."

2ND LIEUTENANT NORMAN DILLON, 14TH NORTHUMBERLAND FUSILIERS, 1896-1997

Our training consisted mainly of route marches. There were no uniforms at this time and authority had only been given for the local purchase of boots. As a result, the men's clothing was a scandal, shirt tails sticking out of old trousers. One day I was drilling my platoon when Brigadier General Armstrong rode up on his horse and abused me because my men were clad in rags and tatters. There were plenty of uniforms available in the stores and I had only to ask for them. This was untrue: we did not receive any uniforms for some time after this, and then they were dismal affairs of blue, mass-produced in haste.

PRIVATE JAMES WILLIAM WILSON, NO11727, A COMPANY, 7TH LEICESTERSHIRE REGIMENT, 10 SEPTEMBER, 1896 – FL.1998

We were sent to Aldershot, where we were quickly sorted out and began training the first day we arrived. Physical exercise was undertaken on Salisbury Plain, and parades outside the barracks in civilian clothes. I was

only a kid but a number of men in the battalion were real tough Yorkshire miners. We had no uniforms and our civilian shoes soon wore out before we ever received boots, in fact the miners said they would refuse to parade again if they didn't get proper boots. After a time, we were given uniforms but not khaki, there was no khaki to be had, so they gave us a red uniform with navy blue cuffs and white braiding, ceremonial uniform you might say. At Christmas we were allowed to go home, and I can remember it to this day, I was walking up Granby Street, fancying myself a soldier, and an elderly gentleman stopped me and said, "Excuse me, Sir, are you going to France in that uniform?" I said, "I've got no other." Do you know, we didn't get khaki until March 1915.

LANCE CORPORAL VIC COLE, 7TH QUEEN'S OWN (ROYAL WEST KENT REGIMENT), 1897-1995

The signals officer approached a sergeant and told him he wanted some men to be signallers, so the sergeant said to us one by one, "Well, what are you? Boy Scout? Good. OK, you. What are you?" And he came to me and I said, "Wireless operator." "Oh, we don't want you," he said, dismissing me out of hand. He didn't know anything about it, didn't know there was such a thing as wireless. I thought, "That's funny," until the officer said, "Right, is there anyone else?" And I said, "Yes, Sir, I know morse and semaphore," so he said, "Why didn't you say? OK, well, come on then!"

We practised morse code using flags. We'd go out with the section and form a square and signal to each other. I had messages all written out, "Enemy attacking such and such, send reinforcements" and this would be signalled round the square and we would see if the same message came back. The blokes were pretty good because they used to like it and it was better than company drilling, marching up and down all day. As the training progressed, the telephones came in, and morse became morse by sound instead of sight. The telephones came with thin copper wire, number 18 size, just japanned over black. On manoeuvres it used to get entangled in everything and the infantry used to curse us as they frequently got emmeshed in the stuff. Later, we got D3 cable and a dry cell battery to which you added water to make it active, and they lasted about two or three weeks.

Because of my knowledge, I was made a lance corporal, and on my suggestion we went out for a bit of a march with the signals section around Purfleet. It was an agricultural area, fields bounded by dirt road tracks and telegraph poles, plenty of room to muck about. We had two sets of climbing irons so we could scale the

> Damn it, you couldn't get into the ruddy army, there was such a rush to get in and defeat the enemy, and prevent him from taking over this country.

telegraph poles. There were two terminals on the D3 telephone, and we put wire round one terminal on the phone. One terminal went to the line and the other went to earth or was clipped onto some railings. Then one man would scale the telegraph pole and clip onto one of the telephone wires and the rest of the section would go up the road a couple of hundred yards and clip onto the wire to see if we could get through.

There was a permanent current on the wire and when we tuned in, we could listen to civilians talking on the telephone. It was great fun.

We had call signs: "Is that AK1?" and we would hear:

"I say, Gladys, whatever's that terrible noise on the wire?"

"I don't know, it must be the soldiers, dear."

"Er, sorry, madam, um, troops on manoeuvres."

2ND LIEUTENANT NORMAN DILLON, 14TH NORTHUMBERLAND FUSILIERS, 1896-1997

My company commander and his second in command chose two furrows next to each other, and, like the rest of us, got some fitful sleep. There was no more rain, and as it was only late September, it was not too cold. However, next morning when we gathered shivering round a small fire and had some tea and bully beef, my No.1 complained of heavy rain. "It must have been wet last night. I was lying in a furrow next to Jones and when I woke up my trousers were completely soaked." Nobody said anything, but our suspicions were confirmed when his second in command arrived and said, "My word, it was cold last night, it affected my bladder. I couldn't be bothered to get up so I just turned over and let fly."

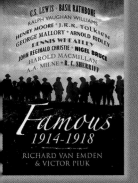
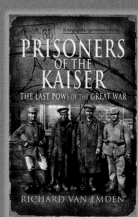

THE FINAL WITNESSES:
INTO ACTION WITH THE GERMANS BEFORE CHRISTMAS 1914

Even before the nucleus of a New Army began to form in Britain, the regular army was venturing towards the Belgian town of Mons. Ahead of the infantry rode the cavalry, which cautiously moved forward, probing for evidence of the enemy who, they were reliably informed, were marching south in huge numbers.

On the night of 21 August, C Squadron of the 4th Dragoon Guards were sent north to see if contact could be made. Among their number was a sixteen-year-old trooper. He was about to witness the first action of the British Expeditionary Force on the continent.

TROOPER BEN CLOUTING, 4TH (ROYAL IRISH) DRAGOON GUARDS, 1897-1990

All four troops of C Squadron were on outpost that night with two troops on standby, saddled up, ready to move at a moment's notice. Our troop was in a

cornfield, along the back of which ran a wood. Everything was still and quiet; everyone was tense. We tied the horses' reins round our wrists, while those too nervous to rest talked to each other in whispers. A few of us slackened our horses' girths to let them breathe freely. But silence was the order, and, as horses were prone to play with their loose bit bars, we held or tied handkerchiefs around the bars to muffle any sound.

At about 6.30am, we arrived at a farm on the corner of a staggered crossroads and began watering our horses in a trough. There were already a few people about and, as we waited, a farm worker came in saying he'd seen

Men and mounts of the Cavalry Division, British Expeditionary Force, after arriving in France in August. Trooper Ben Clouting, 4th (Royal Irish) Dragoon Guards would be among the first into action at Mons.

four German cavalrymen coming down the road.

There was a flurry of action, and a plan was hatched to capture the patrol as it passed. Four men from 4th Troop were dismounted and ordered to fire a volley of shots into the patrol at close quarters. This would be followed by 2nd Troop charging forward and bagging the remainder. I believe a man was sent out behind a hedge to signal when the Germans were about to arrive, but in his excitement he ran to grab his horse and gave his position away.

The Germans turned their horses to go back and the 1st Troop of C Squadron, led by Captain Hornby, went after them, while the rest of the Squadron followed on in support at a fast canter. As the Germans retired into the village, they met up with a larger group of cavalrymen, and, owing to the congestion, were soon caught by the 1st Troop. We arrived after the Germans had scattered, with the main body splitting off and carrying on up the main road. We continued to give chase, our horses slipping all over the place as we clattered along the square-set stones of the road.

Our chase continued for perhaps a mile or more, until we found ourselves flying up a wide tree-lined road. The Germans, reaching the crest of the road, turned and, though they were still mounted, began firing back down

German Uhlans passing through a burning Belgium town.

the hill. The order came, "Action front, dismount. Get the horses under cover!" In one movement the Troop returned their swords, reached for their rifles and dismounted, dashing for cover. Glancing up the hill, I saw several Germans filling the road. They made a perfect target, and Thomas, the first into action, shot one from his horse.

As far as I am aware, we came out of the action with three prisoners, all suffering from sword wounds. We suffered no casualties except among the horses, one of which had a bullet wound to her stomach. She managed to bring her man out, but she was finished, and was poleaxed in a nearby village.

[Ed. The first shot fired by the British Army on mainland Europe since the Battle of Waterloo ninety-nine years earlier, took place outside the walls of a once-grandiose house one mile north of the village of Casteau, in Belgium. In May 1990, as part of the Old Contemptibles' final pilgrimage to France and Belgium, Ben revisited the spot where the fighting had taken place and stood next to the field where he had taken the horses under cover. It was the first time he had returned there in over 75 years. Ben was seriously ill but he was determined to make the trip and never once let on how poorly he was. On his return, he went into hospital where he died ten weeks later.]

PRIVATE MICHAEL LALLY, 2ND MANCHESTER REGIMENT, 2 SEPTEMBER 1894-13 APRIL 1999

We were meant to be deployed along the Mons-Condé Canal, but in the end we were held in reserve, so we didn't see much action that day and our casualties were light. The battalion received orders to fall back from the Canal to a little village nearby called Dour, from where we could see fires burning in the direction of Mons, and people were streaming away from the fighting, trying to get away with whatever they could carry with them on farm carts and prams. They were terrified and we felt that we had let them down.

TROOPER BEN CLOUTING, 4TH (ROYAL IRISH) DRAGOON GUARDS, 1897-1990

There was complete confusion during the retreat from Mons, for no sooner had the BEF been forced to pull back than the roads became clogged with entire families on the move. Horses, trucks, handcarts, and carriages poured onto every highway, accompanied by the old and the young, all carrying anything they could manage, and all moving at walking pace. We felt sorry for them, but there was nothing we could do.

It was hot, dry and dusty, and very quickly the horses began to look exhausted and dishevelled. Where we could, we rode along the road's soft, unmetalled edges, for the paving stones were very hard on their legs, but our horses soon began to drop their heads, and wouldn't shake themselves as they normally did. Many were so tired, they fell asleep standing up, their legs buckling and taking the skin off their knees. To ease the horses' burden, excess kit was dumped. Shirts, spare socks and other laundry were all thrown away along with our greatcoats.

PRIVATE MICHAEL LALLY, 2ND MANCHESTER REGIMENT, 1894-1999

Michael Lally.

As we retreated down the road, the Military Police were asking, "What division? What regiment?" It was a bloody shambles. That retreat from Mons was the worst part of the war. As we marched south our feet became horribly blistered and sore, I had to wrap puttees round my feet. Later I saw other lads throw their boots away. We ended up in a field just south of Le Cateau. After taking a message on the field telephone, the captain came over and said, "We're all on our own now, lads. Keep going."

TROOPER BEN CLOUTING, 4TH (ROYAL IRISH) DRAGOON GUARDS, 1897-1990

The infantry reservists found the going unbearable. Many had been called up after five years on the reserve and had not marched in all that time. Their feet simply weren't up to the stone-set roads, in stiff, unbroken boots. Blood oozed through shoe soles, or from bits of rag tied round blistered feet. In grim determination, they hobbled along in ones and twos, often hanging on to our stirrup leathers to keep going. At any halt, men fell asleep instantaneously, and required a good shake or the prod of a sergeant's boot to wake them again. History judged the Retreat heroic, but from where I was sitting, it was a shambles.

[Ed. The regular army fought a rolling retreat to the River Marne, south east of Paris, before the tables were turned and the German army, exhausted and over-stretched, was forced to retire to the Chemin des Dames. Within weeks of the outbreak of war, Britain would require its territorial forces to take the field, the first units leaving for France in September. Others followed soon after.]

CORPORAL G B JAMESON, 1/1ST NORTHUMBERLAND YEOMANRY, 1892-1999

We rode into Zeebrugge. It was dead quiet, blackout everywhere, but the clatter of the horses' hooves soon brought the people out. "Oh, they're British", and they flung open every blessed place and showered us with oranges and apples and plied us with wine and loaves of bread. We made a triumphant arrival into Zeebrugge,

girls kissing us, we had a marvellous time.

Towards the end of the day, the squadron was quartered in a field, with the horses tied up on picket lines in a square. It was a beautiful evening, a lovely azure blue sky, dead quiet. We lay there, with our heads resting on our saddles, our waterproof sheets on the ground with a blanket and greatcoat on top. There is nothing more thrilling than to sleep out and then wake in the fresh air of an early dawn. There was no thought of a war. Suddenly, away to one side somebody started to play an air from Cavaleria Rusticana on a fiddle and then presently a light baritone took up the refrain and started to sing. These two men were both members of Gosforth Troop: one was Billy Elliot, he had been an associate of the Gosforth Amateur Dramatics Society in Newcastle, the other was Alf Carrick, a member of the operatic society. To lie there with that lovely sky above you and hear that beautiful music wafting all around, and the chomp, chomp of the horses eating, I've never forgotten that, nothing like it, amazing.

[Ed. Eleven Old Contemptibles made the final pilgrimage to the battlefields in 1990. Even fifteen years ago, the average age of those who went was over 95. As well as Ben Clouting, G B Jameson, Frank Sumpter, Joe Armstrong and Fred Dixon also made the trip. G B had dislocated his hip but despite being in great pain, he was determined to go back and although he was forced into a wheel chair for the first and only time in his life he, like Ben, never once complained of his discomfort.]

British cavalry resting up during the etreat from Mons.

LANCE CORPORAL JOE ARMSTRONG, 1ST LOYAL NORTH LANCASHIRE REGIMENT, 1895-1997

We were jogging along on the train, some of us on the footboards and some on the roof, when a couple of hundred yards ahead I saw some beautiful peach trees, I got up and quickly made my way along the top of the train towards the engine, where I climbed down to the footboards and jumped off. The trees belonged to a house and in the garden was a mother and a daughter. I pointed to the peaches and the mother pointed to my cap badge. Without arguing, because I'd got the train to think of, I let her have my cap badge and I grabbed a few peaches, just managing to leap onto the footboard at the back of the train.

CORPORAL G B JAMESON, 1/1ST NORTHUMBERLAND YEOMANRY, 1892-1999

Naturally, wherever we went we were looking for food. It was very chancy, as we were so often detached from our supplies and to a large degree they were very slow coming forward. Anyway, as a corporal I was told to take my patrol up the Menin Road and to push on as far as I could and look for Germans. Under no circumstances had I to get embroiled, but to find and ascertain the enemy's strength. Anyway, we arrived at Gheleveldt Château and I said to my fellows, "Go downstairs and see if you can find some food," while I went upstairs. I remember seeing two small bronze medallions which had fallen off a wall. One showed the Cloth Hall in Ypres, the other showed a man called Edward Pecker. I took those medallions as souvenirs and carried them right through the war. The Château was spick and span, but there was no food at all, not a scrap

in the place anywhere, but what we did find was champagne in the cellars. So, we helped ourselves to a couple of bottles each and stuffed them into the strapping round the saddle. But champagne doesn't ride well on horseback and as we rode off, the corks began popping, champagne spewing all over the horses' flanks and in the end we lost the lot.

LANCE CORPORAL JOE ARMSTRONG, 1ST LOYAL NORTH LANCASHIRE REGIMENT, 1895-1997

The company officer decided to have a kit inspection while the battalion was out on reserve. We had to show our tin of bully beef, packet of biscuits and tea and sugar, well, by this time, half of us had eaten them. We had to be punished, so what did the officer do? He turned to Regimental Sergeant Major Thompson and ordered him to bring two earthenware jars, each containing two gallons of rum – the nights had been getting cold and he'd started putting rum in the early morning tea – and he ordered the RSM to take the cork out and pour the four gallons onto the ground. He should have been shot.

Out on reserve, Thompson had his own little dugout. Next morning when he got up, he found a tent peg and attached to it was a field postcard, on which was written:

This place marks the spot
Where many a young soldier lost his tot
It was poured out in damn dirty fashion
Because he had eaten his emergency rations.

Thompson went crackers.

TROOPER BEN CLOUTING, 4TH (ROYAL IRISH)DRAGOON GUARDS, 1897-1990

Clean water was of great importance to a regiment on the move, and whenever possible, water bottles were kept topped up. On one occasion, the Squadron turned into a stream, and the horses, tired and thirsty, went to drink, but we were told to "Ride on", so on we went. The water was less than a foot deep, clear and inviting, and it seemed such a waste. Several troopers did try to get water into their enamelled bottles, removing the cork and slinging them over into the stream as they rode, tipping and dipping them in the water, but with little success.

ABLE SEAMAN ALF BASTIN, HAWKE BATTALION ROYAL NAVAL VOLUNTEER RESERVE, 1896-1997

The first job when we got settled in the trenches was to post guards, and, my name being Bastin, I was at the top of the bloody list. At 11 o'clock at night I was called out and stood on a corner on guard, rifle ready. I could see

France 1917. Lieutenant G B Jameson, MC, serving in the Royal Field Artillery. He survived over four years' fighting in France.

a bit of firing going on round about, but nothing near us, and from where I was standing I could actually see the boats in Antwerp harbour all alight. It was beautiful to see. An officer came round occasionally for reports. "Anything doing?" "No, Sir, plenty of firing going on, you can see for yourself, Sir."

It was shortly after this, that things began to liven up. Without warning we were ordered to mount the trenches and fire twenty rounds straight ahead, point blank, on open range, which meant we didn't have to use the sights. We didn't know what we were firing at, no idea at all, but as soon we'd finished, we were given orders to fall in on the road and were marched off to a yard and told to board cattle trucks. When we were all loaded up, off we went, where to, no one had any idea.

CORPORAL G B JAMESON, 1/1ST NORTHUMBERLAND YEOMANRY, 1892-1999

Before the Battle of Ypres, the squadron was taking shelter in Sanctuary Wood. The Germans were shelling the wood at the time, with splinters of hot metal flying about. The infantry were filtering up through the trees to dig trenches. I was holding my horse, and one of these fellows said to me, "Give me a light, chum." I struck my tinder lighter and leant under the horse's head while he lit his cigarette, just as a shell burst overhead. The man immediately fell dead while my horse had a chunk of shrapnel down its nearside. I discovered too that a chunk of metal was also embedded in the rolled greatcoat strapped to the back of my saddle, and the canvas water bucket that was slung over the sword hilt was punctured and no good. I was untouched but my horse had a nasty gash from about the girth to the stifle down its ribs, as though somebody had taken a red-hot poker down its side. I was lucky. My war might have ended in its first week.

LANCE CORPORAL JOE ARMSTRONG, 1ST LOYAL NORTH LANCASHIRE REGIMENT, 1895-1997

We were told to fix bayonets because we were going to charge. I was behind a hedge with a chap next to me ready to move off, when there was an explosion and he was hit in the knee by a piece of shell. I looked and could see his leg was hanging on with a few bits of skin. I got hold of him and dragged him to safety. He emptied his water bottle as I used his bandage to stem the flow of blood; he then emptied my water bottle and I used my bandage. I'm only sorry now I didn't know about tourniquets. I got him on my shoulder and made off towards our lines, when I heard somebody shout, "Go back you bloody fool, go back." In my confusion I had been walking towards the German trenches. They could have shot me easily, but they must have taken pity on me. I walked back and put him behind a tree, but what could I do? I'll always remember that the man was a cockney because he turned to me and said, "Gor blimey, mate, you aint half a toff." And with that he just got hold of his leg and tore it off and threw it round the tree. I had to leave him; no doubt he died. There weren't stretcher bearers around, but perhaps the blood would have congealed enough to save his life, I don't know. By the time I got back the bayonet charge had been made.

"Go back you bloody fool, go back." Joe Armstrong, hoplessly confused, had been walking in the the wrong direction. Here a Tommy runs for cover.

When I got to the German line, the men were already busy reversing the trench, building up the parapet with dead bodies.

PRIVATE FRANK SUMPTER, 1ST RIFLE BRIGADE, 1897-1999

Frank Sumpter.

The Germans were eighty yards on the far side of Ploegsteert Wood. We were inside the wood, dug in, when General Hunter-Weston turned up. He appeared to object to us being inside the wood and having listening patrols out in front. He wanted us at the front of the wood instead, so he ordered an attack. "We won't get to Berlin like this," I actually heard him say that to one of our platoon officers.

The next morning over the top we went. I hadn't gone twenty yards when the man next to me got a bullet through his head and his brains splashed right across my shoulders. That was my first experience of war. We rushed forward but when we got outside the edge of the wood we found we couldn't get into the fields beyond because there was a ditch full of water, so we lay down and kept up a field of fire until we were told what to do. It was noticed that further along, there was a gateway with a culvert going over the ditch into the field. Orders were given to do mutual advance, one man at a time.

Our officer gave the command, "Get ready, go!" and each time up the man would get and run like hell and go through the culvert and drop the other side. All the time, our officer lay with his revolver over his arm to frighten the boys into going. As soon as a man got up, the bullets came zup, zup, zup, like a shower of needles from a pine forest when the wind blows, and inevitably two or three were hit as they ran forward into the ploughed field beyond. Half the platoon had gone over when it came to my turn. I ran because nobody refused and because I knew the officer was there with his revolver if I didn't. Once across, we opened fire so that the other half could come on until the entire platoon was across and lying in the mud. Then the order was given, "At the sound of the whistle, you'll go forward at the double." But you couldn't double because as you picked your feet up there was half a hundredweight of clay stuck to your boots. We got as far as we could, and no further. We'd done nothing but got ourselves into a mess.

ABLE SEAMAN ALF BASTIN, HAWKE BATTALION, ROYAL NAVAL VOLUNTEER RESERVE, 1896-1997

We'd gone about thirty miles when all of a sudden the train stopped in a railway siding. "What the hell is going on here?" we wondered. We soon found out. We were surrounded by Germans. Orders were issued to get out of the train and line up on the road, giving up our arms and our bayonets as we did so. We'd been captured and

Alf Bastin.

we were dumbstruck. There was one officer with us, Lieutenant Hanson, a naval volunteer, something to do with the Breweries, and he started going mad. This officer did not hand in his revolver and when we got orders to march off, he suddenly stood up in the middle of the road and shouted, "Come on, boys, let's make a dash for it!" and started firing his weapon. What a bloody fool he was, because he was immediately shot and we all quickly lay down in the road. He was carted off, dead I presume, and we were marched away. I suppose there must have been at least a thousand of us on that train.

PRIVATE FRANK SUMPTER, 1ST RIFLE BRIGADE, 1897-1999

Early in the morning, I did a foolish thing. I was only sixteen, it was dark and I put my hand round and felt a skin of frost coming onto the clay. "If my rifle bolt freezes and they counter attack, I won't be able to fire", I thought, not knowing in my ignorance that the bolt wouldn't freeze. So I opened the butt trap of my rifle and took the oil bottle out and on top of the bottle there was a spoon. I oiled the bolt; I tried it and it was lovely. I got the bottle and looked round for the lid but couldn't find it. I must have squashed it into the mud, so I put the bottle back into the butt trap of the rifle closed, it down and thought, "Right, I'll tell the Sergeant Major tomorrow and get another one." At 3am we got the order to retire.

On the way back, we were told to pick up the wounded. A pile of stretchers had been brought up to the edge of the wood, and every four men were to take a stretcher. We found one man wounded in the leg, but there was another fellow whom we wouldn't touch. His stomach had been torn and his intestines were exposed, so they used his webbing to try and bolt him in, to keep his stomach from falling on the ground when they took him away. We carried the other man, but it was an awful thing to do, to carry a stretcher through a forest with all the earth churned up and with roots sticking out of the ground. One of the team would slip and the wounded man would fall off the stretcher. We'd put him on again and then someone else would fall. What a job!

LANCE CORPORAL JOE ARMSTRONG, 1ST LOYAL NORTH LANCASHIRE REGIMENT, 1895-1997

After the bayonet charge, two companies were told to dig in, and not to retire and not to advance, no matter what happened. The other two companies consolidated the position behind. My company was forward of the other two, and I said to an officer, "Are we right at the front, Sir?" And he said, "Oh yes." It was dark then, perhaps eight in the evening and I said, "Well, I can hear voices just over the top." "They'll be Germans," he replied.

At first light, I saw a few Germans a hundred yards away running from hedge to hedge and I took a few shots. Then, shortly after, we heard a hullabaloo on our left and we learnt that the Germans had broken through the Northamptons; in fact they'd swept right past us and captured the artillery and the headquarters. We'd been ordered not to retire but when we saw the Germans coming round the front of us, our officer did a bunk but only ran straight into the arms of the enemy.

When you join the army, you're not told what to do when you're captured. When I was ordered to climb out of the trench, I still had my rifle and bayonet in my hand and narrowly avoided having a bayonet run through me because I didn't drop my weapon quick enough, very close indeed.

They marched us away from the trenches and put us in lines of five to be counted. I had an unlit pipe in my mouth. An officer was counting us, and when he came to me, his hand came up and tugged at the pipe. "This is my blinking pipe," I thought and I stuck to it.

Corporal Taylor, who was behind me, shouted, "Let go of that bloody pipe, you fool." Good job I did, because as the officer tugged at my pipe with one hand, he was about to screw his revolver round my temple with the other. A moment later, I would have been dead.

ABLE SEAMAN ALF BASTIN, HAWKE BATTALION, ROYAL NAVAL VOLUNTEER RESERVE, 1896-1997

After we were captured, we were put in closed cattle trucks and taken away to Germany. We had nothing to eat for days and we were starving by the time we stopped at Cologne railway station. The Germans had been told

that the British Navy had been captured and they wanted to show us off, so they opened up the trucks to public scrutiny. I could see that the platform was crowded with people, mostly women. They just walked along and looked at us, throwing mildewed bread as an insult. This, of course, we were only too glad to eat as we were hungry, and we tore off the bits that weren't so mouldy. We were all bewildered, we'd been on the road for three days, then taken on this train, and we wondered what the hell we were coming to. They were shouting at us in German, "Englische Schweinhund!" spitting and swearing, then out of this tumult, I heard one voice shout out, very distinctly, "Englanders, bloody f...ing bastards!"

PRIVATE FRANK SUMPTER, 1ST RIFLE BRIGADE, 1897-1999

My platoon went in twenty strong and eleven came out. We'd had nothing to eat since 2 o'clock the day before, so you can bet we were pretty all out tired when we got back to our billet. Sergeant Webb spoke to us. "When the Company Officer is available, we'll get our instructions where to assemble. In the meantime, we'll go into this schoolroom." So we got in to this building and threw down our equipment to get some rest, just as our platoon officer turned up. He'd come out from Sandhurst, about nineteen years of age, brand new and full of discipline. He turned to the Sergeant. "These men will fall asleep, but we can't move until we get orders. What do you suggest, Sergeant?" "I know, Sir, have a kit inspection." Unbelievable! We'd just come out of action, we were exhausted and now we were to have a war-time kit inspection, each of us laying our kit out in the ordinary barrack-room fashion.

When we'd done this, the lieutenant went along for an inspection until he came to me. He looked at my kit:

"Where is the stopper of your oil bottle?"

"I lost it last night in the attack, sir."

"Fiddlesticks!" he said. "Put him on a charge."

So I was put on a charge for losing, by neglect, an article of equipment; failing to report the loss of equipment; rendering myself an inefficient soldier, and conduct to the prejudice of good order and military discipline.

These were serious charges, and when they went before the Company Commander, the Captain said, "I can't deal with this, he'll have to go in front of the Colonel." So I was marched in front of the Colonel, but when I started to explain what had happened, the Sergeant Major barked, "Speak when you're spoken to!" Nobody spoke to me, so I couldn't speak. The Colonel said, "This is very serious, a very serious charge, I can't do less: a regimental entry, eight days No1 Field Punishment." I didn't mind the punishment but what I didn't like was that a regimental entry goes onto your paybook and onto your records and is assessed when they make up your gratuity when you leave the army. In my case, No1 Field Punishment amounted to nightly jankers, one hour tied to a gun wheel and then carrying ammunition back up to the trenches, taking another risk with your life.

THE FINAL WITNESSES:

IT WASN'T OVER BY CHRISTMAS 1914, BUT THERE WAS A TRUCE

Soldiers in France and Belgium were facing their first Christmas away from home and for a few days trench life had been relatively quiet. On Christmas Eve, mysterious lights began to appear in the enemy trenches, then Christmas trees, and, out of the dark, carol singing, and calls to Tommy across the trenches to come over.

An impromptu Christmas truce began to take place, but it would require an astonishing consensus from both sides to be successful.

CORPORAL G B JAMESON, 1/1ST NORTHUMBERLAND YEOMANRY, 1892-1999

On Christmas Eve, we were withdrawn from the line. We thought we had struck it lucky getting out of the trenches for Christmas Day. I landed the job of duty corporal so I couldn't wander away from the billet when some of the ration party heard about this Christmas Truce. Two brothers, Keith and Philip Ridley, came dashing up to me and said, "The Jerries are walking around on the top, singing carols and exchanging cigarettes." I couldn't believe it. He said, "These ration party fellows who I have just been talking to are quite certain they are." "Well," I said, "I'm tied here, but you can go up if you like. Go and find out." So off they went with another fellow, Les Wood, up the front line. Some time after, Keith came back with a *Landwehr* hat, which I tried on, while Philip had a water bottle and Les a fistful of cigars. "It's marvellous," they told me, "wandering about, and they're dishing out all sorts of things and kicking a football around!"

G. B. Jameson

[Ed. In 1990, G B Jameson returned for a nostalgic visit to the town of his childhood, Newcastle upon Tyne, where he was introduced to 94-year-old Jack Irving, a sergeant in the Gateshead Troop, B Squadron, Northumberland Hussars. Both men had served throughout the campaign in 1914, including the Christmas Truce, and although they served in different squadrons, they vaguely remembered each other. Later that day, G B visited the Northumberland Hussars' Museum where he met the curator. While looking around the museum, he spotted a picture of Keith Ridley. "I mentioned the fact that Keith had come back from the front line with this hat. The curator took me to the other side of the museum and said, "There's your Landwehr hat", and it was, in a case, given to the museum by Keith. I said, "That's damn funny, the last time I saw that hat, I had it on my head on Christmas morning, 1914."]

PRIVATE FRANK SUMPTER, 1ST RIFLE BRIGADE, 1897-1999

We heard the Germans singing "Silent Night, Holy Night," and then they put up a notice, "Merry Christmas." Then they started singing, and our boys said, "We'll join in." So we joined in with a song and when we started singing, they stopped. So we sang on and then we stopped and they sang. The Germans waved their hands, "Happy Noel, Tommy", and we shouted back. One German took a chance and jumped up on top of the trench and shouted out "Happy Christmas, Tommy!" No one fired a shot, which was marvellous, as before then you couldn't put your finger up without it being blown off. Of course our boys said, "If he can do it, we can do it." The Sergeant Major came along and said, "Get down there, get down there." We stuck our two fingers up at him. "It's Christmas!" and with that we all jumped up and the Germans beckoned us forward to the barbed wire and we shook hands. I spoke to one German and he said, "Do you know Islington?" He could speak very good English. "Do you know the Jolly Farmer's pub in Southgate Road?" and I said, "Yes, my uncle has a shoe repairing shop next door, and he said, "That's funny, there's a barber's shop on the other side where I used to work before the war." He must have shaved my uncle at times and yet my bullet might have found him and his me.

The officers didn't join in; they hid themselves. They'd given the order, "No fraternization," and turned their backs on us. Nobody tried to stop it, they knew they

A CHRISTMAS TRUCE.—BRITISH AND GERMANS FRATERNIZE. DECEMBER 1914.
Soldiers of the rival armies exchanged sweets, cigars, and cigarettes, and sang carols and songs in unison.

"It's Christmas!" and with that we all jumped up and the Germans beckoned us forward to the barbed wire and we shook hands.' Frank Sumpter experienced the spontaneous truce of Christmas 1914. British and German soldiers pose for photographs together.

couldn't, the boys weren't in the mood. We didn't talk about the war, other than how long it would last, and our families. I stood there about half an hour and then I'd had enough and came back. I was young and wasn't very interested, but most of the boys stayed there the whole day and enjoyed the curiosity of walking about in No Man's Land.

PRIVATE FREDERICK DIXON, NO9775, C COMPANY, 2ND LEICESTERSHIRE REGIMENT, 1895-1991

What a glorious feeling, to be able to relax, not to hear a shot fired, or to stand in trenches half-full of water. Two days before Christmas, we'd been relieved and marched out of the trenches to a quiet area of civilization. We halted in a disused farmhouse and were billeted so many to a room, squeezing in. It was a lovely house, hardly damaged, fully furnished, with lovely pictures and full length mirrors everywhere, but no beds. The owners had rushed out of the house when the Germans approached and had no time to take anything. On Christmas Eve, we explored. Poultry and pigs had been turned out to fend for themselves in the open. The poultry were roosting in the trees, so we shot them as we wanted. The pigs were finding what food they could in the garden and fields. It seemed too good to be true. We had been living on bully beef and hard biscuits for a long time and here was pork in abundance. So we shot a beautiful porker. Our cooks drew no rations that day, we supplied all their needs and we all mucked in preparing it for cooking. The pig was dressed by us old farm hands, and the poultry plucked, perfect. Then we raided

the garden for the necessary vegetables for stuffing. I never did enjoy a dinner quite like it in all my life. Over seventy five years later, I can still taste it.

Then we went and spoilt it. The lads found some wine in the cellar under the house. It was full of bottles, we tried first one then another and soon we were hopelessly drunk. I did not drink much, so kept all right, but some of the lads tried everything including something that turned out to be mentholated spirits and that finished things completely. Several of the lads were very ill and two of them died, so our little celebration eventually became a funeral party.

[Ed. The success of the recruitment drive that drew so many into the army in the first months of the war tailed off by the year's end. Many of those young men who resisted enlisting did so for good reason; often commitments to ill or dependent parents or siblings put paid to any immediate thought of enlistment. Yet the pressure to appear patriotic was never far away, and when the opportunity finally arose, most young men were not found wanting.]

SAPPER STANLEY CLAYTON, NO480143, 457TH FIELD COMPANY, ROYAL ENGINEERS, 62ND DIVISION, 27 OCTOBER 1894-17 MARCH 2000

On Christmas Eve 1914, I was with my girlfriend and I told her I was going to join the army. "If you are," she said, "we'll make a pact, we'll have our photographs taken and I'll carry your photograph and you carry mine."

You'd be called a scabber if you didn't join up. The girls would say you were frightened. First one lad would volunteer, then another and another, and they'd say, "You're frightened, you are." My brother had been very ill with Bright's Disease, a form of kidney disease, then just after Christmas 1914 he died. We buried him on the 3 January 1915, and my mother was crying and I said, "Look, mother, I'll soon have to join the army in any case, so I might as well go and you might as well cry for two. I'm going to join the army," and all she said between the tears was, "All right, lad, all right."
[Ed. As promised, Stan carried the picture of his girlfriend all through the war, indeed right up until his death in 2000 that same picture remained secreted within his wallet. His marriage to Kate lasted nearly seventy years.]

PRIVATE ARCHIBALD LEE RICHARDS, NO200862, D COMPANY (D7), HEAVY SECTION, MACHINE GUN CORPS, 7 JANUARY 1897 FEBRUARY 1998

I was scared I might be called up and pushed into something I didn't want, so I came home and had a few days' holiday. Before I enlisted a recruiting agent came to Upton Cross, and he said, "Well, there's a list here of things you can join."

You'd have thought that I wasn't very much for King and Country. I didn't fancy joining the local regiment,

the Duke of Cornwall's Light Infantry. I'd heard a little bit about what was going on abroad, that the infantry had been badly cut up and how many were being killed or wounded, and I thought, "I'll plump for the Garrison Artillery, perhaps it'll keep me at home." Not very patriotic, was it? Heavy guns, back out of the way, but it was up to me what I joined and I took hold of that. I'd

Archie Richards.

made a pledge, to serve, and I knew I couldn't back out, so I just resigned myself to it and said, "Well, if I'm lucky I'll come through, if I get killed, I get killed." I would go through with it; I was patriotic enough to do that.

TROOPER ALBERT ELLIOTT 'SMILER' MARSHALL, NO1771, SOUTHEND TROOP, A SQUADRON, 1/1ST ESSEX YEOMANRY, 15 MARCH 1897- 16 MAY 2005

I had been working as a groom and I decided to go where my mates were, because all the farmers' sons round where we were joined the Essex Yeomanry. Of course, everybody in the

Albert Marshall.

countryside could ride then, the butcher, the baker, the candlestick maker, they all had a pony; cars were almost unheard of. So a little before Christmas1914, I goes up to Colchester, to the Essex Yeomanry office, and knocks on the door, and the sergeant major called me in. He says, "Good morning," and asks my name, and all the rest of it, you know, were my parents English, and then he asks my age. So I told him I was seventeen. "What year were you born?" I said, "1897." He says, "I think you've made a mistake." "Don't be funny," I said, "course I haven't, see." "Well," he said, "you just go outside that door and think it over and then come back and see me." I goes outside into a passageway and there was a chap from Colchester. I got talking to him, and told him the sergeant major had sent me out for making a mistake with my age. "What did you tell him?" "I told him I was seventeen." "Well, you can't get in until you're eighteen." So I goes back in, as if I'd never been before. "How old are you?" he asks. "Eighteen," I told him. "Oh yes, um" and then he says, "I'll tell you what, it's nearly Christmas, come back here in the New Year and you attest then," and that's what I did, on 5 January 1915.

London Metropolitan Archives

London Metropolitan Archives holds records for Greater London and the City, dating back nearly a thousand years.

Discover more about London from 1900 to 1920 and the people who lived and worked in the capital. Sources include maps, photographs, prints and drawings and records from London County Council, businesses, schools, hospitals and charities.

Find out more about our services, including talks and activities at:

www.cityoflondon.gov.uk/lma

Opening hours:
Monday, Wednesday and Friday 9.30am-4.45pm
Tuesday and Thursday 9.30am-7.30pm

Please note LMA is closed for stocktaking from 2 to 14 November 2009

London Metropolitan Archives
40 Northampton Road, London EC1R 0HB
Tel: 020 7332 3820

Designated as an Outstanding Collection

CITY OF LONDON

LONDON METROPOLITAN ARCHIVES

40

1915 – A YEAR OF LEARNING THE ART OF WARFARE

Christmas 1914 had been a remarkable interlude in an otherwise monotonous time at the front. War, in terms of actual fighting, had been put on hold. Men stood in the trenches, stomped their feet and patted their bodies to generate heat, and performed the repetitive and menial tasks that formed daily life in the line.

Offensive operations were suspended during the winter months: the ground had become so churned up, so water-logged and impassable, that to fight was a waste of energy. It required colossal expenditure of time and money to force the long columns of wagons and trucks, mules and horses, along frost-covered roads to re-supply the men at the front. The regular army had taken on the might of the numerically-superior Germans and fought them to a standstill, but at a heavy cost. The arrival of the first territorial units in September and October 1914 had helped to stabilize the front, but it was time to rebuild and wait and bide one's time until spring, when the weather would be better suited to offensive action.

On the Western Front, the BEF announced the end of the winter hibernation with the launch of its first major offensive. On 10 March, the British Army undertook an operation at Neuve Chapelle, as much a demonstration to the French of the BEF's willingness to fight than an attack of strategic importance. The aim was to seize the high ground which looked across to the German-held town of Lille. In the event, the three-day onslaught met with initial success, but early gains were not exploited owing to problems of coordination and supply. This offensive set the tone for the year, as army commanders wrestled with the increasing scale and complexity of operations while bowing to pressure from France to undertake supporting operations before they were ready. On 9 May, troops were ordered again to attack at Aubers Ridge in a one-day operation which was followed on 15 May by an ill-fated attack near the village of Festubert. Both actions were hastily conceived and poorly executed, and proved very costly at a time when the BEF was engaged in a defensive operation at Ypres, a little further to the north. The fighting in the Ypres Salient was a short-lived affair undertaken by the Germans and as it turned out, it was the last such operation they initiated against the British Army for nearly three years. Deciding to concentrate on operations against the Russians in the east,

the German High Command sanctioned only attacks that were limited in scope against the BEF. The offensive around Ypres in April and May was such an endeavour. Nevertheless the German attack used, for the first time, the new weapon of poison gas. In fierce fighting, British and Empire troops were forced back almost to the gates of the city. If it had fallen, it might have opened up the way to the main railheads and vital lines of communication and perhaps eventually the coast itself.

Throughout 1915, the Germans maintained their superiority in ammunition and men, using poison gas and flame throwers. The second attack at Aubers Ridge had thrown into sharp relief the lack of firepower available to British forces, which had had to restrict their preliminary bombardment to just forty minutes. The desperate shortage of ammunition, evident since the first months of the war, caused a political storm back home when it was portrayed by elements of the press as the reason for failure. Britain, it was felt, had to shed the mantle of the amateur and don the clothes of the professional when it came to fighting a European war. In May, a new Ministry of Munitions was established to deal comprehensively with the issue of armaments, while in France troop numbers rose dramatically, the BEF doubling its size from 350,000 in January to more than 800,000 by the end of the year.

477. La Grande Guerre 1914-15. - Les ruines de Neuve Chapelle après les combats de Mars 1915. Visé Paris 477.   IMP. BAUDINIÈRE, NANTERRE   « PHOT-EXPRESS »

1915 – OFFENSIVE OPERATIONS

In February 1915, a combined Anglo-French bombardment of the Turkish forts in the Dardanelles had signalled the opening moves which in April led to a full-blown invasion of the Gallipoli peninsula, and the opening up of an alternative front to that in France.

The Allied campaign at Gallipoli began with landings at Helles and Anzac Cove on 25 April. Heavy casualties ensued, but a foothold was gained. However, attempts to break out were frustrated by poor planning and dogged enemy defence. Despite opposition from commanders in France, the Gallipoli landings were reinforced by more men from Britain and the Empire, and a second offensive was launched at Suvla Bay further up the coast. The landing itself was almost unopposed but British forces failed to push on and the initial momentum was lost. The campaign ground to a halt once again. Increasingly, the Gallipoli operation was deemed an expensive failure. With offensive operations about to begin in France near Loos, and another front due to be opened in Salonika, there were no more troops available for a failing campaign, indeed, many of the troops required for Salonika would have to be drawn from Gallipoli. There was no alternative to drawing down the forces on the Turkish peninsula.

At home, Kitchener's New Army continued training.

Over the winter and spring months, camp life across the country had gradually improved from the appalling conditions suffered by keen volunteers in the late autumn of 1914. Hutted encampments had been erected, and uniforms and equipment issued to most volunteers, now proud to wear khaki and 1914 pattern leather equipment instead of the hotchpotch uniforms of the previous year. The days of broomsticks had also gone, and for the most part even antiquated rifles such as the Boer War vintage Lee Metford and the Japanese Arisaka had been replaced by the highly efficient and superbly-manufactured Short (Rifle) Magazine Lee Enfield No.1 Mk III. The supply of live ammunition was still woefully inadequate, restricting the time and opportunity that men had on the ranges, but most volunteers were fit, healthy and well-trained. By May, the first Kitchener Divisions were deemed ready to sail for active service to support the depleted regular and territorial armies. The 9th, 14th and 15th Divisions were taken into the line around Ypres, while in August the 18th Division sailed for France and went directly to the Somme, a region previously held by the French but taken over in the summer by Britain as part of her expanding commitment to the fighting.

In September, an Allied offensive was launched in

British troops landing at Anzac cove

LEE ENFIELD MK III

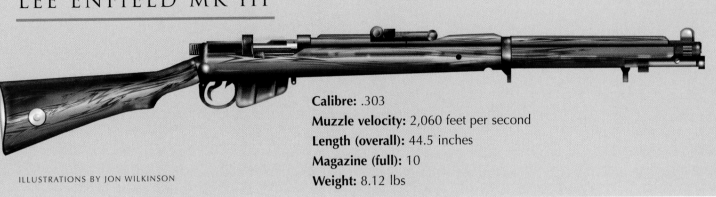

Calibre: .303
Muzzle velocity: 2,060 feet per second
Length (overall): 44.5 inches
Magazine (full): 10
Weight: 8.12 lbs

ILLUSTRATIONS BY JON WILKINSON

what was the first truly concerted effort on the part of British and French troops to break the German line. In the north, in the coalmining district around Loos and Lens, the British were ordered to attack over a seven-mile front, while the French, much further to the south, attacked in the region of Artois. The BEF were to go into action with six divisions of infantry, around 72,000 men. Unlike earlier attacks, this one would be supported by a five-day bombardment, the consequence of improved ammunition supplies. The initial onslaught would be undertaken by regular and territorial units but would be developed by Kitchener Divisions in their first major action.

1915 was a year of radical change for the British Army on the Western Front, finding its way in a new form of siege warfare where open spaces proved lethal and machine guns and artillery forced men to dig trenches. Back in 1914, nobody anticipated how long British forces would have to stay put, or how far the British economy would have to be adapted and re-designed to supply men with all the material they required, not just to prosecute a war but to survive for prolonged periods with little prospect of an early victory. The British entered 1915 wholly unprepared for war on an industrial scale; they ended the year with a radically different outlook.

PRIVATE TED FRANCIS, 16TH ROYAL WARWICKSHIRE REGIMENT, 1896-1996

These route marches were sometimes very long, perhaps twenty miles. Of course we had rests of ten minutes every hour, but when you march with a rifle and kit, you get very tired and fed up, and all the time the officers are saying, "Keep in step", and then one says, "Let's have a song, boys, you know, to buck us up", which was often as we were nearing a town or a village. It was to impress the inhabitants but it didn't impress us. We were almost forced to sing. "Sing, you blighters, don't put your heads down, march properly and sing!" At times, in the summer weather, we were very pleased to start our own singing, we'd sing in good voice, but, as I say, we objected very much to being told. But when you're in the army they can order you to do anything, and you've got to do it smartly, or else.

LANCE CORPORAL VIC COLE, 7TH QUEEN'S OWN (ROYAL WEST KENT REGIMENT), 1897-1995

We marched from Codford in Wiltshire to a vast open field near Stonehenge. Men with worn clothing were issued with new tunics, trousers and puttees, and we were ordered to carry rags or brushes in our haversacks to clean the dust off our boots before the General, I forget which one, came round. When we eventually arrived, the whole Division appeared to be there, the 18th Division on three sides of an enormous square, Battalions of the West Kents, the Queen's, and the East Surreys, while the supernumeraries were grouped centrally. A senior officer advanced right into the middle on a lovely horse, stood up in his stirrups and shouted "Attention!" We all sprang to attention and were ordered to present arms, and they kept us like that while the General came round with the King. The King was mounted and there were a couple of Generals and other

The officer rides and the men march during the advance and then during the long withdrawal.

red tabs. King George V with his beard and his little legs came past, and I was in the front rank at the end, and the General said, "West Kent Regiment, Sir." The King said, "Ah, my mother's favourite regiment," but I reckon he said it to every battalion he passed!

PRIVATE ARCHIE RICHARDS, D COMPANY (D7), HEAVY SECTION, MACHINE GUN CORPS, 1897-1998

I joined the Royal Garrison Artillery and did my physical training on the Hoe at Plymouth, where local people lined up and laughed at us as we made mistakes. Then a group of us were sent to Garden Battery, a six-inch battery at Devonport. I didn't like the training, it was like going back to school again, maths, and sights, ranges and velocity, oh no, I didn't like it one bit, and I and others took pains to show it, acting like dumb schoolboys. They in their turn probably believed we'd never make good artillerymen, so they sent a group of us to Bisley to train on the Hotchkiss machine gun. We trained for several months, and then one day they sent us to Thetford in Norfolk, what for we didn't know. We assumed we would be sent to the trenches with machine guns but we couldn't understand why, when there were the Vickers and the Lewis machine guns, we were training so intensively with the Hotchkiss. Then one day they lined us up and said, "Well, here you are, here's this new weapon and all you people are going to crew them." It was the latest secret weapon, what we called armoured crawlers, tanks in other words, and we were the first to train on them.

PRIVATE TED FRANCIS, 16TH ROYAL WARWICKSHIRE REGIMENT, 1896-1996

We enjoyed the training, enjoyed it very much. We had three months' camp in tents in Malvern and it was more like a holiday than training for war. The fact that our troops were having a rough time and actually getting wounded or even killed never entered most of our heads. We thought, "The war isn't here, we want to go to France." I was a soldier, I had a rifle, there was a war on – what more could a young lad want?

The great day came, after five or six months, when we were issued with rifles. We were all waiting for that; some of the boys would rub that rifle, clean it, brush it, worship it, like a mother with her newborn baby, but for me the greater thrill was when we had real bullets to fire at a target. Now that was something.

CORPORAL ERNEST DORAN, 2ND LONDON REGIMENT (ROYAL FUSILIERS), 1893-1996

In February 1915 we occupied some trenches up at Ypres and all we doing was filling sandbags to keep the sides up, because we were up to our thighs in mud and water. They issued us with waders which you had to button to the top of your trousers, but the water came over the top. I was given quite a cushy job. I had to walk from the trenches to Ypres where I dug up floorboards and removed beams and turned them into duckboards for the bottom of the trench. They pulled Ypres to pieces for wood, quite honestly.

TROOPER BEN CLOUTING, 4TH (ROYAL IRISH) DRAGOON GUARDS, 1897-1990

The trenches were little more than shallow ditches joined together. There were no neat traverses, no proper firesteps or parapets, there was only a quagmire of shallow holes filled with oozing mud and water, for so shallow was the water table in the Ypres area that it was impossible to dig down more than a couple of feet without hitting water. Trench foot was a major problem. The constant cold and wet affected the blood's circulation to the toes in particular, causing men's feet to swell disgustingly. I deliberately took size eleven boots instead of my usual nine. This way I could pack my boots with lengths of straw to keep my feet warm, just as I had seen French peasants do with their clogs. If straw wasn't available, newspaper would do just as well. When the weather was bad, it was common to see a man with sandbags wrapped around his feet or puttees to protect his legs. Trench waders were issued in just two sizes, with two pieces of string that we held on to if we walked anywhere, for the suction power of the mud was

Shelling the Turks, a battery of British 60-pounder field guns in action at Gallipoli.

Terrain over which men were ordered to attack.

so great that without them our feet would simply have left the boots.

[Ed. The weather gradually improved and offensive operations resumed. On the Western Front, the British Army launched its first offensive of 1915 near the village of Neuve Chapelle. Four divisions, part of General Haig's First Army, attacked along a two-mile front.]

PRIVATE FRED DIXON, 2ND LEICESTERSHIRE REGIMENT, 1895-1991

I shall never forget the morning of 10 March. After a sleepless night, I was out at the front line. Captain Weir was a few feet away, and I was watching Colonel Gordon with his watch in his hand. He was shaking like a leaf as the minutes ticked away, then he shouted "Charge!" at exactly 8am. "Come on, Dixon," said Captain Weir, and climbed the ladder to get out of the trench. I followed at once, and we scrambled over our own barbed wire entanglements and made for the enemy. We had orders to ignore their main trench, which would later be attacked by support forces, and to advance as far as we could.

There was no opposition as we jumped over that Jerry trench, but I could see a number of Germans crouched in the bottom of the trench; they had had a battering most of the night. I stuck to Captain Weir until we were both tired out. He then said, "I think we will stay here and dig in; pass that down the line." But I said, "There is no line; there is only you and me." I looked round and there was nobody but us two. I saw a partly-dug trench so I pointed it out to him, and we decided to work on that. He then said, "How far do you think we have come?" I said, "Almost a mile." So he said, "Go straight back to Colonel Gordon and say we have advanced about three-quarters to one mile, and we want reinforcements." Then he surprised me by holding out his hand and saying, "Goodbye, Dixon." I shook it, "Goodbye, Sir", then turned round to plot my way back, and that was the last I saw of him.

How different a plot of land looks when you have seen it from one way and then turn round and look at it front to back! At last I spotted the stump of Richebourg St Vaast Church, and knew if I made for that, I could find my old trenches and Colonel Gordon.

There were lots of bullets coming from somewhere as I plodded along in the sludge, and I could not travel very fast under those conditions with my equipment and rifle. However, I kept going, thinking one of these will get me yet; but I was lucky to drop straight into the trench from where I had started out, and I found Colonel Gordon. I gave him the message exactly as Captain Weir had told me and the Colonel said, "Go straight back to Captain Weir and tell him to hold the position at all costs – and we have no reinforcements. Off you go!" The Colonel dived back into his dugout. My thoughts were unprintable.

As I went up that ladder once again and my hands reached the top rungs, a machine gun opened up from the enemy trench we had left alone: they were waiting for me – no doubt they realized I was carrying messages. Something told me I was not going to get back safely this time, and I dropped back into the trench to wait a bit. If there was ever a time when I felt like being a coward, it was just then. I didn't want to go on, but I thought if I don't go, I shall be shot by my own side as a coward, so I may as well go and chance it. So I plucked up courage, and went as fast as I could, even though I was tired out. As I passed that first German trench again, I saw several men together, but one in particular was carefully taking aim at me, the others looking on. I heard the bang as he fired; and felt the bullet go through my knee joint like a red hot needle. My leg just stopped and I fell full length with my face in the sludge. I had gone off unconscious, but I awoke to realize I was being fired on again; a German officer was firing at me from a communication trench. Two bullets hit the ground each side of my head and I kept perfectly still, thinking, "He'll get me next time", but he dare not expose himself too long, and no doubt he thought he had done enough at me, so he went away. I lay there all day until about 6.30pm when I was found by a stretcher-bearer party from a Scottish regiment.

PRIVATE FRANK SUMPTER, 1ST RIFLE BRIGADE, 1897-1999

We went over and took about two fields and a couple of lines of trenches. As soon as they saw us, down went their rifles and up went their hands and we took them prisoner. The Provo Marshal had them all put in a pen with his men round them and he put a German officer in charge to talk to them, to tell them to go one way or another. I saw the German officer standing there and a man came up to him and the officer said something to the man. He can't have received a polite answer, because he slapped him round his face. I was talking to a couple of Germans and said if he did that in the British army, he would be finished as an officer. They said, "Don't talk rot," and I said, "I'm telling you. If a British officer slapped a man in the face he would be cashiered." They couldn't understand it. They said, "But he's an officer!" as though that answered everything.

V Beach Helles Landing.

GALLIPOLI

Killing, or at least neutralising, the enemy would require, according to some, a new, more inventive plan of attack. The decision to assault the Gallipoli Penninsula was taken in the face of heavy opposition from senior commanders in France who felt that the war could be won only on the Western Front. Others disagreed, and a rift was created between those who counselled continued fighting in the west, the so-called "Westerners", and those who sought to expand campaigns elsewhere, the "Easterners". The latter argued that if an Allied force could wrest Turkish control from the Dardanelles Straits, then a passage to the Black Sea could be opened up between Britain and France and their ally Russia. Equally, if Turkey herself could be knocked out of the war, then Germany's strategic position would be greatly undermined without the need for further heavy losses in France and Flanders. The plan, though well conceived, was poorly executed. The campaign lasted from April 1915 until January 1916, when the Penninsula was finally evacuated, a decision that appeared to vindicate the views of the "Westerners".

2ND LIEUTENANT NORMAN DILLON, 14TH NORTHUMBERLAND FUSILIERS, 1896-1997

In spite of the dismal failures at Neuve Chapelle and later at Ypres, the Higher Command still believed we should smash a hole in the German line and get on with the sort of war they seemed to consider the gentlemanly thing to do. Infantry in long lines, attacking under cover of their own fire and their officers cantering up and down shouting "Up and at 'em". It did not work like that and it cost many thousands of lives.

2ND LIEUTENANT RICHARD HAWKINS, 11TH ROYAL FUSILIERS, 1895-1994

The casualties were enormous. I can't remember the number, it's all been written down. People say that the Generals were wrong in making us go and fight the enemy as we did. Dammit, we couldn't sit there forever. You couldn't sit there in a trench, you might still be there. We'd got to get on with the job and kill the enemy.

PRIVATE ROBERT RICHARD 'DICK' BARRON, NO1629, 2ND LONDON MOUNTED BRIGADE FIELD AMBULANCE, ROYAL ARMY MEDICAL CORPS, 19 OCTOBER 1895-14 FEBRUARY 1999

We were on field exercises when one night, practically with no warning, we were entrained with all our equipment. We found ourselves next morning in a drizzling rain at Southampton Docks and there looming above us was the *Aragon*, a Royal Mail Steam Packet Liner which had been converted to a troop ship. Just before we were about to start, something happened which I will never forget. The whole of the ship's company from the top deck right down, including ourselves, suddenly burst into song. "Homeland, homeland, when shall I see you again, land of my birth, dearest place on earth, I'm leaving you, oh it may be for years and it may be forever. Homeland, homeland." Up to then the whole thing had been most enjoyable, but my heart stood still. I suddenly realised that this was warfare – I might not return.

ABLE SEAMAN WALTER BURDON, ZT90, B COMPANY, NELSON BATTALION, ROYAL NAVAL DIVISION, 26 JUNE 1895-MAY 1992

Because I was a signaller, I had access to a telescope and a pair of glasses. We weren't due to land on Gallipoli until the 26 April, the second day of the assault, so instead I watched the first landings from our ship. Looking through the telescope, I could see the Australians in action. There were people running all over the place, while others appeared to be lying down, stationary, as one of our big ships, the *Queen Elizabeth*, bombarded the shore. "I hope we'll be getting some of that," I said to a man next to me. You don't realize at the time that you might be going to your death.

Soon after that, we got orders to get ready to disembark, ready for landing. We got onto a destroyer and we went in as far as we could, towing about a dozen rowing boats behind us. The destroyer stopped and we climbed into the boats. That was the most terrifying moment for me because we had to descend a rope ladder trailing down the stern of the ship. The stern curved away, and as we clambered down with rifle and ammunition, the ship rose and fell in the water. It was clear to all that if you slipped you would not come up again, you'd sink like a stone.

As we rowed into shore, I could see the hull of another ship, the *Majestic*, upside-down in the bay. At this time we were under fire but not a great deal and we were certainly not as badly off as the Australians, who had got mowed down the previous day. When we came ashore, I was carrying two three-foot flags and a six-foot flag: the smaller flags were for semaphore and the larger for morse. I saw the Australians lying there, and I was sitting beside them, when one said, "You're a flag man, are you? Then take those two flags off that boy's back." He pointed to this lad who was dead with a pack on his back, attached to which were two much smaller flags. "Yours are no good, they are too big. You stand up to use those, you'll never live, throw them away." I took his advice.

PRIVATE DICK BARRON, 2ND LONDON MOUNTED BRIGADE FIELD AMBULANCE, ROYAL ARMY MEDICAL CORPS, 1895-1999

We knew nothing at all about what was going on. We had spoken to the wounded coming from Gallipoli, but we still had romantic notions until we got to see the place for ourselves. When we landed at Suvla Bay. I was in a state of nervousness, I had too much imagination, I could imagine myself all lacerated. However, I saw a

couple of old sweats who had served in the Boer War and they were sitting down smoking, as calm as anything, and I took strength from them.

PRIVATE ADOLPHUS ARTHUR JAMES PRICE, NO1751, A COMPANY, 1/8TH HAMPSHIRE REGIMENT, 13 NOVEMBER 1893-NOVEMBER1993

On the way back from a dressing station, we saw this fellow from my own town of Shanklin on the Isle of Wight. I knew him as being a bit simple, we used to call him Dotty Fred. I don't think he'd done any work in civilian life, but he'd got into the army all right and gone to Gallipoli. He was laid there, dead, and his mouth was wide open and it was black with flies. Many years after, and to my great shock, I saw Dotty Fred back in Shanklin. He told me he had been suffering from typhoid, so he must only have been asleep when I saw him.

PRIVATE DAVID WESTON, 1/5TH BEDFORDSHIRE REGIMENT, 1895-1998

These Gurkhas had been lying out for three weeks and we were detailed for the job of burying them. We went out at night. I say bury them, but you couldn't dig a hole; the ground was so hard you couldn't bury bodies, you had to cover them over with stones. So we did the best we could, but you needed a drill to penetrate the ground. There were twenty or thirty dead on this ridge, dried-up corpses coloured deep brown. We had to cut off their identification discs and all the time we were doing this the stench was awful. The next day, as the weather got hotter I actually saw the legs of these Gurkhas coming out of the ground, bodies we'd buried under stones. The heat of the sun had made them swell and rise up into the air only to sink back down again at night. I said to the sergeant major, "If you put me on a job like that again, I will refuse to do it," and I would have done, too, it was a wicked job. I smelt of those dead Gurkhas for weeks after that.

PRIVATE DICK BARRON, 2ND LONDON MOUNTED BRIGADE FIELD AMBULANCE, ROYAL ARMY MEDICAL CORPS, 1895-1999

The London Yeomanry were crossing the salt lake at Suvla Bay in waves. I was attached to a medical officer and more or less followed him. We were attacked by shrapnel bursting all over the place. Casualties were falling, and I was staggering forward, bewildered more than anything else. The first casualty I dealt with was my old friend 'Gally' Lee; he got hit right next to me. We didn't have steel helmets then and I was shaken by the burst that caught my friend; he was hit in the head and his brains were more or less hanging out. He was unconscious and I looked at him and I could see his brains on the top of his skull and all I could do was to push them back and put a bandage on, a first field dressing. I knew he'd had it but you can't imagine seeing your mate like that, I don't think you're in a normal state. That evening the shrub on the dry salt lake caught fire and there were wounded out there, so we had to try and rescue those we could. You get into a state of mind where you just behave like an automaton.

ABLE SEAMAN WALTER BURDON, NELSON BATTALION, ROYAL NAVAL DIVISION, 1895 1992

My platoon had occasion to move forward during the night; we moved so many yards and stopped. When dawn came, to my horror I was a matter of yards from the Turkish trenches. I could see their bayonets sticking straight up in the air, all the way round, hundreds of them. How we'd got there without being noticed, I don't know. I looked back to our trenches a hundred yards away where the Australians were, and I saw a man, he'd a real heart because he must have seen the predicament we were in, jump up on top of the parapet and pepper the Turkish line with machine gun fire to cover us.

If we'd had a few grenades we could have cleared that trench, but we had nothing to help us, so I said to the fellow next to me, "We have no chance, I'm getting out of it." By this time a Turkish machine gun had opened up. I waited until the gun paused and then I was off, up and away like hell across the valley. The machine gun began again so I got down behind a little hillock, and I could hear the bullets whistling overhead. When a machine gun stops, it takes about half a minute to put a new belt on. You get to know when a belt has been used up, intuition. I scrambled up again and ran, weaving about, in full view of the enemy, towards the Australian trenches, and I jumped down, my bayonet going right between the legs of an Australian who was sitting at the bottom. I asked for a periscope and just got it above the trench to see one of our fellows running along the gully down which I'd just come. I don't know if he made it because the periscope was shot out of my hand.

A fellow beside us, a New Zealand machine gunner, threw his gun over the top and jumped over. He wanted to cover those who were left out there but he was killed straight away, his body being left on the parapet as a sandbag. That's the way things were. There were two lads crouching there, just below the parapet, young fellows and one's bayonet was red with blood, and he had a bandage round his head, and he was saying, "Come on, come on, let's get at the bastards, come on!" They were not a very disciplined lot, the Australians, but they were fighters, fine fellows.

PRIVATE DICK BARRON, 2ND LONDON MOUNTED BRIGADE FIELD AMBULANCE, ROYAL ARMY MEDICAL CORPS, 1895-1999

We were carrying a man down and could not get him round a trench as it was too narrow, and after a while I said, "I must have a rest, my arms are coming out of their sockets." Men get very heavy when you carry them

> When a machine gun stops, it takes about half a minute to put a new belt on. You get to know when a belt has been used up, intuition.

on a stretcher. There were a few spent bullets buzzing around but not many. Anyway, we lay down under some cover when all of a sudden a bit of shrapnel flew past us and this man leapt off the stretcher and ran down and lay beside us. I looked at him in amazement. "You can bloody well walk the rest of the way," I told him. I saw the MO and said he was as fit as we were.

ABLE SEAMAN WALTER BURDON, NELSON BATTALION, ROYAL NAVAL DIVISION, 1895-1992

We moved down to Cape Hellas and on 5 June I was shot in the head. We were told to advance so far and dig in. We'd got down about eighteen inches when an officer joined us and said, "Prepare, prepare, enemy right". We lifted up our rifles and pointed them and just as I was about to fire, something caught my attention and made me turn and I got a terrific whack at the side of the head. A bullet or a piece of shrapnel had hit my rifle and disintegrated into small pieces of metal. When I came round, I was bleeding like a sheep. I said to these fellows, "Can I get out, can I get past?" but they said, "We're not getting out, we're not standing up, we'll get killed." I had blood pouring down my face and bullets flying about, so I couldn't blame them. I said, "Would you lie down and I'll crawl over you." This was to get to the end of the trench where the parapet was a little higher. I crawled over them to a sort of seat, sat down and passed out. When I came round, there was a right melée going on, they were in a real battle. My own officer, Sub Lieutenant Bookless, was killed just then. I woke to see him standing with two mills bombs in his hand, shouting "Get that machine gun!" but the machine gun got him, and I watched as his batman carried his body away.

While I was unconscious, my hand must have been protecting my face because when I put my hand down, blood poured out in a torrent from my sleeve. A first aid man came over. "You've been peppered this time, mister," he said, and got me down to the first aid shelter for further treatment before I was eventually taken down to the beach for evacuation.

I was in hospital for months while they removed the metal fragments from my head. My nerves were also bad and I was eventually deemed no longer fit for service. During the time I was in hospital, I dropped a line to the family of Sub Lieutenant Bookless to tell them I'd seen him shot. I got no answer. He was a member of a wealthy fruit family and they must have thought I was on the scrounge, but I wasn't. I was just letting them know that someone had seen him killed.

As for my rifle, I spoke to a man afterwards and he said he'd never seen owt like it, my rifle, it was just bits.

[Ed. Not all the metal could be removed from Walter's head. Even in 1992, when Walter was aged 97, he still had two fragments embedded in his skull, one to the side of the head and the other on the crown.]

BRITISH BUILD UP IN FRANCE

Ed. By May 1915, with the expedition well under way at Gallipoli and with losses spiralling on the Western Front, the first Kitchener Divisions were required to embark for France, and take their place in the field, much earlier than Lord Kitchener had foreseen. That month the 9th Scottish, followed shortly after by the 14th Light Division, landed in France, to be joined throughout the summer months by more New Army Divisions as they were required.

LANCE CORPORAL VIC COLE, 7TH QUEEN'S OWN (ROYAL WEST KENT REGIMENT), 1897-1995

Vic Cole..

We went to France, embarking at Southampton aboard the cross-Channel packet Mona's Queen, of the Isle of Man Steam Packet Company. It was a good trip as far as I recall, nine hours in all. We were buoyed up by the spirit of adventure, which helped those of us who suffered a bout of sea-sickness on the way, packed as we were like sardines below deck. We arrived in excellent morale at Le Havre and were observed with great curiosity by stolid German prisoners working on the roads under the watchful eyes of French sentries. French reservists also patrolled the railway lines, occupying sentry boxes every two or three miles up the track. As we passed, one of these gents saluted us in baggy red trousers and a blue frock coat and wearing a Kepi rather rakishly, I felt.

PRIVATE JACK DAVIS, 6TH DUKE OF CORNWALL'S LIGHT INFANTRY, 1895-2003

We didn't know where we were going or how long we would be on the train, and as most of the lads had been drinking before they got into the carriages, they soon needed the toilet. Anyway, those who were further up the train, where I was, just opened the window and urinated. When we eventually stopped, some of the lads further down who had stuck their heads out of the window were saying, "Oh, you could feel the steam from the engine", but it wasn't that at all!

LANCE CORPORAL VIC COLE, 7TH QUEEN'S OWN (ROYAL WEST KENT REGIMENT), 1897-1995

After forty-eight hours of incarceration in cattle trucks, we were detrained at Amiens. A short rest here and then we took to the roads. French roads were mostly cobbled across the crown, leaving four or five feet of soft going on either side. When marching in fours and keeping to the right of the road, two men of each four would be on the cobbles, number three would have one foot on cobbles and one foot on soft ground and number four would be altogether on the soft going. A halt was called at the end of every hour and a change-over made: the outside man went to the inside and the others moved up one place.

At night the western skyline was lit continuously by flickering star-shells and the glow of Very lights, while the intermittent thunder of guns became louder and louder. The sector we were heading for was held by the Regiment's First Battalion, and we, the Seventh, were to go in with them for instruction in trench warfare. For the first time, I began to realise what I had let myself in for.

PRIVATE JACK DAVIS, 6TH DUKE OF CORNWALL'S LIGHT INFANTRY, 1895-2003

On 12 August 1915, we were going to take up our forward positions ready to occupy the front line. There were four companies, and one was to occupy each of various points just behind the line: the Ramparts, Salicourt Bridge, the reserve line and the cellars of St Martin's Cathedral. I was in D Company and it was a toss-up between C and D who occupied the Cathedral down below in the cloisters. I had a charmed life. C Company went in and they'd only been there, settling in, for about ten minutes when the Germans shelled the place. They had a 17-inch gun on a railway line at Dickiebusch, what we called the Dickiebusch Express, which was shunted up into position. There was a direct hit on the Cathedral and our boys were underneath, tons of masonry falling on top of them. Working parties were immediately sent from various battalions as well as

Jack Davis.

our own regiment, trying to get these boys out. We had ten minutes to get to them before the next shell came. This went on all through the night. We couldn't reach them, couldn't move the mass of masonry, blocks of stone weighing several hundredweight, and we had only our hands, no other means. I don't think we got many out and much of the company was killed, including the second in command, Major Barnett, and many more wounded. Their bodies were not recovered until after the war.

PRIVATE JOHN REA LAISTER, NO1222, 2ND KING'S ROYAL RIFLE CORPS, 14 MAY 1897-1999

We were ready to go into the trenches and the order came to go up the communication trench. We go down into thick slimy mud, it goes into your boots, creeps up your legs, goes around your privates, gets to about waist high. We're relieving the French, who were noted for burying their dead in the side of the trench instead of removing them. So anyway, we're in this mud with no gumboots and you had to keep pulling your leg up, all the way along, and the snow is coming down, and all of a sudden an arm hits you in the face, buried in the side of the trench. You pass the word along, "Arm 'ere", you go a few more yards, you see a head hanging out, "Head 'ere", until you reach the front line. When you were out there a week, you forgot all thoughts of ever coming out, a week in those trenches, a week, and you're never coming home again, you took it for granted, and from then on you didn't care a damn. That was the feeling and it stayed with me all through the war.

PRIVATE TED FRANCIS, 16TH WARWICKSHIRE REGIMENT, 1896-1996

The news flashed around in the first line of trenches, this fellow had been killed coming up a communication trench carrying food and water. Parts of the trench had been knocked down by shellfire and he was a bit careless. Instead of bobbing down, he'd walked by standing tall and a sniper had got him in the head. We were in the front line and the news was flashed round the whole battalion very quickly. It sobered us up and kind of put a doubt in our minds about this soldier business. We were not playing at soldiers now and people were getting killed.

2ND LIEUTENANT NORMAN DILLON, 14TH NORTHUMBERLAND FUSILIERS, 1896-1997

I was full of curiosity and the foolishness of youth. I was about to put my head above the parapet to have a look, when an old hand pulled me down. "We've lost several doing that," he said. "Use a periscope." So I did and hardly had I put it up when a bullet came through it.

PRIVATE JACK DAVIS, 6TH DUKE OF CORNWALL'S LIGHT INFANTRY, 1895-2003

There was a sergeant and his brother in the same company as me. The Germans had a fixed rifle centred on part of the our trench and every now and again

they'd fire this, which kept making a hole in the sandbag parapet and it had to be built up every night. At Stand To the next morning, this brother of the sergeant said he'd spotted the sniper and he got up on the parapet and put his rifle up to fire but the sniper got him first. The bullet hit his thumb and went through his mouth and out again without hitting his teeth. How lucky can you be? Anyway, we stuck a cigarette in his mouth and off he went down the line.

[Ed. No Man's Land had become too difficult and dangerous to occupy or cross and alternative approaches to conducting hostilities had to be found. The war underground was every bit as vicious as that conducted across the trench lines above. It grew from what had almost been a cottage industry in 1914 to a sophisticated weapon of war employing thousands of men, working in cramped, airless conditions to mine under enemy positions in order to blow them up.]

2ND LIEUTENANT NORMAN DILLON, 14TH NORTHUMBERLAND FUSILIERS, 1896-1997

I made friends with a Royal Engineers Tunnelling Company officer who was mining under the German front line positions. This was difficult work, because the water table was high and the workings had to be kept clear by constant pumping. One advantage of mining in the clay was that it was almost soundless, so much so that we broke into a German tunnel, which was found to be partially flooded. As we listened, the noise of a pump could be heard. This was a great opportunity for a bit of fun, and as the River Lys flowed close by, it was easy to put a large hose from the river into this gallery. The water flowed by gravity and the Germans spent some weeks pumping the river through their mine, until they realized what had been done.

An officer uses a folding trench telescope to view the German trenches.

PRIVATE HARRY NORMAN EDWARDS, NO2912, 1/6TH GLOUCESTERSHIRE REGIMENT, 13 JANUARY 1894-21 SEPTEMBER 1999

In front of Ploegsteert Wood it was reasonably quiet, when all of a sudden there was a most enormous blast and our Sergeant, Bertie Harris, a schoolmaster from Manchester, poked his head out of the dugout. He hadn't got his trousers on because he was having a sleep, although he shouldn't have taken any clothes off in the front line trenches. "What's to do, lads?" he asked and I said, "As far as I can make out, a mine's been blown under the Hampshire Tee Trench down the road." "Oh blimey," he said, "any of our men on duty there?" I thought there was, but by this time there was such an uproar, with all the guns going and shelling, I'm not sure he heard me. After a while the furore gradually died down and we were able to go along with a trench periscope to have a look. The Germans had mined out to this isolated part of the trench system, and had blown a hole twenty feet deep and thirty feet across. Fortunately from our point of view, they'd been out in their reckoning and instead of blowing up the Tee, we could look over the trench wall with the periscope and right down into this great hole. We'd been lucky and suffered no casualties but our trench was now right on the lip of the crater.

2ND LIEUTENANT RICHARD HAWKINS, 11TH ROYAL FUSILIERS, 1895-1994

You never knew when you might be blown up by a mine, and that knowledge put a tremendous strain on the nervous system. When we were down at la Bassée, the Germans were forever driving tunnels under our lines and blowing us up. We of course tried to counter-mine, or blow up their trenches too. We had an Australian mining engineer posted to us and he used to come round at 4 o'clock in the afternoon to let us know what was happening. "Are you in charge of this section?" "Yes." "Well, um, a mine's going up here tonight, probably about two in the morning, not quite sure. I should clear these trenches, if I

were you. The mine's been overcharged and the whole thing is going to go up and there won't be a lip. Good afternoon and have a good evening," and off he'd potter. Wonderful. That night I was writing, sitting in the dugout on a little stool, 2am, situation normal, then woosh, the ground absolutely rocked backwards and I'm sent crashing to the floor. Anyway, he'd stopped the Germans mining out to us for a while, that was for sure. Damn clever chap, that Australian.

TROOPER SMILER MARSHALL, 1/1ST ESSEX YEOMANRY, 1897-2005

Our intelligence could tell that the Germans were ready to blow a mine and we were told to evacuate the line but we didn't go far enough. They made a bloody great crater, hundreds of tons of dirt blew up into the air. Two of our fellows were almost completely buried, another was caught up to his legs, and I had my feet trapped. The weight was so great, I tried to pull myself out but couldn't. One chap had just his head sticking out of the earth and a message was passed round from this man, "Is Smiler all right?" That came round to me and I said, "Yes, but I can't move, I'll have to wait until our lads come to dig us out." "Well, for Christ's sake will you sing "Nearer, my God, to thee."" My Sunday school teacher went down on the *Titanic* and we had grown up hearing that was the hymn they sang in great peril, and when in trouble I have always sung it. So I sang this hymn until they dug us out:

> Nearer, my God, to thee
> Nearer to thee
> Just like the wanderer
> When the sun goes down
> Darkness comes over me
> When my rest was a stone
> Yet in my dreams I'll be
> Nearer, my God, to thee
> Nearer, my God, to thee
> Nearer to thee.

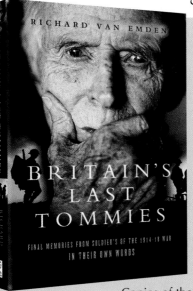
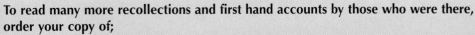

We realized that we were in for a battle, no doubt about that. Everything was building up to such a vast scale that we were all convinced that this was the push, the 'Big Push' that was to end the war.

1916 – THE BIG PUSH ON THE SOMME

After talks with the British High Command and the new Commander in Chief, Douglas Haig, it was agreed that the two allies would launch a joint offensive, and the region chosen was the Somme.

Standing shoulder to shoulder, the British and French troops would attack over an extended front, smashing through the enemy's deep defences and allowing the cavalry to wreak havoc behind the German lines. This would be the Big Push, starting an advance that would begin the wider drive to retake northern France and push the enemy back to her national borders.

As the build-up began, fresh British divisions arrived in France, swelling the number of troops from one to one and a half million. New divisions, such as the 31st Division, had been training abroad in the heat of the Egyptian desert; others, such as the 34th, had been on Salisbury Plain, enjoying the comforts of country living in Wiltshire and Somerset. To guarantee future troop requirements, conscription had been introduced in January, bringing into the army whole swathes of men previously employed in civil industry.

As far as the British were concerned, the rest of 1916 would be dominated by the offensive on the Somme. The logistics in preparing such a battle were enormous, culminating in a round-the-clock bombardment of the enemy lines, intended to last five days but, owing to poor weather, extended to seven. The enemy trenches, it was assumed, would be smashed before the infantry attacked on 1 July. Then, just prior to zero hour, a series of mines dug under German strongpoints would be detonated before the infantry went over the top. In all, around 120,000 infantrymen would advance on what turned out to be a glorious hot sunny day.

The German infantry, secreted in dugouts forty feet below ground, were far from obliterated, and when the British barrage lifted, they swarmed up and cut down the advancing troops. Around 50% of the men deployed that day were either killed or wounded. Only in the southern sector of the front did British soldiers meet with any visible success.

A battle of attrition ensued and continued for four and a half months, as the Germans fell back to defend new lines constructed little more than a mile behind those they had been forced to give up. As individual woods and villages were contested one by one, the losses on both sides mounted. The British adapted, deploying new battle tactics and weapons to break the stalemate. Their introduction met with varying success, most notably the introduction of the first tanks in September. However, the hoped-for breakthrough that would return the war to one of movement remained elusive, and the offensive bogged down in the winter mud just six miles from where the troops had started, back in July.

PRIVATE THOMAS 'TOM' ALFRED DEWING, NO85196, 2 SECTION, 34TH DIVISIONAL SIGNAL COMPANY, ROYAL ENGINEERS, ATTD. 101 BRIGADE, 21 APRIL 1896-1 FEBRUARY 2001

On the first day of January 1916, the first sections of our Company embarked for France and we were sad to see them go. The next day we left, and cheered like mad as we made for Southampton. But it wasn't an adventure.

I think by the time we actually embarked for France, we were all feeling a bit sad – it's hard to say after all this time, but yes, I would say that we were definitely feeling sad, and as we went down the Solent we all stood and watched the shores of England fading into the darkness.

PRIVATE ERNEST WILLIAM FORD, 10TH QUEEN'S (ROYAL WEST SURREY REGIMENT), 1896-1995

After the usual messing around, we were eventually stowed into cattle trucks, 'Tommies' Pullmans' bearing the trade-mark, Hommes 40 Chevaux 8, from which we inferred that a horse was worth five men. Whoever was responsible for this sign must have been a very optimistic person. I doubt whether it would have been possible to put 40 men, with all their impediments, into one cattle truck without making two layers of them. Anyhow, there were 28 in my truck and there was not sufficient floor-space for us all to lie flat. We piled our legs down the middle of the truck and endured a 19-hour journey followed by a nine-mile march into billets.

PRIVATE TOM DEWING, 34TH DIVISIONAL ROYAL ENGINEERS SIGNAL COMPANY, 1896-2001

Our accommodated consisted of wooden huts with pitched roofs of tarred felt. Each hut had a door at one end and a slow combustion stove at the other. There was a battery of field guns nearby and it was an interesting experience when we heard the first shells. One morning the Germans started shelling the battery and we all rushed out to watch. A shell burst fairly near the huts and a piece of shell whirred past us. We followed the sound with our eyes. Presently a second piece went through the roof of an empty hut and we all rushed to find this bit of shell. I found it and I carried it in my haversack for months.

PRIVATE ANDREW BOWIE, NO22693, D COMPANY, 1ST CAMERON HIGHLANDERS, 3 OCTOBER 1897-26 2002

I had an uncle who happened to be an agent for bullet-proof vests that looked similar to a thickly padded waistcoat. Now these vests would, in theory, stop a bullet, so my sister purchased one and sent it to me. I wore it under my tunic. There was a sergeant major, who was a rather cowardly type. He knew about my bullet-proof vest and he used to say to me, "When you get killed, I'll have that vest." We were out on rest once, and he said, "Come on, we'll try your vest out." So we draped it around a sandbag, went about fifty yards away and fired shots at it. They went right through the padding, after which his eager claim dropped a bit.

LANCE CORPORAL VIC COLE, 7TH QUEEN'S OWN (ROYAL WEST KENT REGIMENT), 1897-1995

In the trenches around Bécourt Château, there had been a German attack in the early days of 1914, and a lot of French had been killed. It meant that when we dug new trenches we came across these bodies, including, I recall, a ghostly hand sticking out where some earth had given way. Yet we just went on, thinking that was the way it had to be. It didn't worry me, seeing bodies that had turned black, you took no notice because it didn't matter, because very soon you yourself would be like that.

Battalion HQ was situated in the very extensive cellars of the Château. The building had been much knocked about but part of the roof was intact, and from there I could just see the 'hanging virgin' crowning the ruined basilica in Albert.

The Château was still habitable on the ground floor, where there was a salon and an old piano. This was played now and again to the accompaniment of machine gun bullets and shells passing overhead. One shell burst in the small library, scattering books. They were torn and dusty but one could see amongst them the beautiful bindings of old volumes mostly inscribed on the fly-leaf or cover with the name 'Comte de Varicourt'.

In the cellar, there were one or two tables and a telephone switchboard into which we plugged the various wires we were using; the plug was the bullet out of a 303 cartridge, the wires were wrapped or soldered onto the cartridge, and the bullet was put head first into whatever cartridge you wanted, to make a connection. It was all very ingenious.

To exit the cellars, we dug a door in the back that brought us out onto a path that led into a wood and down to the communication trenches. In front of the Château, there had been a garden with a well, which we were told had been poisoned. There was a wall each side and iron gates, and we called the square in front of the Château 'Piccadilly Circus'. Out of the iron gates, the communication trench, Dufferin Avenue, led down a slope to a sunken road where our water cart was, and from there up to the support line.

We were well behind the line here but that did not mean we were safe. Death or injury could happen at the most unexpected moments. I nipped down one night to the water cart to fill my bottle just as a machine gun opened up and a shower of bullets smacked into the ground all around the cart. A man beside me groaned and fell. A stretcher bearer came up at the run and we found that a bullet had entered the poor bloke's back in the lumber region and had come out just above his left knee. When bandaged, he seemed to be all right and went off on a stretcher, smoking a cigarette.

PRIVATE SMILER MARSHALL, 1/1ST ESSEX YEOMANRY, 1897-2005

My mate Lenny Passiful was in a different troop from me. I was in the Ardley Troop; he was in the Colchester Troop, but he asked his sergeant if he could come and join me in the same bay of the trench. A German had been using a sniper's shield and we reckoned there was a chance of getting him because when he shot there was a

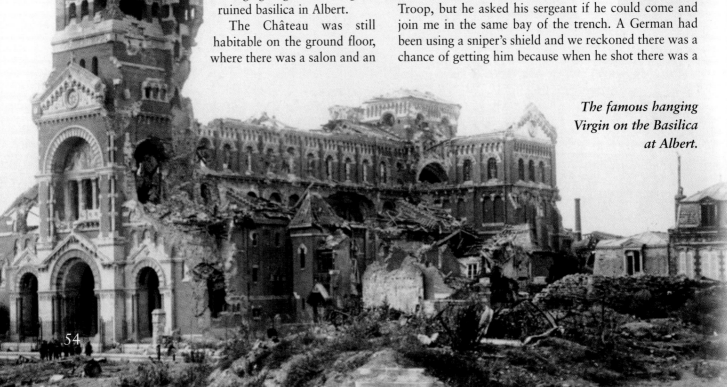

The famous hanging Virgin on the Basilica at Albert.

tell-tale flame from the barrel of his rifle. So what we'd try and do is get ready and concentrate, waiting for the next time he fired.

I'd had five or six shots when my mate Lenny said, "Let me have a go, Smiler," and he jumped up on to the fire step. Now I'm down in the trench watching and he had a shot or two when the German fired and I suddenly saw Lenny collapse. I put my arm out and broke his fall.

He lay at the bottom of the trench and I spoke to him. "Never mind, Lenny, you've got your blighty one. What more do you want?" He coughed up a little blood, but he managed to smile and say "Ta ta, Smiler." I wanted to take him down to the chalk pit, to the first dressing station. "Please, he's my best pal, I'd love to take him, so that I know the RAMC have got him." But Sergeant Geoffrey Weir said he'd take him and as he went along the communication trench, a German mortar came right over and blew the parapet down, blocking the way. He had to take Lenny over the top, so for a couple of minutes he was exposed to the Germans, who opened fire with their machine guns. He got a medal for that.

LANCE CORPORAL VIC COLE, 7TH QUEEN'S OWN (ROYAL WEST KENT REGIMENT), 1897-1995

You could look over the top but you had to be very careful. Sandbags lined the length of the parapet so we'd sew a sandbag onto our tin hats and peer over, just your eyes, so that you were practically invisible to the enemy. Then you'd just rest your arm next to your rifle and you'd be quite comfortable for a while. Then you might see a puff of something over there and wonder for a moment what it was, ch ch ch ch, the sound, you know.

"Trench mortar coming over!" And we'd all dive down the dugouts, and it would come, ch ch ch ch, like a train, a large tin canister turning over in the air, CRAAAASH, and then we'd all come out again.

LIEUTENANT RICHARD HAWKINS, 11TH ROYAL FUSILIERS, 1895-1994

We all had great fun really, tremendous fun. I personally enjoyed the ruddy war, I don't know why. Of course, it wasn't very pleasant when *Minenwerfers* were being thrown in the air, great big five-gallon oil drums, filled with rusty metal, you could see them turning over – where's that going to drop? Which way should we run?

LANCE CORPORAL VIC COLE, 7TH QUEEN'S OWN (ROYAL WEST KENT REGIMENT), 1897-1995

You weren't having a battle but it was a game of wits all the time. Up near Fricourt, there was a German machine gun we nicknamed Banjo Willie; he used to open up every night at 8 o'clock. "Oh, there's Banjo Willie," and he would fire 'tat, tat, tat, tat tat....tat tat' from two different places, then quickly swing his gun round and loose off two extra shots. It was his signature.

We learnt to spot the snipers too. You'd put up a large turnip on the end of your bayonet with a tin hat on it, and so attract the sniper who might fire. If he did, we'd take the turnip down very carefully and take a bearing through the hole that the bullet had made, then do it again further up the trench and get a cross bearing. We didn't fire at him ourselves, rather we would ask the trench mortar people to drop one on him.

British Tommies writing official postcards home after being captured.

PRIVATE SMILER MARSHALL, 1/1ST ESSEX YEOMANRY, 1897-2005

I wrote to Lenny's mum after he was shot. "Expect Lenny home within weeks, he'll be back in England, he's been shot." About four or five weeks later, I got a letter back. "Dear Smiler, you'll be very sad to hear that he only lived three days." They buried him in Béthune Town Cemetery. In his paybook there was about £3 or £4, and they stopped £1 for the blanket he was buried in. What do you think about that? A soldier wounded in the front line, and the army took a pound for the blanket, unbelievable, but that's as true as I'm here.

PRIVATE ANDREW BOWIE, 1ST CAMERON HIGHLANDERS, 1897-2002

When we were in the line, the mail from home was vital to morale and wasn't censored. Mail going home was read by an officer, to see that you hadn't said where you were fighting. If you did, then a big black pencil would go through the offending words. Many people had an understanding with home, a code, so, for example each paragraph would start with a letter which, added up to the opening letters of every other paragraph, would spell a word. "You are in my constant thoughts, "Y". "Present days are very tiring," "P". "Received your letter with great pleasure, "R"...and so on "E" and then "S"...Ypres. So you'd tell your friends at home you were at Ypres.

PRIVATE TED FRANCIS, 16TH WARWICKSHIRE REGIMENT, 1896-1996

I'd written three letters to my father, telling him about the war, and I'd had no replies. I couldn't understand it. Of course, leave was out of the question. Then one day, a letter came for me from a strange hand. It was from a gentleman who had taken over my father's pub and he said, "I've opened a letter you sent and it's obvious to me you don't know that your father is dead – he died six weeks ago from cancer." That knocked me over. He told me that my eldest brother, who was twelve years older than me, had had what he liked of the home and put all the rest to auction, and therefore I'd no home.

When I got leave, I had to find my brother and beg to stay at his place. He wasn't too keen, but his wife said that I could give them a hand and that there was a spare room, so I got lodgings. I had no money at all and I had to rely on my brother and his wife to give me half a crown to go up town and go the pictures or theatre. That was a miserable ten days for me and in a way I was glad to be back in France. That was my only leave in three years.

LIEUTENANT NORMAN DILLON, 14TH NORTHUMBERLAND FUSILIERS, 1896-1997

In 1916 we were issued with steel helmets for the first time. They were uncomfortable because they didn't fit; they sat on one's hair, but they worked. I sent home for a liner which fitted like a bowler hat and was comfortable, but most annoyingly it was stolen. The maker was Lincoln & Bennett of St James. It was interesting how one could order London-made goods in the middle of a war, and what is more, receive them.

LIEUTENANT RICHARD HAWKINS, 11TH ROYAL FUSILIERS, 1895-1994

One of my fellow officers by the name of Lewis wrote to Dunhill and said, "Dear Mr Dunhill, please send us a pipe," and this parcel was delivered by the post office to us in the dugout, the night before an attack. Lewis opened the parcel and there inside were twelve pipes, each in a little box, with a tin of ointment and a spare aluminium tube. Beautiful French Briar, famous they were, and there was a letter, "Dear Mr Lewis, thank you very much for your letter. We don't know what size or shape you prefer, so we are sending a dozen for you to choose from. When you've made your choice, please at your convenience return the remainder, unless of course any of your brother officers would like to buy one." Well, I fell for it, fourteen and sixpence, but it was beautiful.

2ND LIEUTENANT NORMAN COLLINS, 1/6TH SEAFORTH HIGHLANDERS, 1897-1998

To ease the pressure we smoked; almost every man seemed to smoke. Cigarettes were a great comfort and, at the right time, worked wonders. Most of the cigarettes were terrible and were hardly worth smoking. The cheap cigarette was a Woodbine. The Players and Goldflake were quite good, sixpence for twenty or fivepence ha'penny for Players. Although I might smoke up to 40 or 45 cigarettes a day, I never inhaled, so I can't say that I

Norman Collins.

was a great addict, but some men would take the end of a cigarette and relight it and, even though it was saturated in tar and nicotine, they'd enjoy it. Smoking was all part of the camaraderie and of course it relieved stress, no doubt about it.

TROOPER SMILER MARSHALL, 1/1ST ESSEX YEOMANRY, 1897-2005

Most men smoked cigarettes to help relieve the pressure, but I didn't. Instead I would start to sing, to help morale, break the ice, so to speak. It was better than standing there twiddling your thumbs. If you can start singing, you're all right. It stopped the fear, stopped you being mopey or worrying. If everything was quiet and a machine gunner began sweeping your parapet and then the shells, trench mortars and rifle grenades started bursting, and everybody is sitting there, nobody speaking, it doesn't matter what it is, start singing. Everybody will look up, and the whole place will be more lively.

In the front line, we used to sing all sorts of songs, and I made one up about the food we used to eat.

James William Maconochie
Made a monarchy
On his own
Beans mixed up with turnips and carrots
And all sorts of things.
The troops all did a funny 'un
When an onion came to light
But the troops didn't mind
That the man who got fat
Was JWM

PRIVATE JACK DAVIS, 1ST DUKE OF CORNWALL'S LIGHT INFANTRY, 1895-2003

At La Bassée we had no recognized front line. We were operating from saps, dug in the ground, Suffolk Sap, Machine Gun Sap, and Lunatic Sap, which speaks for itself. I had to do a tour of duty with my company officer to supply the other saps along the front with a rum ration. So we were out for more or less three to four hours supplying the ration, after which we came back for a rest until Stand To. One day a young officer joined the regiment, and I was told to take him out and show him the route we took to the other saps. So the first night, all right, no problem. But, being an officer, he was taught to lead, while other ranks were taught to follow. So he said, "All right, I'll lead tonight," and he did, and took us onto the German wire. I was furious because he was insistent. He had only been over this ground once, and I had made regular tours with my Company Officer. What can you say? You don't say, "You're going the wrong way." You don't argue, you've got to follow.

The machine guns opened up all along our front. Self-preservation took over, and I got into a shell hole for cover and I called him and he came in. The Germans traversed their machine gun, and we waited until they passed us and made a dash for it, it was just a few yards to a bombing post, and we got back safely.

The next night he was still not satisfied, he wanted to lead, so he said, "Make sure we take Corporal Hubbard with us." He was in charge of the machine gun, and the same thing happened, we ended up on the German wire. Once again we jumped into a shell hole but the Corporal lost his head. He was running up and down the German wire while they were machine gunning. The officer and I got back, but we couldn't leave the Corporal out there and so I went out again with another man and got into

> He was running up and down the German wire while they were machine gunning. The officer and I got back, but we couldn't leave the Corporal out there and so I went out again with another man and got into a shell hole. We shouted out for him...

a shell hole. We shouted out for him to join us, which he did, and all three of us ran back to the bombing post. However, as Hubbard bent over to get into the post he got a machine gun bullet right across his back, a flesh wound. He was the luckiest man alive, for it was within an eighth of an inch of his spine.

TROOPER SMILER MARSHALL, 1/1ST ESSEX YEOMANRY, 1897-2005

A corporal and some men were going up the line to mend the trenches that had been blown in by a trench mortar. We were selected for the working party, but two lads, John Eade and Harry Jowers, they had the wind-up terrific. They had sweat dripping off their chins. Eade had the wind-up because he had numbered off as 13, so I tapped him on the back and said, "Change places with me. I'll number off 13, I'm not superstitious." We changed places, but they both died. Next morning they were buried a mile or so behind the lines. We'd had leather jerkins issued that night, so they wore them for the first time, and then they were buried in them. They were best mates, close as anything, and would have been together when they were hit.

Every night on the working party the padre used to come up and say a little prayer, and he used to say that it doesn't matter how near you are to death, there's always somebody nearer, so that's what you've got to try and think. Don't think that you might be the next one.

RIFLEMAN ROBERT RENWICK, 16TH KING'S ROYAL RIFLE CORPS, 1896-1997

Corporal Hiddins had gone to the company office and come back fuming, so I asked him what the matter was. He said, "What's the matter? I have to take a man with me and get a sample of German barbed wire." I said, "What are you waiting for?" "Are you volunteering?" he asked. "Yes, and I have a set of wire cutters." So off we went over the top. I then suggested that there was plenty of wire about without going anywhere near the enemy line. I picked up a length and cut each end clean, and of course we spent a bit of time sitting in a shell hole. The wire was accepted as being German and I thought we were fully justified in dodging the order.

PRIVATE ANDREW BOWIE, 1ST CAMERON HIGHLANDERS, 1897-2002

A captain, who had been the adjutant in Invergordon, came out to the battalion and went out on patrol, as ordered, from his part of the trench. Another patrol under a young lieutenant called Stephenson went out as well, and they were supposed to go along No Man's

Land and meet and come back again. Stephenson came in and said he had not met the captain, but the captain said he had gone right along there as ordered but hadn't seen Stephenson. The captain had told a deliberate lie, because the men who had been with him told the truth and said, "He never did that, we were with him and we just went over into No Man's Land and we all sat down and came back in again. He never did his patrol." That was very serious, of course, he could have been court martialled. The other men backed Stephenson, that he'd gone along all right but nothing had been seen of the captain. He was a pure coward and the men had a nasty feeling about him.

2ND LIEUTENANT HERBERT ERNEST BRIGHTON, 10TH SOUTH WALES BORDERERS, 20 NOVEMBER 1896-29 SEPTEMBER 1997

We'd lie flat out in No Man's Land when the Very lights went up, then we'd move. We took rifles and fixed bayonets. I always wore an other rank's uniform with just the pips on my shoulder to show my rank. Whenever I was out on patrol I took a man called Davenport, a reliable man. It was his manner, if we got close enough to the enemy trench, to always spend a penny on their barbed wire entanglements. He was a brave and a grand man. Just to show his contempt for the Germans, that's what he said.

PRIVATE JACK DAVIS, 1ST DUKE OF CORNWALL'S LIGHT INFANTRY, 1895-2003

My Company, A Company, were to take part in a bombing raid so we were taken out of the line to a field a couple of miles away. There they had a plan of the German line all mapped out in tapes, and we practised

A British Lewis gun team prepared for a gas attack.

attacking the line for 10 days before the raid took place. I was made bayonet man, which meant I was on the extreme left of the line when we went over. I personally carried six mills bombs, a bandolier of ammunition, rifle and bayonet, two four-pound tins of high explosive amanol to blow up the German wire and two stokes bombs with two five-second fuses to bomb the dugouts.

To give the signal for our advance, the light artillery opened fire on the German wire, but in the event they fired short. We had to take evasive action and I found myself right on top of a Lewis Gun team that was meant to give us cover. My first instinct was to get rid of some of this arsenal, to avoid being blown sky-high, but the guns lifted and we made for the German line.

On reaching the enemy trench, the section commander got up on the top of the parapet, brandishing his revolver. As soon as the Germans knew we were going to attack, they panicked and rushed their machine gun down into their dugout. This was stupid, because a stokes shell went down after them and blew the whole lot up. We took a prisoner at this point: he was the fellow who had operated the machine gun, and as he'd tried to make a getaway, our officer shouted and the German was so terrified that he stopped. They collared his rifle and stuck it up the side of the trench, and they sent him back with two men to our lines for questioning at headquarters.

At this point, we still occupied only a small portion of the front line so we spread out, bombing all the dugouts and if possible capturing anything of any use. As bayonet man, I went to the head of their communication trench that led straight out under the la Bassée road. Covering me were three men with mills bombs, which they had to lob from behind me towards the enemy who were now trying to advance.

The raid lasted twenty-five minutes before the signal to retire, which was a Very light fired from the back of our lines. By this time I'd got no support, as the bombers had all been injured, and I was entirely on my own. It was extremely cold that night but I was sweating like a pig. The Germans must have sensed that the raid was ending and tried to rush the communication trench where I was now the only bloke to stop them. Fortunately they'd difficulty getting round a corner of the trench while I kept up a rapid fire. I was very excited, knowing this was a case of self-preservation. I was fortunate. The Germans' fire suddenly subsided and I knew they'd given up.

Before we left, the stretcher bearers had to move in to evacuate the wounded. I had to stop until all the raiding party had got out. When I was ready to go, my section officer stopped me and said he wanted the German rifle that was stuck on the top of the trench, and then he said, "Oh, and pick up all the unused bombs that are left there." There was nobody else now, I was the only one in the German front line. I had to get out quick so I grabbed what I could, then scrambled over, tearing my uniform on the wire as I went. We'd lost 26 men on the raid.

PRIVATE JOE YARWOOD, 94TH FIELD AMBULANCE, ROYAL ARMY MEDICAL CORPS, 1896-1995

Joe Yarwood.

As a rule we didn't go in the front line, we were left in the second line at what was known as a Relay Post. It was a monotonous job, and there were long periods when there was nothing happening and you were bored to the pants. Very often the regimental men were the people who administered first aid to their wounded before we'd pick them up. The first case I ever took out of the line was a man shot through the head. We were at a place called Cheerio Dugout.

We dashed down and the poor devil was lying up on top behind the parados. He'd been concentrating on a sniper and he'd been shot through the head. The regimental stretcher bearers had dressed him before we lifted him off the parados with the nasty feeling we were going to get bumped off any moment.

We found we couldn't carry the stretcher down the trench as it was frightfully narrow; it had been dug by the French and they hadn't done the job properly, so we carried that poor devil out with great difficulty, holding the stretcher in the crook of our elbows, as the trench narrowed. One fellow walked behind, hanging on to the casualty's wrists, for we found there was a tendency for them to grab at their bandages. At one point where the trench widened, we stopped for a moment and put him

down, and as we did so, sure enough, he snatched the bandages off and his brains and blood went all over my tunic. He then vomited. What a mess! I had felt sorry for the poor fellow and put my tunic under him.

When I got back to headquarters, I had to indent for a new tunic, and when the colonel heard, he told me I was a bloody fool and that if I did it again I would have to pay. My paybook was bloodstained all round the edges and yet I carried that through the war.

The poor fellow was called Corporal Hazeldine of the East Yorks. I heard from others that he survived with a metal plate in his head but I find it hard to believe.

SATURDAY 1 JULY

PRIVATE TOM DEWING, 34TH DIVISIONAL ROYAL ENGINEERS SIGNAL COMPANY, 1896-2001

We realized that we were in for a battle, no doubt about that. Everything was building up to such a vast scale that we were all convinced that this was the push, the 'Big Push' that was to end the war.

We had a Norfolk sergeant with us, Sergeant Britcher, an old soldier, and he wasn't so keen. He said, "I ain't a-going to be in no big push, I'm going back to England."

To us that seemed extremely unlikely, but Britcher had it all worked out. So he claimed to the doctor that a tumour on his face, which he had had for years, was making him deaf. The doctor said it could not possibly be the case but Britcher persisted and it became increasingly difficult to hold a conversation with him.

The officer knew perfectly well he was swinging the lead, so did we all, and he knew that we knew. One evening we were in an estaminet and one of the lads went quietly up behind him. "Would you like a drink, Sergeant?" Britcher glanced round to see nobody was watching, "It ain't no good you saying would you like a drink, 'cos I can't hear you."

In the end he managed to convince the authorities that he was deaf, even though the doctor was adamant he was shamming, and Britcher was sent back to England to train other troops.

LANCE CORPORAL VIC COLE, 7TH QUEEN'S OWN (ROYAL WEST KENT REGIMENT), 1897-1995

If you didn't want to do something, or you got fed up, you went sick, or tried to go sick. If the medical officers knew you'd had a rough time they were lenient with you, but if you were trying to swing the lead, as they called it, they would just give you a No.9 pill, a mild laxative, and send you back up the line.

I was on my way back to the battalion after a short leave. The battalion was due to attack on 1 July, and the bombardment was on. I was in the village of Meaulte, just behind the lines, when about midnight I was wrenched into wakefulness by the roar of an explosion. Extricating myself through clouds of dust and debris, I discovered that my trousers were wet with blood from a gash above the hip-bone. I was packed into an ambulance and sent to a convalescence camp. I had an idea that they didn't want to send me home, but rather to a hospital around Amiens. Anyway, I had been told that if you chewed a piece of cordite it would give you all the symptoms of a heart attack. I had some strips of cordite because I had been opening brass cartridges to make a telephone switchboard in the cellars of Bécourt Château. So there I was lying in bed, and I cut off a quarter of an inch – I didn't want to cut off too much just in case it blew my head off – and chewed away. I quickly frothed a bit at the mouth, and my heart started racing. The nurse, she'd just come out from home, and she said, "Whatever's the matter?" I said I felt terrible and she called for a doctor, saying, "Look at him!" She persuaded him that I should be sent down the line instead of Amiens Hospital, and I got all the way back to England just as the offensive got into full swing.

LIEUTENANT RICHARD HAWKINS, 11TH ROYAL FUSILIERS, 1895-1994

One of our objectives for the 1 July was to take some German guns close to a wood, I forget the name now. We were practising for the attack near the village of Maricourt and my dear friend Adie was with his platoon, lying out in a field, when General Maxse rode up. Adie should have been going for those guns, but for some reason he'd failed to do so. I don't remember the whole story, but it ended up with words I'll never forget. "Lieutenant, write home to tell your mother you made General Maxse cry."

LIEUTENANT NORMAN DILLON, 14TH NORTHUMBERLAND FUSILIERS, ATTD 178 TUNNELLING COMPANY, ROYAL ENGINEERS, 1896-1997

Our job, as officers, was to keep underground watch with primitive sound detectors, some form of electrified earphones, and note what was going on. It was not possible to keep the mining silent. In the chalk, sounds were bound to be made.

So long as one heard digging, one could be moderately sure that it would continue in one place, indicating the formation of a chamber, and later there would be the sound of dragging sacks of explosive. This was a signal for a possible blow, and the staff were informed so that precautions could be taken against the usual surface attack subsequent to the blowing of a mine. It was a very nerve-wracking business, sitting fifty feet down in the chalk and wondering if the filling of the chamber had been completed or whether one would never know at all.

We worked in shifts round the clock, two to three hours each in tunnels three feet high and two feet wide. However, digging in chalk required very little support as regards props and so forth. The chalk was carried out in sandbags to maintain silence while bellows and pipes were used to provide ventilation. It wasn't very pleasant and we had a very high casualty rate.

While I was on relief duty, the Germans blew a camouflet, a small explosion designed to eliminate the enemy and his tunnel but not to destroy the trenches above. It killed an officer and two other men, but that was part of the accepted risk. You tried to refrain from blowing such a counter-mine because you blew your own tunnel same as the enemy's. We only did it when absolutely necessary.

PRIVATE JOE YARWOOD, 94TH FIELD AMBULANCE, ROYAL ARMY MEDICAL CORPS, 1896-1995

We were in the line several days before the attack on 1 July, and everyone was optimistic. I was sent up on 28 June to join the three squads who would deal with the wounded. I took the place of a man who had gone sick. He had been in the Boer War, and was old enough to be our father. He went sick and poor old Joe had to take his place, which I wasn't happy about, as I had to endure the bombardment. You can take it from me, it was hell. The lads had blankets there in which to sew up the dead, and when I arrived they said, "You, you long bugger, you'll need more than one blanket," and they were actually measuring me up to see whether two blankets would be sufficient, as a joke, of course, they were being funny, but it wasn't particularly funny to me.

Close to where we were, was a place called Euston Dump and nearby there was a battery of guns that were going night and day for the whole period, only stopping to let the guns cool. Every so often, I would pass through the guns just as they opened up again, wooossh!, and my tin helmet

"We worked in shifts round the clock", Norman Dillon was attached to 178 Tunnelling Company RE.

would fall over my face with the shock. The only relief we had was the knowledge that the Germans were going through hell over there, and that made it easier for us.

LIEUTENANT NORMAN DILLON, 14TH NORTHUMBERLAND FUSILIERS, 1896-1997

I had heard that my battalion was going to take part in the attack and I wanted to be in it as we believed this was the big one. I couldn't see any future to tunnelling if open warfare was going to resume and we were on the move, as I hoped we would be. So I put in a request to go back to my unit and they had no grounds to refuse it.

The 14th Northumberland Fusiliers, being pioneers, had to follow the leading troops at some distance, the object being to help consolidate the newly-won positions, but on the day it was all badly managed. We were to enlarge scrapes in the ground or turn captured German trenches round to face the other way, so that the parados became the parapet, and then put out barbed wire.

On the morning of 1 July I was half a mile away when these huge mines were exploded, and the ground shook under my feet. The first waves went over the top and made some progress. I saw a field gun battery galloping up and putting its guns into position and firing just behind what had been our front line. Those guns soon had to limber up and gallop off again because they came under fire; they were too close. I went forward with my company about half a mile, and found one of the junior subalterns, Second Lieutenant Walker, had been needlessly killed after being brought up, then doing nothing, before he was hit by desultory bursts of machine gun fire on our flanks. The truth is we hadn't much idea what we were to do that day because everybody expected to be miles ahead.

PRIVATE TOM DEWING, 34TH DIVISION, ROYAL ENGINEERS SIGNAL COMPANY, 1896-2001

On 30 June, the day before the attack, two of us were sent to an observation post called Smiths Redoubt. This was a small dugout with a slot that enabled us to look over the German lines. There we were joined by the Brigade Intelligence Officer, Lieutenant 'Blanco' White, and various runners. We were also connected to Brigade Headquarters by telephone, and had a powerful telescope that could be mounted on a tripod.

Shortly before 7.30am on 1 July we felt the ground heave from the explosion of the mine at La Boisselle but we could see nothing. In the first place, there was a certain amount of mist and then when you add to that the enormous amount of smoke from the barrage, a great deal was hidden. Then when the mist and smoke cleared, we were able to see the infantry going forward in open formation as if on the parade ground. In many cases the men didn't get very far, they were just wiped out. One of the officers in our dugout had some field glasses which he allowed us to use from time to time, and looking into the crater we could sometimes see a German getting up, raising his rifle and firing. During the attack, a signaller, Corporal Bone, and one or two other men followed the infantry to their first objective.

They set up a heliograph, as the weather was ideal for its use, and we waited anxiously for the first flash. When it came, we were thrilled; they had reached their objective. They sent our call sign, 'ZJA, ZJA'. Z stood for Brigade, J was the tenth letter of the alphabet, A the first, so we got 101st Brigade. We waited for the message that was to follow but it never came. The enemy had seen the flashing and opened up with a machine gun.

> The first three lines were being mown down. I walked forward in a daze. Near the crest of the slope, I saw the reason for the carnage: Jerry had manned every single post. As I neared the enemy wire, I felt a sharp thud accompanied by a pain in my chest and I fell.

SERGEANT WALTER JAMES POPPLE, NO14134, 15 PLATOON, D COMPANY, 8TH KING'S OWN YORKSHIRE LIGHT INFANTRY, 16 JANUARY 1896-CIRCA 1990

1 July promised to be a beautiful day. The sun had risen high in the sky and we could hear the birds singing. I stood on the firestep and scanned the scene. Jerry had been pounded for a week and would be decimated. What few were left would not be able to offer any real resistance. I recall wondering if that was true as a shell burst in the trench 40 yards away, and an officer and three men were killed outright.

A loud blast on a whistle and the first wave began the attack, as the barrage moved forward. Then it was time for my platoon to go. A line had been cut in the barbed wire the night before, through which to advance, but as I did so I could scarcely believe my eyes.

The first three lines were being mown down. I walked forward in a daze. Near the crest of the slope, I saw the reason for the carnage: Jerry had manned every single post. As I neared the enemy wire, I felt a sharp thud accompanied by a pain in my chest and I fell.

PRIVATE CLARRIE JARMAN, 7TH QUEEN'S (ROYAL WEST SURREY REGIMENT), 1896-1996

That morning we turned out our pockets, dumping postcards of naked French girls to ensure they weren't sent home with any personal effects should we be killed. Then the trench ladders were put into place and on the blast of whistles, and after wishing our chums the best of luck, over we went. It was like a dream, lots of the lads were shot down just going over the parapet.

We advanced, each platoon forming a star. Only when we got close to the German line would we move into extended order. But of course it was just a shambles; it was every man for himself.

I was a bomber. I was staggering along with 250 rounds of small arms ammunition, a rifle and a fixed bayonet, seven mills bombs on my chest and seven on my back and a pick and shovel, going along in a dream-like state. All the while you could hear the machine guns, tak, tak, tak, tak, tak.

Lieutenant Haggard had taken us over, one of two brothers in the battalion. The last I saw of him, he was bending over a local chap, Arthur Spooner, who had lost an eye, and shortly after, about half way across, I got hit. I went down straightaway and crawled into a deep shell hole, dumping all my equipment. I had a look round the battleground and as far as I could see, there were our lads lying out dead, wounded and dying. There were some lads in a shell hole near me and when they saw me looking over, they said, "Get your head down" and I did and didn't know any more. The shrapnel had shattered the bottom part of my right leg and for much of the time I was unconscious with the loss of blood. There was no pain and I lay there all that day, about fourteen hours.

It was getting dusk when a lad from the RAMC happened to come my way looking for wounded, and in a very faint voice I called to him and he heard my call. I was lucky to be picked up.

LIEUTENANT RICHARD HAWKINS, 11TH ROYAL FUSILIERS, 1895-1994

We moved up into our front line trench, and in the early hours every man was given a good breakfast and packet of woodbines, stupid thing to say, but I went over smoking an Abdullah cigarette. It was a lovely morning and over the top we went at zero hour. We had a marvellous day, and got right into their first and second line trenches. The Manchesters to our left were held up and the battalions were held up on our right too, otherwise, someone said, we could have walked through to Berlin.

I was keen to get on and beat the enemy. I didn't really think I might be hit at any moment. My batman, named Good, followed me over and he was hit early on; we were great friends, damn good chap. He slumped to the ground and appeared to have been shot through the lungs. I thought he was dying, but I had to leave him, I'd got to get on with the war.

You hadn't time to mourn the dead, sorry old thing, very sorry, poor old so-and-so being killed, damned bad luck, never mind, let's get on boys, let's get on with the job. People were being killed all day long.

PRIVATE JOE YARWOOD, 94TH FIELD AMBULANCE, ROYAL ARMY MEDICAL CORPS, 1896-1995

We were taking the wounded from a relay post at the end of the communication trench across Euston Dump to the main road, where the dugouts were. Some of the injured had blighty wounds and you could almost see the satisfaction on their faces. The machine gun bullets were flying all around, all the time. If a chap was able to walk, it was much better for him to walk than to occupy a stretcher, and where we could, we would carry his equipment and escort him down. I met one poor devil injured in the face. He had been a walking wounded case and he was an elderly man, too, and I felt very sorry for him. His face was bandaged but his wound was still bleeding, and the whole of his chest was covered with a

British Tommies cross a communication trench during an attack on the German lines.

thick mat of congealed blood. I thought he would go down any minute with loss of blood. I couldn't help him because I'd already got a case with me, but I got him carried out on a stretcher because, had he collapsed, he might well have died. And that's what I was doing, all day long, simply going backwards and forwards like an automaton, you didn't think much. If we'd been winning, that might have been some consolation, but we hadn't even got that.

There were so many more lying out in No Man's Land, but we couldn't reach them. We talked about it. One team tried to clamber out over the top, but one of the lads was shot straightaway, a bullet smashing his thigh, and the rest of the team scrambled back in. We were amazed that Jerry was able to survive the bombardment.

SERGEANT WALTER POPPLE, 8TH KING'S OWN YORKSHIRE LIGHT INFANTRY, 1896-1990

Walter Popple.

Running footsteps to my rear seemed to bring me back to reality. Then came the sound of a falling body, and with it the certain knowledge that a sniper was about. A German was firing from an advanced post, picking off anyone he saw, including the wounded. As I glanced upwards, he saw me. He fired, a bullet taking the heel off my boot. My rifle was somewhere around but my shoulder was so stiff that I couldn't handle it. Then there were the two grenades in my tunic pockets but I couldn't throw them that distance. All these thoughts flashed through my mind with the ugly realisation that any pot shots might easily set off the grenades.

I came to the terrible decision that it was better to get it over with quickly and die, rather than to be picked off piece by piece so I raised my head and pushed myself upwards, almost kneeling to look straight down into the muzzle of his rifle. A sharp crack, and my helmet flew off and my neck stiffened. I sank to the ground. Utter silence. The hours passed by. At first there was a buzzing sensation in my head and then sharp piercing darts of pain. Had I been killed as I first thought? I dared not lift my head and there I remained through the heat of the day, wondering if in fact part of my head had been blown away. Night came, and I cautiously turned over and began to take stock. I gently lowered the bandolier full of ammunition from my shoulders, and the two hand grenades. Moving on my hands and knees, I crept to a large shell hole and despite the bodies around it, began to make myself comfortable. The bullet, I realized, had hit flush on the front of my helmet but instead of killing me outright it must have ricocheted upwards with such force that it ripped the straps from the flanges on my shrapnel helmet, sending it spinning into the air. The

Germans, of course, would have assumed that I was dead.

The next day followed the same pattern except that we were shelling Jerry's front line trenches with high explosive shrapnel that at times crossed the shell hole where I was sheltering, wounding me in the right leg and shoulders, some seven more wounds in all.

LIEUTENANT RICHARD HAWKINS, 11TH ROYAL FUSILIERS, 1895-1994

General Maxse came to see us afterwards. He was about five foot six tall and, rather stupidly, we thought, he had a guardsman as his aide-de-camp, Captain Montague, who was about six foot three.

Maxse spoke to us: "Morning, gentlemen, damn good show, thank you very much, you did very well, marvellous. Tell me, where would you expect to find a group of officers congregated together in the middle of the biggest battle there has ever been?" "Ooh," we thought, "now, wait a minute." "I'll tell you," he said. "walking about on the skyline looking for souvenirs! I saw them through my field glasses." Well, there wasn't anything else to do, all was peace and quietness where we were and I managed to pick up a marvellous German pickelhaube.

We had a good day on 1st July, no doubt about it. As for my batman Good, he was picked up later in the day and the wound was nothing like as bad as I'd feared. He wrote to me from hospital about my new batman, a Northerner. "I hear you've got Green doing for you now, Sir, he's a good lad but it's a pity he don't speak our language." Marvellous fellow. Became a police sergeant on the other side of London somewhere.

[Ed. The 11th Royal Fusiliers were one of the more fortunate battalions in action that day. Casualties were relatively light and German resistance in the trenches attacked by the Fusiliers was less determined than on other parts of the front.]

PRIVATE TOM DEWING, 34TH DIVISION ROYAL ENGINEERS SIGNAL COMPANY, 1896-2001

We didn't realize what had happened until afterwards, until the next church parade. At Brigade Headquarters we had regular church parades, and on this occasion, instead of the troops coming along as they usually did, there was just a handful out of each battalion. We felt sick. The colonels were sitting in front of what was left of their men, sobbing. The service was taken by Padre Black, who later became Dr James Black, Moderator of the Church of Scotland. He was a man we all respected; he was more likely to be found in the trenches than in the officers' mess. Before the attack started, he had said that he would go over the top with the stretcher bearers but the message through our signal office said, "If Padre Black goes over the top, he is to be arrested and sent down the line for a court martial." Instead, he did the next best thing. He stayed at the first field dressing station.

How he managed to take that service, I don't know.

His text was "I will restore unto you the years that the locusts have eaten". He meant every word of his sermon, and we knew it. There were so few, so few men left. How can you describe a mere handful of men where you used to see about a battalion? It must have been a great ordeal for him to conduct that service. It is an occasion that I shall always remember.

LIEUTENANT RICHARD HAWKINS, 11TH ROYAL FUSILIERS, 1895-1994

I was lying out on the night of the 1st of July in the dark, half asleep, happy and with nothing to do, and a voice in the dark said, "Hello, had a good day?" "Oh," I said "yes." "Do you know where the 12th Middlesex are?" I said, "I don't know where the hell they are, somewhere on the right, I think." "Oh," he said, "I'm Colonel Maxwell and I've come to take over the 12th Middlesex." He'd come up in the middle of the night to see where the battalion was. Oops, in the dark I didn't realize he was a Colonel. He couldn't wait until his battalion came out of the line, he had to come up and join it, not because he had to, but because he could not keep out of the battle.

PRIVATE JOE YARWOOD, 94TH FIELD AMBULANCE, ROYAL ARMY MEDICAL CORPS, 1896-1995

The next day the wounded were still waiting to be moved away, but we were lacking convoys. All these elephant dugouts had been turned into aid posts. There were piles of wounded lying on stretchers waiting for ambulances to move them.

I had just left the dressing station when we were shelled, but they landed with a pop not an explosion, and then I got a whiff of it, it was tear gas. I rushed back to lend a hand in getting as many under cover as I could.

They couldn't get their gas masks on, so for an hour or so it was pandemonium trying to get these poor devils out of harm's way.

Our Colonel, an Irishman by the name of Stewart, was a bit of a martinet and inclined to shout and bark and call you a bloody fool. He was very ambitious, a doctor in civilian life, and he held the DSO and MC and you don't get those for nothing. A brilliant officer, no doubt, but he was, to my mind, a little conceited, haughty even, you get it with some officers who take a large size in hats. Anyway, when we were leaving the trenches, he sounded like a benevolent father, pleased and very pleasant for once because we'd broken all records with the number of wounded we'd shifted, although he couldn't quite show his gratitude.

We were told to clear out because our lot was decimated. I saw a battalion leaving and there was a band in front and then about three or four ranks of soldiers, and that was all that was left of a thousand: thirty or forty men.

Just around there I recall one poor devil who had been buried in the bottom of the trench, but not deep enough, with the result that the top of his skull was exposed just level with the top of the trench floor. There was a bald patch right down the centre of the poor fellow's skull where troops had marched and worn the hair off his head. My God, what would his relatives at home think if they knew that had happened?

SERGEANT WALTER POPPLE, 8TH KING'S OWN YORKSHIRE LIGHT INFANTRY, 1896-1990

The third day I was exhausted, and it was on this day that a thunderstorm broke the terrific heat. By this time all the bodies around me had turned black. One of them had a waterproof sheet protruding at the back of his pack. I formed a ridge and the water trickled down into

"There were piles of wounded lying on stretchers..." Joe Yarwood recalled the misery of the wounded.

my mouth. The fourth day was relatively quiet but I realised time was getting short and unless help arrived soon, I was finished. I made up my mind that, whatever happened, I must reach my lines by morning. Crawling throughout the night, I got to within a few yards of our trenches by daybreak. By a sustained effort, I rose to my feet and hopped the necessary distance. Machine guns opened out, but I held my course and was lucky to enter one of the lanes cut for the attack. A sentry shouted, "Who's there?" I croaked "KOYLI." To hear my own tongue being spoken was nectar. "And yours?" "Middlesex" came the reply, "anyone else out there?" I told him no.

[Ed. Walter arrived back in the front line on the morning of 5 July, and must have been one of the very last men wounded on 1 July to have remained on the battlefield unattended. The bullet that hit him in the shoulder was removed and he kept it as a souvenir. However, the psychological effect on Walter's health was devastating. He lost weight and looked gaunt, and although he recovered from his wounds medically, he was in no fit state to return to active service. In 1917 he was removed from a parade of men due to return to France, as he was clearly in distress. He never returned to the firing line. The memory of those days haunted Walter, before in 1986, aged ninety, he finally returned to France and the Somme battlefield.]

CORPORAL NORMAN EDWARDS, 1/6TH GLOUCESTERSHIRE REGIMENT, 1894-1999

We took over the sector behind the village of Serre on 5 July from the 94th Brigade and at night time, when I looked out, the flares were all going up, and between the lines, in No Man's Land, there were twinkling lights everywhere. I thought, twinkling lights, what could it be? I found out afterwards the Pals

Norman Edwards.

Battalions of 31st Division had arranged that every man would carry a triangular piece of tin on the back of his pack so that when he was crawling forward, attacking, our own airmen looking down could see the depth of the advance. All those twinkling lights were literally hundreds of men who had been killed on that morning, before breakfast, awful slaughter. You can understand what a man felt like to see that. I just thanked God we hadn't been ordered to attack, although had we been ordered to do so we would have done our duty, I would think, because we'd got to win the war.

[Ed. After a brief respite, fighting resumed on the southern sector of the Somme battlefield, where the attacks on 1 July had seen a modicum of success, two villages, Montauban and Mametz, having fallen that

first day. On 2 July, the Germans abandoned another village, Fricourt, and a day later fresh attacks resulted in the talking of La Boisselle. Assaults of a limited nature continued, before a major night attack was conducted on the 14th on the German second line with positive results; a further phase of the Somme campaign was opened up on the 23 July.]

TROOPER SMILER MARSHALL, 1/1ST ESSEX YEOMANRY, 1897-2005

The Ox and Bucks arrived between five and six in the afternoon and were billeted close to where we were, in broken-down houses in Mametz Village. They were to attack the next day. Zero hour was 6.30am and their objective was not far from Mametz Wood.

It was the worst place I ever saw; there was more dead laid there than I ever saw anywhere, and we buried them. The Ox and Bucks went over the next morning at 6.30am and by 8am there was hardly one left. The next night we were sent up as a working party to help bury them, one, two and three in a shell hole. I didn't go through their pockets, that wasn't my job, but one of these dead chaps, he had pictures of his girlfriend and his mother, letters with his address, and these were all sticking out of his pocket or lying on the ground by his body, because shrapnel or machine gun bullets had ripped it open. I took his new boots off and put him in a shell hole, and threw my old boots in the shell hole with him, and took his. A while later I wrote to his mother in High Wycombe, Turner, I think the name was, and I got a nice letter from her. She said he had been reported missing in action. I said that I was on a burying party and told her he was killed near Mametz Wood and that we buried him in No Man's Land. Blimey, it was a rough job, poor buggers, but you just had to get on with it and not think.

We were taken on working parties for several nights and I got hit through the hand, because the bullets and shrapnel were flying around, battle or no battle. You don't know what caused it until you see the blood running onto the ground. I was sent down to the casualty clearing station, walked down. There must have been some dirt as well because my whole hand turned to poison, and it got worse and worse and ached all up my arm. Eventually I got sent to Rouen and then back to England and Newcastle. I nearly lost my arm.

RIFLEMAN ROBERT RENWICK, MM, 16TH KING'S ROYAL RIFLE CORPS, 1896-1997

All the woods round the Somme were hard fought for, Mametz Wood, High Wood. It was after my battalion had attacked High Wood and lost a lot of men, that I was sent to France on a draft just in time for an attack on Delville Wood, or Devil's Wood as it was called, and for good reason.

We were due to go over at a specific time but our bombardment fell short onto our lines so the officer said, "I'll be damned if I'll see my own men knocked out by our artillery," and he took us out and led us into shell

Robert Renwick.

holes. We waited for the barrage to lift and we advanced. The wood was just a mess, there was no undergrowth at all. A number of men were falling and I looked around to see a man hiding his corporal's stripes. I think he thought he wouldn't be targetted by the Germans without them. Then, as we dodged about from shell hole to shell hole I had a strange vision. I saw myself back at school and our schoolmaster was coming down his garden path to the wicket to call us in and line us up. I said to myself, "I think if ever you see that place again, you'll be lucky."

After the battle, we were sent back to bury the dead. Being sent back to bury your own pals, I think they did that to harden us up a little bit, but I thought it was rough. It was mainly men from the new draft who were sent to do it, but I thought men from a labour platoon should have done it. We took the dog tags off, and buried the men in their groundsheets.

One of the dead was a lad who had a web belt and a purse with a golden sovereign in it. He'd showed it to us a few times but I couldn't bring myself to take it out. That lad was buried with the sovereign. Later in the war, I would have taken it out, but not then.

A curious incident happened after this. There was a lad who got home wounded and he wrote to my parents explaining how I'd been killed. During the attack he had shouted to me that so-and-so had been injured and was in his shell hole, and he told my parents that I'd come across to see if there was anything I could do. Then he shouted back to my mates, "Renwick's been killed now", and he wrote all this in a note to my mother and father. I don't know how that happened. Perhaps there was another lad of the same name.

I remember the incident but I certainly wasn't killed. My father read the note first and then handed it to my mother, and she got a terrific shock. Then he said, "Look, we've had a field card since this date, so this cannot be right." It was a mystery, that one.

PRIVATE DICK TRAFFORD, 1/9TH KING'S LIVERPOOL REGIMENT, 1898-1999

The rations were being dished out when the sergeant came up with a loaf of bread and some jam. The loaf was divided up and we held our mess tin lids out for our jam ration just as a shrapnel shell burst overhead. One bit of shrapnel went through the jam and my mess tin lid, another chunk cut part of my thumb off, and I had three other wounds on the same hand. The man next to me got a piece through his back, which killed him outright. Another chap was shocked but all right, but the fourth lad, Joe Shaw, he jumped up on top of the road and ran off towards the end of our line, shouting and bawling, waving his arms. We couldn't really make out what he was saying because he was shell-shocked, but this was right in front of the German lines and that was the last we heard of him. We thought naturally that the Germans would get him; he made a good target for any machine gunner.

About three months later, I was on leave in Ormskirk and I was walking down the road, just as a chap in a postman's uniform crossed in front of me, all smiles. "Hello, Dick, don't you know me?" I says, "I know the voice," and it was this Joe Shaw. I said, "I thought you were dead."

During the fighting, the army had a little place in a wood about three miles back from the trenches, where they could put these sorts of cases temporarily, to see if they could recover. However, Joe was sent down to the dressing station, but there were that many wounded, he was bundled in with the others onto a train and sent down the line to hospital. He was shell-shocked, there was no doubt about it, and in the end he was considered of no further use for the army and was demobilized.

[Ed. On 15 September, a completely new weapon of war was introduced to the battlefield: the tank. It was used in what was designated the third phase of the Somme Battle, a major attack on a six-mile front during which 49 tanks of C and D Companies, Heavy Section, Machine Gun Corps were used to spearhead the last concerted effort to break the German line in 1916. However, owing to mechanical problems, only 32 tanks reached the start line that day and of these only nine can be said to have inflicted heavy casualties on the Germans.]

LIEUTENANT NORMAN DILLON, 14TH NORTHUMBERLAND FUSILIERS, 1896-1997

Our Division was staging an attack and we were in reserve near the village of Flers. It was a stinking night. The Germans were putting over everything they had, including a lot of gas shells. My sergeant and I were sitting by the roadside when we heard a shell "woo wooing" down very close and a gas shell hit a couple of yards behind us. At the same time, a queer object crawled over the mud and there it was. The first tank in action.

PRIVATE ROBBIE BURNS, 7TH CAMERON HIGHLANDERS, 1895-2000

The gunfire was terrific but then I heard this brrrrr, and I thought, what on earth is that noise? It got louder and louder, so I stood on the firestep and saw something moving. I said, "Look!" and we all started to peer over. An attack was going in and at that moment some of the men got up on the parapet to look, and the Germans too were up on the parapet to see what was happening. Behind these tanks were five or six soldiers crowded together with bayonets fixed, taking cover. We could see more than one of these tanks, one would disappear and wouldn't seem to come back up, then another fell onto its side, and all the time we could hear this gentle brrrr of the engines. We didn't know what they were for, perhaps for taking down barbed wire, we thought.

PRIVATE ARCHIE RICHARDS, D COMPANY (D7), HEAVY SECTION, MACHINE GUN CORPS, ATTD. 41ST DIVISION, 1897-1998

It was a hot September that year, and the stink – oh – the smell was terrible, terrible. Arms and legs were sticking out of trenches, and rotting bodies. The Canadians, Australians, the British and the Colonial regiments had all taken part in attacks long before the tanks put in their appearance, and they were lying about, the Scottish in their kilts, and there were stretcher bearers, scores of them, picking up the dead. We were moving up for this first attack, and we had to go over the old trenches, and bodies and everything else. I expected war to be dreadful, but I was seeing it in the raw. I felt grateful that we had the tank to cover us a bit; that gave us hope.

On 15 September, all hell broke loose. At about six o'clock in the morning, our barrage opened up. You couldn't hear yourself speak, shells flying everywhere, and the Germans were retaliating. We were scared, really scared, but we just resigned ourselves to putting up with it. We had orders to move down to a village and onto the first main road, a hard cobbled road. The Germans had not shelled it because they had brought up supplies on it previously, and we did not want to shell it now because we were using it for the same reason, so the road remained quite sound, just a shell hole here and there.

PRIVATE ARCHIE RICHARDS, D COMPANY, HEAVY SECTION, MACHINE GUN CORPS, 1897-1998

Our officer sat at the front with the driver and signalled what he wanted, and the tank would swing round to face the target. The tank would turn on its own in a wide circle, but with two gear changers you could turn it in its own length. The engine was quite powerful and vibrated the machine somewhat, but it was the movement that was worse, up and down, this way and that. I had a job sometimes to set on my target to shoot. I'd just get set and ready to fire, and bang, the tank would lurch somewhere, throw me right off. The targets were the trenches, anywhere we thought there'd be machine gun posts.

There was no choice but to drive over the dead, you couldn't pick your way through. If they fell in your way, you had to go over them. We never deviated the tanks for anything except targets. When we went into action, the infantry kept tucked in, clustered behind our tanks for shelter, then as soon as we captured a trench, they took over, going along the line and ferreting the Germans out. I only saw Germans when we got right on the trench, with our guns laid on each side. They had never seen anything like the tank before, and when they saw we were armed with small guns and machine guns, they gave up straightaway. A few of their machine gunners got away and we could see them silhouetted against the sky with their guns on their shoulders, going like hell back to their third lines.

[Ed. The Somme offensive was officially closed down on 18 November on a damp, cold day. The severe weather throughout much of October and November meant that the battlefield was a quagmire and there was little point in continuing hostilities. Once more, both armies battened down the hatches for winter. In the meantime, divisions in need of rest were withdrawn to billets behind the lines and brought up to strength with new drafts.]

The tank. On 15 September, a completely new weapon of war was introduced to the battlefield:

1917 – A YEAR OF THE OFFENSIVE SPIRIT AND WAR WEARINESS

It was not evident to anyone, least of all the soldiers in the line, but the tide of war was beginning to turn against Germany and its associated powers. True, it would take almost two years to win the conflict, but German forces were not just on the defensive but more often also on the back foot.

The Somme had been ruinously expensive for all sides in terms of lives lost, and Germany could afford the losses least of all. At the same time, the growth in war production in Britain afforded to the soldiers at the front artillery support undreamt of eighteen months earlier. Artillery could be used to pulverize and demoralise the enemy, breaking up counter-attacks, and softening them up prior to an advance. The tactics as well as the lessons learnt during the Somme and those further developed in 1917 would be used to break the line decisively the following year.

The winter of 1916-17 was as cold as anyone could remember for thirty years, with weeks of unbroken frost. Horses became bogged down in the mud and were unharnessed in favour of mules with their smaller, daintier feet, picking their way through the morass created by an army going nowhere. The Somme mud mixed with chalk created a glue that was worse, according to many veterans, than any met elsewhere, even at Ypres; clinging to the feet and legs, it ingratiated itself onto every bit of uniform, especially the greatcoat which hung heavy with filth. Out of the line, uniforms, if they were removed, froze solid; both friend and foe suffered, and fought the weather rather than each other.

The soldiers who were sent to France and Flanders in 1917 were overwhelmingly conscripts, lads who had been called up in designated age groups since the middle of 1916. They included Arthur Barraclough, an apprentice hairdresser from Bradford, called up at 18 for training. His flat feet might have precluded his service in the heady days of 1914, but not any more. He was sent to France in January 1917 with the 2/4th Duke of Wellington's Regiment, a territorial battalion. Another new arrival

Harry Patch.

Cecil Withers.

was Cecil Withers, aged eighteen, a lad from London. Cecil had enlisted in the days of the Derby Scheme, when the Government made a final attempt to revive voluntary enlistment. The Scheme invited men to enlist, but allowed them to return to civilian work until the army required their services. Cecil enlisted under age without his parents' consent, and left for France just prior to Christmas 1916, joining his battalion in the small French village of Grand Rullecourt. Harry Patch would also arrive at the front in 1917. An eighteen-year-old apprentice plumber turned conscript, from Somerset, he already had two brothers in khaki and was a reluctant soldier, having heard about the terrible nature of the fighting from his eldest sibling who had fought at Mons.

For the Germans, other issues were more pressing than fighting. Their desire to defend their position in the west necessitated a tactical manoeuvre: a limited retreat. Their army, worn down by the fighting in France, was too thinly spread to hold the whole line in depth. By retiring to newly-constructed positions forty miles back, they could shorten their lines and therefore proportionately increase the number of troops holding the front. In mid-March, in the face of the British forces, the Germans retreated to the Hindenburg Line, begun in September 1916 by the then new Chief of Staff, after whom it was named and Ludendorff, his Quartermaster General. This was just one of a series of positions held by the German army, that stretched from the coast to Metz, east of Verdun, but it was the most complex and believed to be the most difficult to break, characterized by vast belts of barbed wire and strong points that supported one another.

The German withdrawal came as a surprise to the Allies, who were preparing a renewed offensive in the spring. The French, under their new Commander in Chief, General Robert Nivelle, wanted a joint offensive, and British forces were temporarily placed under this charismatic officer, who promised a surprise attack and victory within forty-eight hours. For the forthcoming offensive, Nivelle would launch a massive attack in the south on the Aisne while the British would go forward with fourteen divisions in front of Arras.

On 4 April, a furious bombardment of the German lines began, utilizing over 2,800 guns of all calibres. On 9 April, the British attacked with fourteen divisions, including four of the Canadian Corps, ordered to storm the formidable height of Vimy Ridge. At the northern end of the British line, the attack was an overwhelming success, as infantry supported by tanks tore into the German lines covering almost three miles. Vimy Ridge was captured as well as ten thousand prisoners. At the southern end, the resistance was stronger, and for five days the fighting raged as the Germans threw in reinforcements to halt the British advance. On the 14 April, the British attack was halted to allow the French to advance on the Aisne but here the offensive turned to catastrophic failure. Mutiny began to spread through the French ranks; by mid-May, fifty-four divisions were affected, as men refused to undertake further offensive operations, while there was a general complaint of poor pay, poor conditions and cancelled leave. Nivelle was ignominiously sacked and Petain, the hero of Verdun, was made the new C-in-C.

The offensive spirit of the Allies knew little rest in 1917. No sooner had the Arras offensive petered out than the Germans were attacked again, this time on the Messines Ridge, southeast of Ypres. This attack, launched on 7 June, was one of the most audacious of the war: the Ridge, held since 1914 by the Germans, was captured in one morning when nineteen mines dug under German trenches were detonated at 3.10am, literally blowing the enemy off this important strategic position.

Such was the devastation caused, so demoralizing the effect, that the attacking British and Empire forces found that they were able to occupy the entire Ridge within hours and at minimal cost. The Germans launched several half-hearted counter attacks over the following days, which were all beaten off. Third Ypres was the last great battle of attrition on the Western Front. Haig's aim was to break out of the Salient, pushing British forces towards the German submarine bases along the Belgian coast, from where the German navy had been conducting a successful war against Allied shipping in the Atlantic. Haig also believed that the German army was in a parlous state and was likely to collapse if one last great offensive could be mounted. A conventional ten-day bombardment prior to the assault prepared the way for a successful attack on 31 July.

Once again, there were significant gains as the enemy was thrown back. However, the weather was about to come to their rescue. In the afternoon, a downpour drenched the battlefield, churning up the ground into a quagmire made worse by the preliminary bombardment that further destroyed the drainage ditches. All attempts to renew the offensive came to grief as men, animals and tanks floundered in mud. Haig pressed on and made localized assaults whenever there was a break in the

Three despondent looking soldiers rest up on deck boards as they make their way up to the front.

weather, but the gains grew smaller and smaller. Ultimately, the village of Passchendaele, on the last of the low ridges that surrounded the town of Ypres, was taken, ninety-nine days after the offensive began. The costs were terrible on both sides, but it was the Germans who could not afford such like-for-like attrition, and therein lay a marginal, if hollow, victory for the Allies.

In previous years, the approach of winter had been the cue to close down major military operations until spring, but Haig did not want to do so now. One last assault would be launched at Cambrai, involving over 300 tanks in an attack over better ground. It broke the German lines in a single stroke and forced the Germans into flight. Yet in the aftermath of Third Ypres the army simply had too few resources to capitalise on the breakthrough. As the Germans fell back on their reserves and supplies, so the British became overstretched. A German counter-attack on 30 November won back all of the land gained in the previous week and a half. The year finally drew to a close, with all sides in need of recuperation.

LIEUTENANT RICHARD HAWKINS, 11TH ROYAL FUSILIERS, 1895-1994

Our forming-up place was just in front of a depression known as the Gully and our target was Boom Ravine a short distance ahead, seizing the high ground in order to provide observation over the upper Ancre Valley.

I was commanding D Company and on the night of the 16 February we began to move up. There were two routes to the forming-up line; both were very congested and in the dark it was almost impossible to get the men up. The journey was made more difficult by the weather. For at least three weeks it had been freezing hard, indeed, that winter was one of the coldest periods I can ever remember, but this night a thaw had begun to set in. We waded through the mud and slime to be in our positions by 4.45am and were harassed all the way by artillery and machine gun fire, causing a lot of casualties just to get my company into position.

At 5.30am I went round the line with some rum and gave all the men a good tot, chatting to them as I did so. I finished about 6am. The only thing I could do then was to establish my headquarters at the top of a small ravine that ran at right angles to the main objective, Boom Ravine. At 6.20 I clambered to the top of the ravine which was 25 or 30 feet high. I just managed to see from my watch that it was 6.25am; it was still dark. The time went on, 6.26, 6.27, 6.28. It was 6.29 when the biggest bloody barrage I had ever been through suddenly descended on us. It was obvious that the Germans had wind of our attack. Captain Collis-Sandes, who was commanding B company, turned up at my side. "I think this is going to be a pretty awful show." "Yes," I replied, "I think I am going to get myself a rifle and a bayonet," and I collared one from a fellow who was dead.

At 6.30 our barrage opened with a blinding flash behind us. We were still bogged down with the German barrage when there was another flash and Collis-Sandes

Richard Hawkins in a trench on the Somme 1916.

fell dead and I was hit in the shoulder. It was like being kicked by a mule. As the force spun me round, I lost my balance and fell right down the ravine, crashing into some barbed wire at the bottom. I lost consciousness for a while. I awoke as it was beginning to get light, to hear a cockney voice say, "Cor blimey, 'ere's Lieutenant Hawkins, the poor so-and-so is dead." "No, I'm not," I replied, "but I shall be if you don't get me out of this lot."

I'd lost a lot of blood but they helped me to my feet and took me back a couple of hundred yards and there I met dear old Doctor Sale, from Australia. He stripped my tunic and put some dressings on before he called over three German prisoners, "Here, come and get hold of the end of this stretcher." He needed a fourth man and, looking round, he saw a German officer. This German officer was a good looking young fellow with a ginger moustache and he explained in fairly good English that it was not the job of a officer to grab hold of a stretcher with three private soldiers. Dr Sale was a pretty busy man, and he hadn't time to argue, so he just repeated himself, "Get hold of the end of that stretcher!" The German said "Nein." Dr Sale was a very good rugby three-quarter and he stuck his boot into this fellow's behind and he took off. They started to go round in a very big circle, down in the shell holes, and up the other side, the doctor launching a kick at this officer every few yards and missing practically every time because of the impossible state of the ground. In the end, dear old Sale caught him and kicked his backside several more times, after which the officer decided he would take the end of the stretcher after all.

71

Harry Patch.

PRIVATE HENRY 'HARRY' PATCH, NO29295, C COMPANY, 7TH DUKE OF CORNWALL'S LIGHT INFANTRY, 17 JUNE 1898-25 JULY 2009

I didn't want to join up but I was conscripted, so there you are. I came from a very sheltered family, the youngest of three brothers. The army didn't appeal to me at all, and when I found what a rough and tumble life it could be, I didn't like it one little bit. I had no inclination to fight anybody. I mean, why should I go out and kill somebody I never knew? We had a week's embarkation leave and then we were sent in an old paddle steamer from Folkestone to Boulogne. Then up the hill into camp. I wasn't carrying enough, so they gave me a fifteen-pound pack of bully beef. On arrival, we were separated and drafted to various regiments. I had a chum with me who came from the same village; I went into the Duke of Cornwall's Light Infantry, and he was drafted to a regiment in Egypt, and we never met again.

You were scared all the time. You couldn't deal with the fear. It was there and it always would be. I know the first time I went up the line, we were scared; we were all scared. I would get a butterfly in my stomach and my hands would shake, so for a moment or two I would have a job to coordinate my nerves to do anything. We lived hour by hour; we never knew the future. You saw the sun rise, hopefully you'd see it set. If you saw it set, you hoped you'd see it rise. Some men would, some wouldn't.

PRIVATE CECIL WITHERS, 7TH EAST SURREY REGIMENT, 1898-2005

You see when you're in the trenches, your life's measured by the second. You never know one second to another whether you're going to be blown to bits. It's so imminent that you never trouble your head about it, it's too terrible to think about.

"Don't forget to tell mum I died instantly." That was

Cecil Withers.

something every chap would ask. It might be a damn lie, of course, but it was done for the mother's sake.

PRIVATE ANDREW BOWIE, 1ST CAMERON HIGHLANDERS, 1897-2002

You see pictures of men sat on their bottoms doing nothing and because the picture was taken during the day, you think that's what their life is. Far from it. Once it got dark you had to get a move on, you were on a working party and you'd to work like blazes to keep up, wiring, carrying sleepers, carrying duckboards, corrugated iron, all the things you needed to build and maintain a trench. You are working like a slave. And if there were dead to be buried or taken away, you did that too.

One job started with the "you, you, and you" business, about six of us. "There's a dead mule lying outside our parapet," we were told. "Go out and bury it." A dead thing like that always gave off a bit of a stench, and someone decided that it must be buried. That was the order but it was easier said than done. We went out, and I don't know if you have ever handled a dead mule, but we couldn't move the blasted thing, so we took our spades and put mud on it, thinking that would hide it. But the next morning we looked out, and there was the poor beast still visible with these pats of mud on it.

LIEUTENANT G B JAMESON, C BATTERY 72ND BRIGADE, ROYAL FIELD ARTILLERY, 1892-1999

Getting up to the front line, you were all zig-zagging about. When there wasn't a battle in progress, the back areas were always subjected to searching and sweeping by the enemy's 5.9 inch batteries, which would try and hit supplies. You studied where these shells were falling and listened to them for a while, and then you made off in a slightly different direction to get out of the way. You were always weighing up your chances.

When a battle was in progress, you just listen to the various salvos and watch them drop and then take a deep breath and run for the next bit of cover, and wait again. I had to make for the front line during the attack on Vimy Ridge. I was with three telephonists and all their gear, so I spread them out. "Right, you go first and make for that shell hole and dive in there, and when you've got there, stick your hand up and I'll come and get in a shell hole and I'll put my hand up and the next one will come," so we weren't all in the same place. Soon as I got there, I pointed out another place and he'd run there, so that we were leapfrogging each other all the time.

LANCE CORPORAL VIC COLE, 1ST QUEEN'S OWN (ROYAL WEST KENT REGIMENT), 1897-1995

We were up on a ridge near Arras, looking down on this field. We were moving up to what was known as the Brown Line in support, and the Royal Field Artillery had a battery of 18 pounders in this square field, each gun with a dugout next to it. We saw this battery, and they were shooting away, and Jerry must have spotted them because he retaliated. As shells started falling, four chaps came out of a dugout and started playing touch around this field, running around like kids. They must have been at the rum bottle or something, and now and again a shell would land and a fountain of earth went up in the air. It was the most amazing sight, and these lads carried on playing, and no one seemed to get wounded. After a time Jerry stopped shelling and the men went back to their dugout.

British troops resting up during the day.

PRIVATE CECIL WITHERS, 7TH EAST SURREY REGIMENT, 1898-2005

You could see the shells go over, like a misty dark patch going down, then as they hit the ground it was like a bottle of red ink spraying, but all in one direction, all red flames and shrapnel. It meant that if you were standing to one side of a shell-burst, you could remain practically untouched.

ARRAS

ALFRED HENN, 3RD BATTERY, WARWICKSHIRE ROYAL HORSE ARTILLERY, 1897-2000

It was dark and there was a hell of a noise going on, guns firing, shouting, and the noise of wheels rumbling over cobbles. We were going through a very narrow street in the outskirts of Arras when we came to a sudden halt, causing the horses to swerve. The gunners behind started shouting and bawling for us to go forward but we couldn't move. The horses were scraping their feet and neighing, and then came a terrible smell. I couldn't make out what was happening. Then a Very light went up and I saw steam rising up all around me. To my horror I could see that the wall opposite was absolutely blasted by meat, flesh torn from horses and men blown to pieces. The steam I saw was ascending from the blood.

PRIVATE TOM DEWING, 34TH DIVISIONAL ROYAL ENGINEERS SIGNAL COMPANY, 1896-2001

The attack was timed for 6am on 9 April. The day before, a few of us were sent to the advanced signal dugout a few yards behind the front line. We had a very quiet night but promptly at six, a shell from a 16-inch naval gun roared across with the sound of an express train and every gun on the front opened fire. There was no prolonged bombardment but now every German battery was subjected to devastating shellfire. The troops left the trenches and moved towards the barrage, so that when it lifted they were able to jump down into the enemy trenches almost at once. Harry Bradfield had heard that tanks were going over and he wanted to see

them. So when the gunfire started, he ran up the dugout steps and put his head up above the parapet. Presently we heard him shout, "Come here quick, come here quick!" We thought he was wounded, but when we got to the top of the steps we were amazed to see scores of German prisoners hurrying down the communication trench as fast as they could go.

PRIVATE ARTHUR BARRACLOUGH, 2/4TH DUKE OF WELLINGTON'S REGIMENT, 1898-2004

We had been practising for weeks going behind these tanks, a platoon behind each, in two ranks. Now we could hear them coming a mile away, and four tanks got set up in front of our trenches. We set off behind one of them. The idea was that when it came across the German line, it was supposed to flatten the wire and our platoons would open out and attack. The problem was there had been a lot of rain at the time; it was terribly flooded. We had hardly gone twenty yards when the tanks got stuck in the mud, and others went nose down into old trenches. The tanks had bundles of wood tied to their tops and these were supposed to be dropped into the hole to give the tank tracks some grip to get out, but it didn't work that way, the tanks were too heavy and smashed up the wood. None got any further than the first line of trenches and not one of them reached the objective on our bit of front.

LIEUTENANT NORMAN DILLON, MC, 2ND BATTALION, HEAVY SECTION, MACHINE GUN CORPS, 1896-1997

Inside the tank it was frightful. You couldn't hear a word, and so when the driver wanted the gear-changing man to change gear, it was no use shouting, so they had a code whereby they took a hammer or a spanner and rapped on the engine casing, which made a loud clang. One clang meant bottom gear, two clangs meant second gear, three clangs meant neutral. No matter what the temperature was like outside, it was like an oven in there, terribly hot, and of course a lot of chaps lost their lives by opening flaps and sticking their heads out of the top of the tank.

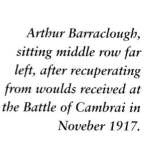

Arthur Barraclough, sitting middle row far left, after recuperating from woulds received at the Battle of Cambrai in Noveber 1917.

As we went forward, bullets hit the framework of the tank and had the unpleasant effect of knocking off, on the inside, a tiny piece of red hot steel, so if there was a lot of machine gun fire in one place on the side of the tank, you got quite a cloud of these fragments, smaller than a pin-head. That is why the tank crew wore masks.

PRIVATE ARCHIE RICHARDS, D COMPANY, HEAVY SECTION, MACHINE GUN CORPS, 1897-1998

The Germans turned these guns on us, particularly on the trap doors, and the bullets smacked against the tanks, causing the metal to splinter. Tiny flakes would fly about and cut you all over. Our faces often bled, and we wore goggles to stop ourselves being blinded.

Inside the tank, the atmosphere was sickening. When you are in action and all the traps are down, the fumes are hardly bearable. There is a thick haze of petrol and gas and cordite fumes. With the engine running, it was incredibly stuffy. The engine was in the centre of the tank and there was a little passage to step around it, but we were very cramped, and you had to watch your head. It was impossible to speak to anybody, so we had to make pre-determined signals with our hands and fingers. I had a good stomach, but others were sick, spewing up all over the place and passing out. You can imagine what it was like, eight men cooped up in a tank with no air for five hours.

Your nerves get worn, the noise and everything, it gradually gets to you. We had two men in the tank and their nerves gave out and they went funny in the head. They had a kind of glazed look in their eyes; the smells were affecting their minds, they didn't know what they were doing and they were unsteady on their feet. But we were all on the verge of collapsing sometimes.

A/LANCE CORPORAL CECIL WITHERS, 7TH EAST SURREY REGIMENT, 1898-2005

The sergeant major came round with the rum jar, and we had a little tot of rum in our mess tins. Soon after, we fixed bayonets and climbed onto the firestep. Before I went, I'd say a little prayer, "Lord help me," you know, a plea for mercy, but sometimes I didn't say anything. We knew our duty but we never calculated what was happening, or worked things out; it was so swift, we lived from second to second not minute to minute.

It was freezing cold, and our arms felt like blocks of ice. We were waiting for the whistle, shells were whining over, bang, bang, crash, crash. Then over we went. As I climbed the parapet, the chap next to me collapsed. "Get up, get up!" someone shouted, but as far as I know he didn't get up, that poor boy, he showed all the signs of a stroke.

As soon as we got on top, we went as fast as we bloody well could, because the quicker we got to the German lines, the quicker we'd be out of the range of their guns which were fixed on our own trench. Even so, we tried to keep in line with each other, not stray all over the place. As we were going, a football appeared, and landed in front of my right foot. So I just kicked it to the

officer on my left, Captain Maxwell, and the first thing he did was kick it straight into the German line, and as he did so everybody rushed forward into the enemy trench which we found was empty. They'd cleared off.

A/LANCE CORPORAL CECIL WITHERS, 7TH EAST SURREY REGIMENT, 1898-2005

Close to the German trenches, near a shell hole, there was a German lying on his back, blood all over the place, dying obviously, and he said one word, "Wasser". I got my water bottle out and poured some of it on his lips and down his mouth as best I could, and I've never forgotten the look of gratitude in that man's eyes, as much as to say thank you. I was just pausing for a few seconds but I was out of line with the wave of men going forward, and I remember the sergeant saying, "Come on, Withers. You ought to give the so and so a bullet, not water."

RIFLEMAN ROBERT RENWICK, MM, 16TH KING'S ROYAL RIFLE CORPS, 1896-1997

I remember the corn was just coming through the ground as we moved to attack the Fontaine Line on 23 April. We went up on the Sunday night, and we were lying out at the side of a quarry, to go over the next morning. It was a surprise attack and the signal to go over was one big shell. Our platoon was held back in support. After some time, Jerry counter-attacked and we got orders to go forward which we did and took their line. I remember Nicholas Dodd, a Hexham lad, and another from Gateshead, Bob Thompson, they both got a bullet through their wrists, and I can hear this Nicholas Dodd yet. "Good luck, Bob, we're off for Blighty." I envied those two men that day, I'll admit that, I really envied them.

After things had quietened down, we were mopping up when a German sergeant appeared from a deep dugout. For a moment he seemed amazed at the sight of our troops and picking up a rifle and fixed bayonet, he had a go at a sergeant of the 2nd Queen's who had somehow got mixed up with us during the attack. He was wounded first in the shoulder, then he got the German in the same place but rather more severely, and the rifle dropped to the ground. Instead of having another go, the Queen's sergeant put his rifle aside, took out his water bottle and had a swig, handed it to the German, put it back, then took out his cigarette tin and produced two cigs, lit up, and gave one away. "Come on with me, Fritz, we are finished with this game." By this time, the German was losing a fair amount of blood and feeling weak, so he put his arm around our sergeant and off they went, out of the trench and on to the open ground towards the dressing station, looking like a couple of friends. There were two men prepared to fight to the death and, when both were wounded, they went down arm in arm to the dressing station. As I watched them I thought to myself, "What on earth are we fighting each other for?"

We were trained to hate the Germans; we called them either the Hun or the Boche but when we took prisoners we called them Fritz.

THE DEAD

DRIVER ALFRED FINNIGAN, 5TH DIVISION ROYAL FIELD ARTILLERY, 1896-2005

I've seen several horrible sights, bodies of which only the trunk remained, head, hands, arms, legs gone. Heads with no faces, empty skulls. I hadn't been out in France long and we were at Achiet Le Grand station, in the railway yard. There was this man and he had been placed out front with his tunic thrown over his face and head. He was a member of a German medical team that had been caught by our artillery and they were just lying around, all dead, in various stages of decay.

I hate to think of it now, but out of curiosity I pulled his tunic aside, and his head was an empty shell, his face had gone.

DRIVER ALFRED HENN, 3RD BATTERY, WARWICKSHIRE ROYAL HORSE ARTILLERY, 1897-2000

We stopped on a road once and there was a German sitting quite normally on the edge of a shell hole, not far away, and I could not understand what he was doing there. So I went over to have a look. He was sitting with his mess tin in his lap. He'd been eating when a shell had split his head open and his brain had fallen into the mess tin. If that isn't sudden death, I don't know what is.

SAPPER STAN CLAYTON, 457TH FIELD COMPANY, 62ND DIVISION ROYAL ENGINEERS, 1894-2000

I came to the remains of a large church and saw a door and steps. I walked down and counted fifty-one steps and found myself in a German headquarters. At the bottom there was a corridor and a series of entrances on each side. I saw a door with a number five on it and I looked in and there was a German lieutenant, sitting at a table, and he had a photograph in his left hand. He was staring at a picture of a woman and a little curly headed girl, about two-years old, beautiful she was. I looked at him. He was white and quite dead. He must have taken poison because he was not wounded at all. I had to drag the picture out of his fingers tips and gave it to an officer. I heard no more about it, but I hoped it might be sent home to his wife, so she'd know for certain that he'd died.

GUNNER FREDERICK WILLIAM TAYLOR, NO207742, 13TH BATTERY, 17TH BRIGADE, 29TH DIVISION, 12 MAY 1898-19 MARCH 2000

It was my turn to go on duty, walking around the silent gun pits, the length of the battery, perhaps one hundred yards in all. We'd only just taken over this position after recent advances, and when I got to No.1 gun I noticed a shell hole half filled with muddy water. In the gloom, I made out a face looking towards me. It belonged to a German. Why his body was still there and hadn't been cleared away, I don't know. But suddenly, as I looked, his face appeared to laugh at me, it was so uncanny,

A water-filled crater holds the remains of a German soldier. Scenes like these were a familiar sight for the men at Passchendaele.

supernatural, that I moved quickly away and kept away for the rest of the night. In the morning, his body was pulled out of the water and taken away for burial. I realized afterwards that a wisp of cloud had passed over the moon and made it look as though the man had laughed. Very scary when you are on your own, I can tell you.

DRIVER ALFRED HENN, 3RD BATTERY, WARWICKSHIRE ROYAL HORSE ARTILLERY, 1897-2000

We were going along the Monchy Road, and we saw a big log of wood and three soldiers sitting there with their hands on the top of their upturned rifles. They'd got their eyes closed and I thought, "Fancy sleeping through all this lot, some men have got a nerve." The next day they were still there – the flash from a shell must have killed them outright, instantaneously, and nobody had bothered to move them.

A/LANCE CORPORAL CECIL WITHERS, 7TH EAST SURREY REGIMENT, 1898-2005

It was pitch dark and there was a chap out in No Man's Land, groaning, right in front of the trench we'd taken, and he was saying, "Mutter, mutter." It was enough to break your heart. A cockney man was going through the trench at the time, and said, "It's no good him calling out for mum, he won't see her no more," and I thought that was a callous thing to say, cruel words. When your mind goes back to these occasions, they come up like a record in your mind, you can't help it. It makes you very bitter. These things stand out so vividly that they make a deep impression on you as an eighteen-year-old, like a pencil making a dent on paper, it's the same on the brain.

There were so many wounded after the attack at Arras and no one left to attend to them, so the sergeant said to me, "Withers, we've no stretcher bearers and this chap's wounded. Would you carry him down to the 5th Southern General Aid Post?" It was dark and while I was going across with my rifle dangling on my left arm, two military police on horseback went by and asked where I was going and if I had my rifle, that was their concern. They saw it and let me go, satisfied I was not a deserter. I made my way to the Aid Post, about two kilometres, and as soon as they took the wounded man off my shoulder, I collapsed. They put me on a stretcher and gave me a dose of sal volatile, a stimulant, a few drops in water, to restore a fainting person. They gave me a half hour's rest on the stretcher and then I went back to rejoin my unit.

PRIVATE ARTHUR BURGE, 1ST EAST SURREY REGIMENT, 1895-1999

Another badly wounded man came in. He was shouting and swearing. I was annoyed, as they brought him in and placed him amongst some sacks where I was supposed to read signals. They dropped this man down and I said, "Don't leave him here," but they said, "Sorry, mate, but we're too busy." On my right, there was a pillbox, the top of which was being used by a surgeon. He wasn't ready for the casualty and he said to the sergeant, "For God's sake keep that man quiet!" The sergeant spoke to the man and said, "Stop that bloody noise, will you?" The man stopped for a moment and started again once the sergeant had gone. The sergeant came back again and repeated himself, and the same happened. The third time he came back, he had a syringe and he rolled up the man's sleeve and gave him an injection, and put him right out. The surgeon had said he couldn't work with the noise, and to my mind he asked the sergeant to finish him off; he was very badly wounded and couldn't have lived.

AIR MECHANIC HENRY WILLIAM ALLINGHAM, NO8289, NO12 SQUADRON ROYAL NAVAL AIR SERVICE,

6 JUNE 1896 - 18 JULY 2009

Henry Allingham.

It was the men in the trenches who won the war. What they put up with, no one will ever know. I've seen them coming out of the line, poor devils, in a terrible state, plastered with mud. They were like hermit crabs with all their equipment on and they'd plonk down in the middle of the road before somebody helped them up. How did they manage? They were at the end of their tether. They were worn out, absolutely done up. They could hardly put one foot before the other, they were gone, depleted, finished, all they wanted to do was sleep, sleep, sleep. Salvation Army there, "Cup of tea?" Further down the road, Church Army. "Cup of tea? One penny."

One day a week, I had some time off and I was wandering about in the town of Poperinge with nothing much to do. As I walked up this road, I saw a chalk message on an old board, all smeared, and there was something about a meeting. "What's that all about?" I thought, and so I walked down the side to find an old stable that was knocked about a bit and there was old Tubby Clayton just making up a lovely bowl of roses. With all the trouble in the world, the sight of those flowers was a right tear-jerker if you were that way inclined. "Aren't they lovely?" he said. "They've just arrived from Blighty this morning." I admired them, and said, "What goes on here?" He was an army chaplain. "There are three or four other fellows in there and I'm going to have communion," and I said, "All right, I'm in." And I went in and took communion.

Tubby was a good man, he did a lot for those boys. They could spill the beans to him. If they'd trouble at home he'd listen and try and iron it out for them, if he could.

PRIVATE HARRY PATCH, 7TH DUKE OF CORNWALL'S LIGHT INFANTRY, 1898-2009

You couldn't relax unless you had the chance to go down to Poperinge into Toc H, that's the only time you could forget the strains of war for a couple of hours. Tubby Clayton ran the place and was the life and soul of the party. He had a deep, almost bass, voice, and he could sing a good song and tell a good tale. He would sing any old chorus including, I remember, the Ivor Novello song "Keep the Home Fires Burning". The only time I heard that song in Belgium was Tubby singing it in Toc H. There were games going on, and you could join in, or, if you wanted to borrow a book, you could, and the price of a book was your cap, which was returned to you when you brought it back. I believe Toc H at one time was used as a grain store, and all the grain had been stored in the upstairs room. I take it the wheat was in the centre, as the middle was a bit dodgy and everyone used to sit around the edge.

The room at the top was his chapel. Tubby upstairs became a different man to the Tubby downstairs. He tried to reassure people in that room, to the best of his ability, that everything was all right. He knew damn well it wasn't. The altar was an old carpenter's bench he'd found somewhere, and he knew, as I think most of the people who went in that room knew, that there were people there who were about to go up to the front line and would not come back.

PRIVATE SMILER MARSHALL, NO195155, 8TH MACHINE GUN SQUADRON, MACHINE GUN CORPS (CAVALRY), 1897-2005

Smiler Marshall was the last cavalryman from the Great War.

The biggest thing is holding your fire. We'll say a German reconnoitering party, perhaps 100 or 120 men, and half are going round one side, half the other with the idea of caging you in, and the officer is telling you to hold your fire, well, that's the biggest shock of the lot, the biggest test, and you get the wind up a bit because they're coming on and you're not allowed to fire. Of course as soon as you fire they scatter, but perhaps you'll only kill a couple, wound a few more, and the rest might scarper back to their trench, well, the officer wants to bag as many as he can.

Then he gives the order and you press that button brrrrr, and you can see them fall or jump for cover, and you don't feel the slightest thing, not the slightest. You are there just on a job. It's either you or them. What are you going to do? You're going to defend your mates, of course you are.

Talbot House, Poperinghe.

PRIVATE HARRY PATCH, 7TH DUKE OF CORNWALL'S LIGHT INFANTRY, 1898-2009

We were a little group on our own, five of us, although we were part of C Company, part of the Regiment, of course. Number 1, he was a lance corporal and he came from Henley on Thames. I was a plumber; he was an electrician. Number 3 came from Truro, numbers 4 and 5 came from Falmouth, one was a shoemaker; the other a grocer. That was our team.

We took our orders from the officers but when we were in the trenches we were just that little body alone, and we shared everything. I used to get a parcel from home about every fortnight, and in that parcel there would be an ounce of tobacco, two packets of twenty cigarettes, some sweets – if the grocer could scrounge them – and a few cakes. Number 4 on the Lewis gun and I were pipe smokers so that ounce of tobacco was cut in half, half was mine and half was his. Cakes, chocolates, anything else, were all divided. If you had a pair of clean socks and a fellow had socks with holes in, he'd have the clean socks and throw the others away.

You looked out into No Man's Land between the firing points, and all you could see was a couple of stray dogs looking for something to eat to keep alive. I thought, "Oh well, I don't know, there they are out there, two stray animals, and if they found a biscuit to eat they would start to fight over who should have a bite. Well, what are we doing that's really any different? We're fighting for our lives, just the same."

AIR MECHANIC HENRY ALLINGHAM, NO12 SQUADRON, ROYAL NAVAL AIR SERVICE, 1896-2009

The friendship in that war was something else, it really was. Everybody was your pal. The man you sat beside, you'd talk to him as if you'd known him for a thousand years, as it were, and he was a complete stranger.

The ground was all colours, it stank and it was offensive. As we moved forward, we passed over Hellfire Corner. There were rats round there as big as cats, and that's no exaggeration. We used to shoot them if we had nothing better to do. You'd shoot at them and if you could hit them end ways, they would be like a tunnel with four legs.

PRIVATE HARRY PATCH, 7TH DUKE OF CORNWALL'S LIGHT INFANTRY, 1898-2009

Roaming around the destroyed villages were not just rats but cats, dogs, mice; you name it, we had it. Stray cats would come into the line, and a stray dog occasionally, and, as a rule, they'd be as vicious as hell.

After the war, I worked with a builder who had a terrier that had been born in the trenches. If you were in the same room as the dog, the only way you could get out was if you had a saw in your hand and you showed him the teeth. He was fierce. It was the way they had to live. They survived on what was dead or abandoned.

PASSCHENDAELE

LANCE CORPORAL VIC COLE, 1ST QUEEN'S OWN (ROYAL WEST KENT REGIMENT), 1897-1995

The battalion went in by night over the duckboard tracks through Zonnebeke and Sanctuary Wood down to the Menin Road. We spread out, two companies on either side of the road occupying a rough line of craters. I had a Lucas signal lamp on a spike with which I was to

flash messages back to Brigade headquarters established in a pillbox on a ridge half a mile away.

When dawn broke, it showed the true horror. As far as the eye could see spread a vast sea of mud and every inch of it lacerated and churned up. Shell craters touched and overlapped on all sides to the horizon, many of them full or half-full of green, slimy water. Beaten down into this mess and half-obliterated were pieces of equipment, fragments of shells, shattered guns and even tanks and the blackened bones and rotting corpses of thousands of men. The new dead lay here and there in khaki heaps. Over this terrible terrain it was our job to go forward and take the next line of pillboxes four hundred yards away.

PRIVATE HARRY PATCH, 7TH DUKE OF CORNWALL'S LIGHT INFANTRY, 1898-2009

I came across a lad from A Company and he was ripped open from his shoulder to his waist by shrapnel, and lying in a pool of blood. When we got to him, he said, "Shoot me." He was beyond all human help, but before we could draw a revolver, he was dead. And the only word he uttered was "Mother". I was with him in the last seconds of his life. It wasn't a cry of despair, it was a cry of surprise and joy. I think, although I wasn't allowed to see her, I am sure his mother was in the next world to welcome him and he knew it. I was just allowed to see that much and no more, and from that day I've always remembered that cry and that death is not the end.

Two or three Germans had got up out of the trench, and one of them came towards us with a fixed bayonet. He couldn't have had any ammunition, otherwise he would have shot us. My right hand was free; I'd just changed a magazine. I drew my revolver and I shot him in the right shoulder. He dropped his rifle but he came stumbling on, no doubt to kick us to pieces if he could. He shouted something to me and I don't expect it was complimentary. I had four seconds to make my mind up. I had three rounds in that revolver. I could have killed him with my first; I was a crack shot. What shall I do?

A half submerged tank in the morass near St Julien.

Four seconds to make my mind up. I gave him his life. I shot him above the ankle, and above the knee. I brought him down but I didn't kill him. For him, the war was over. He would be picked up, interrogated, passed back to a prisoner of war camp, and at the end of the war he would rejoin his family.

LANCE CORPORAL VIC COLE, 1ST QUEEN'S OWN (ROYAL WEST KENT REGIMENT), 1897-1995

At zero hour the regiment went over, slipping and sliding in the mud, bunching up, spreading out, going single file. Meanwhile, our artillery, large and small, with incessant scream and thunder, flung tons of shells towards the enemy. Then came a strange pause in the general uproar, with both sides trying to ascertain the new positions of their respective front lines.

For ten minutes the battlefield was deathly quiet; it was pouring with rain. Then again the sudden rattle of machine guns and rifle fire and the smack-smack of bullets as they passed overhead or sloshed into the mud, followed by the whine of projectiles coming over in counter-barrage. I sent some signals, but whether headquarters received them, I've no idea, because nothing came back. I stuck the lamp into the top of a pillbox that was being used as battalion headquarters and soon after, a lump of metal hit it and put me out of action. A number of stragglers from other units began to accumulate behind our pillbox and there we crouched together whilst the storm of missiles passed overhead.

A kid came over, spewing up blood. There was a concrete hut on the Menin Road, a dressing station about fifty yards from the pillbox, and I took him down. He'd been shot in the chest and I expect he died, but I pushed him down through the mud and shell holes and got him to this first aid post where chaps were lying outside waiting their turn for treatment. I squeezed in and there were men everywhere, and blood, and coughing and moaning, that was enough for me.

I returned to the pillbox where half a dozen men continued to take shelter, and they looked at me with amazement. "They were shooting at you all the way across and you didn't notice!" I didn't. By this time they'd got another man on a stretcher, badly wounded, and they were told to take him down. Everything was in such a mess that as I leant over him to say, "Good luck, old man," the water from my tin hat tipped onto his face. "Get out of it," and he swore at me.

A few Germans began coming across. We had a pot at them round the side of this pillbox before we realized they'd been taken prisoner, and were being left to make

A captured German pill-box. Many were used by the British as battalion HQs and aid posts. Entrances were usually facing the wrong way and in some cases they underwent modification. TAYLOR LIBRARY

their own way back. We stopped shooting and the ragamuffin crew I was with, not West Kents I'd like to say, began nicking everything they could off these poor buggers, making them empty their pockets of watches and money and suchlike, while the rain slashed down in their faces.

From the interior of the pillbox our Colonel emerged. His name was Twistleton-Wyckeman-Fiennes, a wiry grey-faced figure. He was very agitated and was waving his Colt .45 revolver around. Spying me, and practically sticking his revolver in my face, he gave me an order. "Corporal, get hold of these men and take them up to the next line of pillboxes." Apparently our C Company on the south side of the Menin Road had been captured, and there was a hole in the line that we were to help fill.

LIEUTENANT NORMAN DILLON, MC, 20TH TANK BATTALION, TANK CORPS, 1896-1997

I went up the Menin Road with Basil Groves, another Section Commander, to show him the area. There was another attack in preparation, which fortunately did not come off. We got pinned down by shellfire and took shelter in an old German dugout under the road, where we found a two-bunk bed with a dead German in each. There had been a small advance and these poor creatures had been left to die. As we were squatting on the ground, rigor mortis apparently ended and a wet arm flopped over the top bed and caught Basil a clip. We examined the bodies for signs of life, but there were none.

PRIVATE ARTHUR BARRACLOUGH, 2/4TH DUKE OF WELLINGTON'S REGIMENT, 1898-2004

The battalion was being held up in an attack, and we were told to take the Lewis gun and go to the flank and enfilade the enemy. So we found this old building, it was only a few bricks, and we got down and gave them a blast or two. I was lying beside the gun, firing it, and the other two lads were behind, filling the magazines. Within a minute, bullets started flying past us and then shells started to come over and one hit bang in the middle of the four, but all the blast seemed to go one way, taking the gun and the two lads with it. They completely disappeared but the gunner and I were untouched.

PRIVATE HARRY PATCH, 7TH DUKE OF CORNWALL'S LIGHT INFANTRY, 1898-2009

The battalion had been relieved at ten o'clock at night and we were going through to the support line over a piece of open ground, when a whiz-bang burst just behind me. The force of the explosion threw me to the floor, but I didn't know that I'd been hit for two or three minutes; burning metal knocks the pain out of you at first. I saw blood, so I took a field dressing out and put it on the wound. Then the pain came.

I don't know how long I lay there. It may have been ten minutes, it may have been half an hour, but a stretcher came along and I was picked up and taken to the dressing station. There were a lot of seriously wounded there, so I had to wait. I lay there that night and all the next day, and the next evening a doctor came and had a look at the wound. He could see shrapnel buried inside and said, "Would you like me to take it out?" I said, "Yes, it's very painful, Sir." He said, "Got no anaesthetic. All that was used in the battle and we haven't been able to replace it. I shall have to take it out as you are." I thought for a minute and said, "How long will you be?" He said, "Two minutes." So I thought, well, two minutes of agony and I shall get rid of all the pain, so I said, "Okay, go on, take it out." Two orderlies got hold, one on each arm, and two got hold of my legs, and the doctor got busy.

In those two minutes I could have damn well killed him, the pain was terrific. I take it he must have cut his way around the metal and got hold of the shrapnel with his tweezers, so that he could drag it out. Anyway, he got it and asked, "Do you want it as a souvenir?" The shrapnel was about two inches long, broad at one end, and about half-an-inch thick with a sharp edge. I said, "No, I've had the bloody stuff too long already."

I didn't know what had happened to the others at first. But I was told afterwards that I had lost three good mates. The three ammunition carriers were blown to pieces. My reaction was terrible, it was like losing a part of my life. When one day they sound the last post for me, I'm sure I'll be meeting my friends again.

PRIVATE DICK TRAFFORD, 1/9TH KINGS LIVERPOOL REGIMENT, 1898-1999

To go through Passchendaele is to go through hell. There's no other way of putting it. We succeeded at Passchendaele when the Germans left it and said, "Here you are, here's Passchendaele – it's all yours." That's the way I look at it.

Busy comings and goings on the Menin Road during the Third Battle of Ypres. German prisoners can be seen escorted pas a First Aid post. TAYLOR LIBRARY

The whole world shook, all the German guns opened up at once, it was like an earthquake, whoosh, just imagine. We could see very little, and you couldn't hear orders, nobody could hear a word.

FINAL WITNESS: 1918 – GERMANY'S OFFENSIVE AND FINAL DEFEAT

The war entered its fifth year with both sides recuperating from the exertions of Third Ypres and the fighting at Cambrai.

Following events in 1917 the Germans had one major advantage: after the October Revolution and the overthrow of the Tsar, Russia's participation in the war had been rapidly brought to a close in December, first with a ceasefire, then with the negotiated peace treaty of Brevst-Litovsk twelve weeks later. The Germans now had the scope and the opportunity to turn their attention to the west. The Germans began to transport huge numbers of men and materials westwards in order to launch a final, decisive offensive that would win the war before the American Expeditionary Force could arrive in enough strength to tip the balance against Germany.

The German offensive began on 21 March, and was directed against the British Fifth Army, recuperating around St Quentin. A short but devastating artillery bombardment preceded a massive infantry assault that was aided by a heavy spring morning fog. This afforded the attackers an element of surprise far more effectively than any conventional smokescreen. In a matter of minutes, the forward position of the British line was over-run, as the Germans deployed the tactic of rapid infiltration, used successfully for the first time the previous autumn.

German units, rather than attacking strong positions head on, swept around the sides, overwhelming weaker points in the front line before moving on to the second and third lines of defence. They attacked artillery positions, helping to eliminate, or at least throw into confusion, the guns that had been used so frequently to break up and even shatter enemy assaults. Faced with such tactics, huge numbers of British soldiers, unsure what to do, held their ground only to find their retreat was cut off and they were taken prisoner.

The German drive appeared relentless, forcing the release of freshly trained units to France, men and boys with little or no experience of battle. Amongst the eighteen-year-old boys drafted to France in March 1918 was Harold Lawton, a lad from Rhyl, in Wales. A keen member of the army cadet force at school, he registered with the authorities at just seventeen, and was called up for military training a year later. As a conscript, he found himself shunted from regiment to regiment before he was finally sent to the East Yorkshires in France.

Fred Hodges was another *Men of 18 in 1918*, the title of his autobiography. Born and raised in Northampton, the grammar school boy was highly patriotic and eager to serve at a time when enthusiasm for the war was waning and few recruits saw service in France as anything other than a inevitable evil. As the Germans crashed through Northern France that early spring, he and his friends were sent overseas.

Desperate fighting by the British and Empire forces thwarted the enemy's ambitions once again, and the Germans switched the direction of attack to the south, to the area of the Chemin des Dames, east of Paris. The effect of each new offensive, while initially stunning, could only dissipate the strength of the German army, leaving it in control of great swathes of land bulging into Allied lines, salients that were difficult to hold and vulnerable to counter-attack.

The Germans had methodically lengthened their lines a year after they had sensibly sought to shorten them. When their offensive spluttered and then stalled in June and early July, it was only a matter of time before the Allies, America included, were able to regroup and attack a weakened and an increasingly demoralized enemy. The Germans had expended their last major source of reserves and used up vast quantities of ammunition.

On 8 August, British and Empire troops forced a breakthrough on the Somme, driving the enemy back eight miles and capturing huge numbers of prisoners and equipment. Coordinated and honed battle tactics that incorporated air superiority and improved artillery fire, in conjunction with better tactical use of tanks and infantry, proved decisive.

The German Chief of Staff wrote that this was the black day for the Germany army, a tacit admission that the war could not be won. The last hundred days commenced with the Germans being slowly and inexorably being pushed back across the Somme to defend the Hindenburg Line once more. The Allies' storming of the Line on 29 September was hugely significant. The shattering 24-hour bombardment before the assault only underlined the pre-eminence of Allied fire-power.

In October and November 1918, open warfare was resumed and the world of static trench lines left behind. The Germans were now incapable of making a concerted and prolonged stand.

The Allies were in no mood to negotiate. German capitulation could only be a matter of time. Even so, on the morning of 11 November, when news of the Armistice spread, most people, especially those fighting on the ground, were taken aback at the sudden cessation of hostilities.

PRIVATE HAROLD WALTER LAWTON, NO41648, 1/4TH EAST YORKSHIRE REGIMENT, 27 JULY 1899-23 DECEMBER 2005

Father was a tile-fixer. Someone would want a mosaic on the ground, he would do it, but his business tottered and fell during the war. Officer training had been as good as promised me but father had no money to help out with the kit. Instead I joined the rank and file at Wrexham where I met a terrific mixture of boys, lads from Lancashire, a real mish-mash of rough and tumble lads.

We were all aware of the awful lengthening of casualty lists, the news of retreats or bloody battles, sometimes successful, sometimes not, but always with terrible casualties. Shortly after Christmas 1917, we moved from Kinmel training camp in Wales to Great Yarmouth. Here we underwent our baptism of fire when a German cruiser bombarded the town as we trained on the assault courses. The war was getting very close.

PRIVATE PERCY WILSON, NO77033, 21ST MANCHESTER REGIMENT, 14 AUGUST 1899-15 OCTOBER 2004

When they took us out on square drill and called us to attention, our sergeant would say "Right turn" and half of them would turn left, deliberately, because they weren't interested in the army and wanted to make life difficult. The sergeant had been wounded and wasn't fit for further active service, and he would stop and look at us with scepticism, cane under his arm, "When I was a boy, my father bought me a box of toy soldiers. Some got broken and some got lost," then he hesitated for effect, "and now I've found the bloody lot again." He was having a swipe at the conscripts, as he'd found them a lot of rotters, and he was right. They had all been called up and they weren't relishing it. Only a few of us were volunteers. We all knew what the war was about by then. I went to a little village school and six of the lads I went to school with never returned.

PRIVATE FREDERICK JAMES HODGES, NO57043, 2 PLATOON, A COMPANY, 10TH LANCASHIRE FUSILIERS, 18 JULY 1899-10 FEBRUARY 2002

War, to my mind, was a kind of super sport. We were used to hard knocks in football and rugby, and healthy competition in cricket and running, getting into the first three and all that, and war was just an extension of this manliness. If I'd been put down as Class B as a soldier, I would have been ashamed of myself. War was something noble, and we were anxious that it shouldn't stop before we got there. When we took the train down to Dover, we passed a train of German prisoners and they laughed at us. They were safe, going into captivity, and we were youngsters who didn't know what we were going into.

PRIVATE DOUGLAS HENRY ROBERTS, NO11470, B COMPANY, 7TH BUFFS (EAST KENT REGIMENT), 14 JANUARY 1900–2ND DECEMBER 2002

First time we went into the line, it took hours to get forward through the communication trenches. They load you up like bloody camels. I had a two-gallon can of water, three Lewis gun panniers, some toc emma [Stokes Mortar] ammunition and before I got to the end of the line, a sergeant said, "Give that big bastard some more" and they gave me a sack of bread.

"...troops massing on your front. Stand-To!" Signaller Andrew Bowie reported German activities on the morning of 21 March 1918.

GERMAN ATTACK

At 4.40am on a dark and misty Thursday morning, the Germans launched their long awaited offensive. This would be Germany's all-out gamble to win the war. In December 1917 the Germans had fielded 171 Divisions in France and Flanders. However, after the Armistice with Russia, they were able to deploy 192 Divisions, a full 23 more than the combined effort of the Allies. This numerical advantage on the Western Front had to be used to advantage. Three German armies would launch a ferocious assault on three weakened British armies, the Third and Fifth, to knock Britain out of the war.

PRIVATE ANDREW BOWIE, 5TH CAMERON HIGHLANDERS, 1897-2002

We were at Gouzeaucourt on the night of 20/21st March 1918, when a message arrived. I wrote it down and it said: "Prisoners taken report troops massing on your front. Stand-To such and such a time, earlier than usual in any case. All ranks and ratings must be in the front line, a big attack expected." I took the message to the Captain, Captain St Clair Grant. He read it. He was a big tall fellow, and he started to shake. Nerves. He said, "Signaller, what about a wee tot?" He took one himself and he gave me some rum, because I would be nervous too. In the morning everybody stood to, everybody, including signallers, we had to stand in the line just the same. We were in the most precarious position we could be in, we were right out at a point, and it would taken nothing for them to get into our back line.

A/LANCE CORPORAL CECIL WITHERS, 17TH ROYAL FUSILIERS, 1898-2005

It was a very misty morning, and we were just getting ready to be relieved by the King's Royal Rifle Corps when the whole world shook, all the German guns opened up at once, it was like an earthquake, whoosh, just imagine. We could see very little, and you couldn't hear orders, nobody could hear a word. After a while we pulled back. The sergeant caught hold of the officer's mackintosh and followed him down the communication trench and we tagged on, that's how we retreated in the mist, in as orderly way as possible.

PRIVATE ERNEST FORD, 10TH QUEEN'S (ROYAL WEST SURREY REGIMENT), 1896-1995

We had been back from Italy a fortnight when the order arrived to move up nearer the line, as the German offensive had now begun. On the afternoon of the 21st, we marched seven miles to a station and there, in the evening, we entrained, our destination being billets in a village five or six miles west of Albert. About 3.30am we arrived at our destination. The night was black and foggy and we had no idea where we were. We had only pulled up a few minutes when there was a blaze of light and a crash about 100 yards away; this we thought to be a bomb dropped by an aircraft. Five minutes later there

British machine gunners killed whilst manning a hastely put together mobile machine gun post.

was another, followed by a third. We then had the order to detrain and the battalion lined up alongside the trucks. There was a tell-tale swish and another missile arrived with a crash, and I realized that the station was being shelled by one of the enemy's long-range high-velocity guns. We were very puzzled about this as we thought we were 15 miles from the line. Then we discovered that we were at Achiet le Grand, which explained matters to some extent. The German Push had proved much more successful than anticipated. Result: our Division was wanted very much earlier than expected, and instead of halting west of Albert, we were rushed right up to the railhead, seven miles from the line.

The battalion continued to stand along the siding, lined up in fours, while the train was unloaded; meanwhile the shells were arriving with a sudden rush every four or five minutes, and uncomfortably close. We were not at all sorry when the order came to move as it was a rather nervy process to stand still on parade and be shelled and in the middle of an inky night. Although loaded with full packs and blankets, the battalion left that station at quite a remarkable pace!

A/LANCE CORPORAL CECIL WITHERS, 17TH ROYAL FUSILIERS, 1898-2005

The retreat took us back further and further. At one point we went past a canteen. It was what they called the Expeditionary Force Canteen, full of sandwiches, cigarettes, bottles of beer, cigars and tins of fruit, and somebody had burned it all down, a terrible waste, but they had to stop the whole lot falling into enemy hands. I remember there were French people coming down the other side of the road pushing prams and old carts with kettles, saucepans, bedding and mattresses – refugees getting away from the Germans.

We retreated until we got to a small incline and, looking down, we could see a road leading down to the enemy lines and crowds of blooming Germans coming along, rows and rows. There was a little hillock about five feet high and on top was an officer, Brigadier-General Carey, who took charge and ordered us to lie down on the grass on the edge of a copse.

There were officers, even a cook, all sorts of men, mixed up, and he ordered us to fire at the oncoming Germans as fast as we damn well could. I picked up a rifle. I don't know about the other chaps, but my left hand, where it held the rifle, was all blistered because the rifle got so hot. You didn't fire at a man, you fired at the line, blindly, one clip after another. After twenty minutes, perhaps half an hour, I have no idea how long, the General said, "All right, that's stopped the buggers." The line broke and retreated but some had got within thirty yards.

SAPPER ARTHUR HALESTRAP, 46TH DIVISION ROYAL ENGINEERS, 1898-2004

I joined a convoy going up at night from Division to Brigade Headquarters. We had reached a crossroads when a Very light lit up the place, an eerie sort of light, and, as it fell, the darkness came again; then another Very light, and another one, and inevitably the shelling started. The fire was very accurate and in no time there was carnage and carcasses all over the place. The wagon to which I was attached was halted because the leading horse of the team got its left legs in the mud on the side of the road and it couldn't move, and the lead horse on the other side was pawing the air.

Lewis gun on a make-shift anti-aircraft mounting resting on a cart wheel so that a target can be tracked

All the horses were screaming, and there's nothing worse than screaming horses, they are terrifying. The situation was immediately seen by an NCO in charge, and he ordered some of the men to get on the back of the wagon to push and others to get on the wheels to wind them. I was sent to get underneath the horse stuck in the mud. When the order came to move, I heaved and everyone pushed on the wheels and we got the wagon going.

That was my baptism of fire. It wasn't a nice one but strangely enough I wasn't frightened.

AIR ATTACK

PRIVATE ERNEST FORD, 10TH QUEEN'S (ROYAL WEST SURREY REGIMENT), 1896-1995

The amount of traffic on the road was astonishing and gave some slight idea of the size of modern armies and the enormous amount of transport required. I was waiting with the transport at the side of a main road. We were there about twenty hours and during all that time, day and night, there was an unbroken line of traffic moving backwards – limbers, guns and lorries in one continuous stream.

During the morning we heard an anti-aircraft shell burst very low and close to us, and looking up saw a Boche plane at a few hundred feet. It had suddenly dived out of the clouds and evidently intended to attack the traffic on the road. Fortunately the anti-aircraft guns landed another shell right on top of the plane and put the engine out of action (it was very rare for an anti-aircraft gun to score a hit.) The German plane immediately made a hasty landing about eighty yards away from us. We grabbed our rifles, loaded them and made for it (thinking that they might turn on their machine guns) but the occupants, when they saw a horde of armed Britishers bearing down on them, apparently considered discretion to be better than valour, clambered out and did the 'Kamerad' act.

PRIVATE FRED HODGES, 10TH LANCASHIRE FUSILIERS, 1899-2002

I, along with some others, was sent to the village of Mesnil for water. We went to one of those wells where there was a windlass and I fetched a bucket of water up and then tried to pour it into a two-gallon petrol can. I was busily filling the can on top of a steep ridge above the trenches when a German plane came up very close, over the brow, firing at me. What did I do? I ran towards him to shorten the period that I was in his sights rather than stand still or run away. I could see the bullets spraying the ground, passing me. The plane went right over the top and as I looked up I saw the black crosses on the underside of his wings. He swirled round and came back to have another go, by which time I was hiding in the rubble. We watched as he circled a couple of times before returning to enemy lines, whereupon we recovered our water cans and went back to the trenches.

LANCE CORPORAL VIC COLE, 1ST QUEEN'S OWN (ROYAL WEST KENT REGIMENT), 1897-1995

There were all kinds of dogfights we would watch, going round and round, weaving between each other. The ack ack guns would be popping away, and now and again you would see something flash and fall into pieces, and then sometimes you'd see a dot in the sky, and that was the pilot falling to earth. After a dogfight, one of ours would come down "falling leaf" we called it, seemingly out of control, then suddenly flatten out and scoot away home to fight another day.

SAPPER ARTHUR HALESTRAP, 46TH DIVISION ROYAL ENGINEERS, 1898-2004

At regular times in the morning and evening, an observation plane would come over and of course we would take pot shots at it with our rifles. This airman was so low that we could see him using his revolver. As the plane went over, I suddenly felt a bang on the table beside me, and there was a bullet hole in the wood; the bullet had missed me by an inch. No one was hurt in these exchanges and in fact we took it all as a joke and enjoyed it, really.

PRIVATE ALLEN SHORT, 2/10TH LONDON REGIMENT, 1899-2000

Allen Short

One side of the quarry was in darkness but the other was swathed in moonlight. We piled arms and I used my valise as a pillow. A German plane came over and spotted our movement, dropped some bombs and then signalled to the German artillery, which started shelling. A chap close to me, whom I knew casually, was killed just a few yards away as we left our rifles and packs and dived into the shelter of a bank.

In the morning we went back. I found that a large piece of shrapnel had diagonally cut my valise from one corner to another. It broke my toothbrush into three pieces, split open a tin of bully beef, and my face towel was nothing else but a hole with a border around it. My head had been resting on that valise just a second before we decided to flee. Our stacked rifles had collapsed and, above the upper band, a piece of shrapnel had cut a groove that I could get my finger in.

RIFLEMAN ARNOLD MILLER, 2ND RIFLE BRIGADE, 1899-1991

Jerry busted right through. So instead of our draft being broken in gently, in a quiet part of the line, our battalion was rushed up to the front. We were taken up on lorries and we were in no way dispirited because we knew nothing about war. We were full of glory and self-belief: we were going to stop them. The old hands, who had been at Arras and Passchendaele, didn't try and frighten us, but we could see they weren't enthusiastic. That doesn't mean they wouldn't do their job but they knew what kind of a job it would be, and we didn't.

We were near a village called Pargny. There was a canal running across which Jerry was trying to cross. Another fellow and myself had to dig two holes and shoot at anything we saw, which we were quite prepared to do. It was cold and it was foggy and we didn't see anything except the bloke who brought up our rations in the early hours of the morning. We nearly shot him.

Later that morning, we heard a heck of a noise going on a couple of hundred yards up on the right. Nothing happened, so King, the lad who was with me, had a slice of bread and plum and apple jam while I kept a look out. I then cut myself a slice, when he suddenly said, "Run, there's Jerry behind us." He bolted and I never saw him again. The Germans had crossed over the canal and were streaming through about sixty yards behind us. I didn't stand a dog's chance because my rifle was lying on the ground by the side of the hole and I had to climb out of my hole, by which time the Germans were already pointing at me. There was no chance of resistance.

With other prisoners, I was told to pick up a wounded German who was lying on an improvised stretcher, just canvas with a pole through it, and we carried him back under fire from our own guns. We went slipping and sliding through a wood, deep in mud, until we eventually got out into the open where there was a row of field guns firing away like mad. The Germans were very friendly because they were advancing at such a speed, and offered us ersatz coffee while all the time they shouted, "Nach Paris. Nach Paris!"

PRIVATE HAROLD LAWTON, 1/4TH EAST YORKSHIRE REGIMENT, 1899-2005

Harold Lawton

Suddenly all training stopped and we were given draft leave; home, with kitbags and rifles. However, on the second day urgent orders came to return to Great Yarmouth for some frantic kitting out before we made our way to Sheerness and across the Channel to France.

This would have been in the last week of March 1918. Up to this point, I had been in the Manchester Regiment – I had been in the Royal Welch Fusiliers and the Cheshires before then – and now I found myself part of a draft sent to another regiment, the East Yorkshires. This we found near Armentières, resting behind the lines after having a very nasty time. We were the new boys, and the old soldiers took no notice of us whatsoever; they had to get themselves better again. So instead of getting any sort of paternalism shown towards us, that one might have expected from our elders, it wasn't there at all. They told us nothing.

PRIVATE FRED HODGES, 10TH LANCASHIRE FUSILIERS, 1899-2002

I got into the front line and it was all chalk. I sat there on the fire step, and the man I relieved gave me a two-inch square mirror to clip onto my bayonet in order to look over into No Man's Land. I sat there and thought, "Oh, I've got this mirror, I'm not much of a sentry if I don't use it," so I pushed it up over the parapet and all I could actually see was coarse grass and barbed wire. But the mirror must have glinted in the sun because in no time at all a salvo of shells began to burst near the trench, stones rattling off my helmet.

As I sat there, a great lump of jagged shrapnel, as big as my hand, thumped beside me and like a fool I touched it and burnt my fingers, I didn't realise such things would be hot. I looked around and felt like the only man in the trench. I went round the next traverse and people were sat writing letters or playing cards. The sergeant just looked at me and grinned. "That's reet, lad, ta'ake no'a'tice, Jerry'll geet fed oop sooner or la'ter". The boys were quite fatalistic, and during a shelling most people kept quiet and put on a bold front: "That'll do, Jerry. You keep on, you'll hurt somebody."

PRISONERS

Prisoners who were transported to Germany were, on the whole, formally registered as POWs. Messages could then be sent via the Red Cross to loved ones back home who, until then, knew little more than that a son or husband was "missing". Once registered, prisoners became eligible for food parcels sent from Britain, though not all men received them. Prisoners who were kept in France were far less fortunate. These men worked close to the battlefront and were rarely registered and so were "lost" to any help from home. They lived on watery soup and anything else they could steal or scrounge. Frequently, the first news that these men were still alive was when they walked through the door back home, perhaps a year late.

PRIVATE HAROLD LAWTON, 1/4TH EAST YORKSHIRE REGIMENT, 1899-2005

The Portuguese had retreated under heavy artillery fire. We could see them coming back and we wondered what had happened. We were rushed to hold the line of trenches that was little more than a scrape in the ground, and so we had to get digging straight away. We hadn't been there long when one chap, who'd come out with us, looked over our new parapet and he was immediately shot through the head by a sniper.

We were cold and hungry. It was absolute chaos. Not a single British officer came to see us; nobody knew what was happening. The next morning we retreated, but the Germans had already infiltrated our lines and swept around the flanks.

We could hear firing but we hadn't a clue what was going on, not an officer was to be seen, it was shocking. We were stuck. For a while, we lived on our iron rations eating hard biscuits and sipping from our water bottles, hoping all the time that we would be found or someone would tell us what to do.

Eventually, the Germans returned and mopped us up. There were only half a dozen of us, there was nothing to do but put up our hands. What could you do?

RIFLEMAN ROBERT RENWICK, MM, 16TH KING'S ROYAL RIFLE BRIGADE, 1896-1997

We were near Armentières, the Portuguese had fled, and we were attacked from the front and both sides. We kept firing until our rifles were hot, even our Colonel was at it. Orders were given to withdraw one platoon at a time. I was in No2 platoon and being batman to the Sergeant Major, I automatically stayed with him but he had to see the rest of the company out and told me to go. We withdrew about half a mile to a pond where some men went to the left and some to the right. Those that went to the right, about thirty of us, were taken prisoner. The Germans had swarmed ahead, and placed machine guns on the bank side, and so they just lined us up.

At first I couldn't realize what was happening. I couldn't take it in. One Sergeant, Jack Wheatley, shouted to me, "Throw your rifle down, Renwick, or you'll be shot." He had laid his rifle down and that was a sign for the rest of us to do the same. I still had my rifle on my shoulder and on the spur of the moment I made a bid to get away. As I ran, an officer fired his revolver and a machine gun opened up. I'll give them credit, they must have fired overhead as they could have mowed me down. When I got back, the German officer butted me in the ribs with his revolver, "Silly English boy."

Sergeant Henson followed me in flight but they got him in the arm with the revolver. It was a foolish thing to do and I felt partly to blame. Sergeant Henson, always a brave fellow, was standing there crying like a baby. I think the idea of being taken prisoner hurt his pride badly. "When the machine gun started up I shut my eyes," he said. "I never thought I'd see you alive again." I was posted missing, believed killed. It was six weeks before my parents knew whether I was alive or dead.

PRIVATE WALTER GREEN, 1/7TH DURHAM LIGHT INFANTRY, 1897-1998

The Captain came along and said, "I'm sorry, but we're surrounded. There's three alternatives as far as I can see: we can fight it out, a lot of us being killed, or we can lay down our arms, which will mean we will all be captured. The only other way is every man for himself. See that church over there? If you get through, we'll meet there at 12 midnight, as many as are still alive." I asked if I could go. "Yes, you can go, Green," and I picked up my rifle and set off on my own.

I went to the bottom of the trench where I knew there was an old communication trench that had not been used since 1915. It was overgrown and I began to fight my way through. I hadn't been going very long when I came across what we called barbed wire gooseberries thrown into a trench to block it; there must have been eight foot of them. The first one thrown in hadn't fallen to the bottom of the trench so I got down on my stomach

and started to creep underneath when I heard a laugh. I looked up and on top of the trench was an unterofficer, what we'd call a senior sergeant, and two Germans with rifles. As soon as I saw them, I feared the worst, but they gestured to me to come on through, so I crept on and, as I was coming out, one fellow jumped into the trench and put his foot on my rifle and the unterofficer and the other lad came down, got hold of me and lifted me up. As I stood, they unfastened my epaulettes and stripped my battledress off. I stooped to try and pick up my haversack because I'd 250 woodbines inside, but they shoved my hand out of the way.

We came to an opening in the trench and climbed out, and the officer spoke to one of the guards who told me in English to return to where I had started. When I got back, there were seventeen of the twenty-five there, and I asked what had happened. "Two have been killed and five wounded. We were the other seventeen, you're now eighteen, that makes twenty-five."

A German stretcher bearer came along and two of us were told us to follow him. We went back to a field covered in wounded and killed. There, stretcher bearers worked in twos, putting field dressings on the wounded, while dozens of prisoners picked casualties up on duckboards and carried them to a sunken road, three or four hundred yards away to a field hospital. This continued all day until dusk.

RIFLEMAN ROBERT RENWICK, MM, 16TH KING'S ROYAL RIFLE BRIGADE, 1896-1997

Sentries escorted us to the main road where we were handed over to Uhlan cavalrymen who rode up and bumped us with their ponies as we walked. We were marched through Armentières where a few of the enemy were looting and one, the worse for drink, came up and pointed at my cap badge. I was in no position to argue, so I let him have it. It snowed that night and we spent the coldest night of my life in an open cart shed without overcoats.

In the morning we were taken to an intelligence officer. We were questioned; one lad went in first, and when he came out he gave me a wink that I took to mean he hadn't given away anything of importance. I was the second to go in. I must say this German officer was very polite. "Tommy, you are a prisoner of war now, and we would just like a little bit of information about what is behind you in the way of troops." We hadn't eaten for forty hours and I was offered a meal for my cooperation. "Look, Sir," I said, "I'm sorry to be taken prisoner, that's grieving me, but I'm not giving any information. I'm still playing cricket." I said, "You speak English very well. Have you ever heard that remark?" and he said, "Yes, Tommy, I have." He finished up by saying, "We'll be over that ground in a day or two, it doesn't matter much." He then asked if I had been home on leave

There's three alternatives as far as I can see: we can fight it out, or we can lay down our arms. The only other way is every man for himself.

recently, and when I lied saying I had, he suggested that London was very much knocked about by the Zeppelin raids and people were very short of food, which I denied.

PRIVATE HAROLD LAWTON, 1/4TH EAST YORKSHIRE REGIMENT, 1899-2005

The funny thing is, I can't remember them taking us prisoner. All I can remember is sitting on the bank of a ditch without any webbing, and not a soul about. What happened to the men taken prisoner with me, I can't say. From what I could see, I was somewhere near a transport park. I was sitting there, blank, watching these vehicles of one sort or another, and along came a tall, fine-looking man with a very remarkable air about him, and he generously gave me a packet of biscuits.

More and more prisoners started to come in, and we were held in a field for several days before we were taken through Lille to a fortress known as 'the black hole of Lille'. As we marched, the townspeople came out and tried to offer us bread, even though they were hungry themselves.

The fortress was a truly awful place; I hesitate to describe it. Hundreds of men were crowded into cells, men lying on wooden shelves for day after day, six to one bunk, jam-packed, men covered in scabies. You couldn't move in the filthy conditions. Sometimes the Germans came along and we were given half an hour's fresh air. Food was a mug of soup but what was in it, I can't tell you.

Men were dying every day from wounds and dysentery. I was kept for twelve days, and it was a relief to be taken to Germany. Like so many others, I was reported missing, believed killed, and it was some time before I was able to write home.

LANCE CORPORAL VIC COLE, 1ST QUEEN'S OWN (ROYAL WEST KENT REGIMENT), 1897-1995

We got out of the train, and advanced into the sprawling Nieppe Forest in extended order when word came down that we were now the front line. There was no sign of war, the sun shone, birds sang in the trees and startled deer ran leaping off into the brush.

Beyond the forest we came into the open, and there was a field with a chalk road running across and we started along this road. Ahead of me the column veered right, and I thought, "What's up?" In our path there was a complete section of blokes lying in fours, dead. You couldn't help but look, but a voice said, "Come on, come on," and hurried us past. About ten yards away was a little bit of ground with the earth scooped out. It had been a shrapnel shell that had burst, and wiped the lot out.

We moved on up to a hedge and one of the lads said, "There they are, over there in that village," so we dug ourselves a hole and stuck our rifles through the hedge. Then, with a shattering crash, the fun commenced and in a moment the air was full of bursting shells, flying shrapnel and the smoke and noise of battle.

Pulling myself together, I noticed that most of the stuff

was going over our heads and dropping into C Company lines. The world seemed full of the whine and crash of shell splinters. To our front across a ploughed field, the ground rose a little so that we had hardly any real field of fire, then suddenly, quite close, I saw the Germans – at least I saw the tops of their helmets bobbing up and down as they ducked and dodged in our fire. Aiming at these moving blobs, I fired again and again until there was no longer anything to shoot at and the 'cease-fire' whistle brought respite. A battery of our field guns now joined in the game. Concealed in the forest behind us, they fired over our heads. As poor Fritz came on, our guns shortened their range until their shells were falling just in front of our own position. One fell right among our men, then another, and several were wounded.

I tried my best to get through to the battery on our phone but the line had been cut. The Company Commander, Captain Scott, was furious with the artillery and ordered me to take a message back to the guns myself, so I shook hands with my friend Ralph Newman and set off. All kinds and calibres of missiles were crashing all about, shrapnel, whiz-bangs, high explosive, all in a frenzied mix-up and at the back of it the steady tap-tap-tap of machine guns.

I reached a little stream, crossed on the plank bridge and turned into the wood where C Company was dug in. Here I found a signaller complete with telephone in a hole behind a tree, and in a minute or so my message had been passed to the guns and the range had been lifted nicely.

As I turned to leave, something hit the tree behind which we were crouching, there was a blinding flash, a whirling sound of splinters, and there I was lying flat on my back looking up at a startled signaller. I had been hit in the lumber region and was already feeling numb from the waist down. Stretcher bearers arrived and dragged me over to a hole for temporary cover and turned me on my face. One of them let rip a stream of swear-words as he cut away my leather jacket and saw the wound.

My wound bandaged, I lay until the attack slackened off. They lifted me into an empty ration limber drawn by a couple of mules and we rattled off back through the forest. I hardly recognized the place as the same one we had come through such a short time before. Then it had been a lovely peaceful bird sanctuary and now it was a shambles, fallen trees and great holes everywhere.

When I came out of the wood, I looked right and left. There were red caps about fifty yards apart and I said to the driver, "What are they doing here?" and he said, "They're to stop anybody going back."

PRIVATE FRED HODGES, 10TH LANCASHIRE FUSILIERS, 1899-2002

At night you're all alone, you might be the only man in the world. Your battalion's fairly near you, but you and your mate are the only two sentries awake and you look around and there's nothing going on. You look up and notice the stars, and I'd try and remember the names of the constellations. Similarly, in the day you'd see white clouds lazily drifting over the battle front, hear larks singing overhead, and nature just getting on with life, a bank of poppies sheer red, yet all around men were dying, and you couldn't help but be struck by the contrast between the horror that man had created for over four years and nature which proceeded in its quiet, beautiful way, stars, birds, flowers, the humming of bees. I had never lived so close to nature and was acutely aware of life, the abundance of colour and scent.

PRIVATE WALTER GREEN, 1/7TH DURHAM LIGHT INFANTRY, 1897-1998

We were taken to work in an ironstone mine. I worked with another English lad, two Russians and a chap from Luxembourg with a peg leg, who was trained to do the drilling and blasting. We had to break the stone up and load it into wagons all day long, then, during the night, Italians came along and pushed what we'd loaded onto a gantry and it was taken outside. We were awakened at three in the morning, given a bowl of soup and a wash, and then got ready to be taken down the mine to start work at four, for twelve hours, when you came back up for another bowl of soup and bed. The work was very physical, using a seven-pound hammer, a diamond chisel, and a shovel. The hammer had a rosewood shaft which would bend, so as you swung the head to hit the chisel, the effect was to turn a seven-pound hammer into one with the power of a ten, perhaps fifteen pounds, smashing stone three foot square into little pieces. For the first three weeks your hands blistered, and then the blisters got hard, and then your hands got hard.

You weren't conscious of how much weight you lost. You weaken as time progresses, so that towards the end of the day you are told to get on with it or else you're not going to get your quota, in which case you might face a punishment commando. They'd threaten you with all sorts, but the most effective was that if you didn't do what you were told, you'd go down the salt mines.

Mostly, we had soup. It was so thin we used to say that it was 'been soup', not made with beans, but that it was once soup. Lots of men, particularly the Russians, were dying through a disease called octin, which was caused by having too much liquid in the blood with no substance in it. The signs were pain and swelling in your feet, then right up your legs until it got into your body, and then it started to swell your head, and then you'd suddenly die. I was in hospital a week with octin. A cart used to come round, and bodies of those that had died during the night were thrown onto it. I had some advice, to try and strain the soup, if I could, and sacrifice the water and eat only what was left over. It's hard to do when you are so hungry.

The only way to supplement the meals was by scrounging, if you could, but this was difficult for us, being in the mines. If you could get out on a fatigue into a field when food was growing, you could eat raw potatoes to fill up. What won't fatten will at least fill. Those who were working near houses, repairing railway lines or working on goods trains were best off, as they could scrounge around in dustbins for peelings and cabbage leaves which they would bring back to the camp and boil up.

RIFLEMAN ROBERT RENWICK, MM, 16TH KING'S ROYAL RIFLE CORPS, 1896-1997

They had us handling ammunition, and of course we let them know that we shouldn't, that it was against international law. We were loading shells, then handgrenades the shape of an egg, from a light railway truck to the full gauge railway, and a box dropped in between and exploded. Whether it was done on purpose, I don't know, but the whole thing went up in flames. I was in a big truck with a mate and a German, helping. The sentry jumped out first, then my friend, both being wounded. I was unhurt and I dragged my friend to safety, then, spotting a garden, I went into it and had a feed of anything I could find.

The Germans took it that it was sabotage. We were sent to solitary confinement in Fort Macdonald. We had six weeks of confinement in there, during which we lost most weight. It was a terrible, weary time. You were just called out for your coffee and your black rye bread, 1/3 of a loaf for dinner and breakfast, but we were all so hungry that we ate it there and then and had nothing else until the watery soup next day at lunchtime. We had no exercise, we just lay on wooden beds with no bedding, nothing to do, nothing to read. Two dozen to a cell.

I came home weighing seven stone, and my mother

"I won't say we were ill-treated, but we were badly neglected," Robert Renwick.

and sister cried at the sight of us. We were never in a registered camp and as a result we never got a Red Cross parcel. We were shunted from one farm building to another. I won't say we were ill-treated, but we were badly neglected.

PRIVATE HAROLD LAWTON, 1/4TH EAST YORKSHIRE REGIMENT, 1899-2005

Horse-wagons took us to Germany and as the train trundled along we took turns to reach up to the small barred window to get fresh air. Our first camp was in Westphalia, where we were cleaned up, our uniforms fumigated, and our bodies washed. Our boots were taken away and we were given wooden clogs that nobody liked.

Before I went to France, we heard that a local man, well-known in Rhyl, had been taken prisoner, and that he was not having a bad time at all. When I arrived at the POW camp, this man was there and he seemed to be in charge of the place as far as the POWs were concerned. Everybody knew who he was. When I went up to him, I asked if he could get me any tea and sugar, which he did. Then one day we saw a German, a real Prussian, bullying a young man, pushing him around, and this chap from Rhyl went straight over and knocked the guard out with one punch. Of course he was arrested straight away and put into the cells. Everybody knew about it, but when his trial came he was sentenced to one year in Cologne Prison and he was taken away.

A group of us were then taken on to Minden Camp, sifted, and a few of us put on one side to be examined by a friendly German Colonel. He talked English to us one at a time, asking what we were going to do after the war, while a man took notes. He asked me if I was going to university and which one I would like to go to. I told him I wanted to specialize in French and Latin and he asked some very intelligent questions to check whether it was true or not. At the end, he said to the man behind him, "A1 intelligent". What he was going to do with this information, I've no idea, but I've the impression we were given lighter work than the others.

Each morning the guards brought a cylinder of clear liquid, tea it was supposed to be, but everybody used it for shaving instead. I was able to speak to a guard and got a job peeling potatoes, and a group of five of us peeled them in a glasshouse. I still had underwear on under baggy blue trousers, and I used to tie a piece of string round the bottom of my pants, and while peeling, I took some slices and put them down my trousers to cook that night, just enough for myself and one or two others. I had to be careful, walking away, to stop them falling out, as the German in charge, a nice chap really, used to watch us go and I had to walk very steadily. It was awfully difficult to build a fire without raising suspicion, but we managed to boil the potato in a mug.

In time we got Red Cross parcels once a month,

"Tommy, you are a prisoner of war now..." Robert Renwick recalled his interrogation before being transported to Germany in cattle trucks.

cardboard boxes which were administered by the Swiss. Occasionally they were damaged on purpose. Some of the Germans examining them stuck chisels through the contents to check nothing untoward was hidden inside. In some respects we were eating better than they were. They were very short of food and used to look with longing eyes when the parcels came in.

AIR WARFARE

FLIGHT SERGEANT WILLIAM GEORGE HALL, NO216264, 216 SQUADRON ROYAL NAVAL AIR SERVICE, 23 MAY 1898-JANUARY 1999

I was posted to a place called Ochey, near Nancy, at the end of October 1917 where the Squadron took over a French aerodrome. The weather was all against us, raining and snowing, and we were up to our necks in mud. It was a miserable place and we didn't actually undertake operations in our twin-engine Handley Page bombers until March, just as the Germans launched their big offensive.

We never bombed the trenches. If you were only twenty yards out, the bombing would be pointless. At best, you might kill or injure a handful of men and that wasn't worth the effort of flying there and the cost of the bombs. You left that to the artillery. Our targets were anything that helped the German war effort. We bombed Cologne, Mannheim, all along the Rhine, different works, ammunition factories, aerodromes, an important bridge, railway junctions or yards, and, if we spotted anything quite interesting, we bombed that as well. On one occasion, I bombed a train.

There was one thing that worried me. If we were going on a raid on a Sunday night when people would be in church, I knew it was possible that I might kill them. So on one of my leaves I had a word with a clergyman and he told me, "No, you can reassure yourself there, you're doing your duty. If it happens, it is most unfortunate." After that, I never thought about the people below.

When you flew, you watched the pilot all the time, watched his switches, his clocks, you watched how he made manoeuvres, so that in an emergency you could take over. I did feel that I could get a plane down, even if I crashed on landing. We had no parachutes. We weren't used to them so it didn't enter our minds. If people wanted to know what we would do, we told them we'd slide down a searchlight's beam.

If everything was in our favour, we could achieve 70mph, but that was with the wind behind us. I would plot the course before we went. I was navigator and bomber, and the pilot flew the plane and did as you asked him to do. When we took off from the aerodrome, we started off with five planes, half an hour between them, but by the time you got to the objective, the difference could be much longer or shorter.

Bombing Cologne, we'd follow the river to find the city, and as we got toward it, all the city lights would suddenly go out as if there was a switch, so by the time we got there it was all black, and we had to rely on the bridge behind the cathedral to give us a sense of where we were. We knew the city was getting ready. Anti-aircraft guns would start up and searchlights scoured the sky. Once they found us, a dozen beams would concentrate on us, a brilliant light; it was like looking at an oncoming car with undipped headlights, but twelve times worse. We couldn't see a thing below and we used hand signals to tell the pilot how to get out of them, waving to dip or bank. The pilot would immediately dive or fly higher to get out of the beam.

We fired at the searchlights as much as anything to

relieve the pressure but the machine guns were really for defence against other planes. In the dark you couldn't see a plane, only a black mask. On one occasion we'd finished a raid and were coming back, and nearing the aerodrome we could see searchlights, so we knew something was happening. Eventually the searchlights went out, but as we prepared to land I saw a black object below me. I prepared the machine gun, not knowing if it was ours or theirs, before I suddenly realized it was just my own shadow from the moon onto the ground.

As a crew we all sat in the middle of the fuselage. The pilot and the navigator sat forward of the bombs, and the gunners stood further back. They had two guns, one to shoot behind and upwards and one to fire underneath the plane, through an opening. As the navigator, I sat alongside the pilot.

Only as we approached the target would I crawl forward through a hole about two feet by three feet, under the instruments, to the actual bomb-dropping position, right at the nose of the plane. There I'd prepare the bomb sight, adjusting for wind, speed and height. I would approach the town but not go straight for it. Instead I'd go right round and then get the pilot to close down the engines and sail quietly over the objective. That had two advantages: the plane wasn't shuddering or moving so your sighting was steady, and at the same time the searchlights couldn't find you because they couldn't hear you.

Underneath where the pilot and the navigator sat, there was an eight-foot square grid like a box of eggs into which these bombs would fit on hooks. Our plane took sixteen one-hundredweight bombs and to drop each one you pulled a lever that released a hook. The bombs had four wings and, if they had not been properly aligned, the tips could catch in the corner of the fitting and wouldn't drop. When this happened, you had to lean over from your end and the gunner would do the

An FE2b in the progress of being fitted with bombs whilst the pilot and observer look on. Flares can be seen beneath the wing.

same and free them by hand by trying to square them in the fitting.

When we were bombing, we flew at five or six thousand feet, no more or we couldn't see the target. We could see the explosion of anti-aircraft fire in the air and the shrapnel would fly about, making dozens of holes in the fabric, but these were easily repaired. If I heard an explosion, I knew it was very close because our engines, one on each side, created a deuce of a noise, and to hear anything above them meant it had to be near.

Because we approached the target from the rear, we were already on a straight course for home.

AIR MECHANIC HENRY ALLINGHAM, NO12 SQUADRON, RNAS, 1896-2009

I was a mechanic so I wasn't meant to fly, but in the RNAS you were mechanic, gunner and head bottle washer, and so you did anything that was asked of you. You never knew when you might go up; if you'd done a job on a plane, the pilot would point at you and say 'patrol' or 'first flight.' This ensured you did the best job you could on it.

You'd take off just before light in the morning. As we went up, I always had to listen to the engine; the least change of note and you would come back, if you could. There were so many accidents. I've seen aircraft and they'd be going along and suddenly they'd come down, it wasn't very pleasant – I've seen fellows fighting for their lives to keep control as little things went wrong. Very often the lock nuts failed, as lots of them were poorly-designed, and the plane stood no chance, bucket and a spade that's all you'd need for the pilot.

Even when you landed safely, you had to bail out as fast as you could and leave the plane for 20 minutes. It would seem all right, then woosh, it would be all in flames. If pilots didn't get out quickly enough you'd see them burnt alive and you had nothing to put the fire out with, nothing at all. You had to stand and watch and their arms would slowly rise into the air. There were no fire extinguishers whatsoever.

When you were flying in the Ypres Salient, you could see our line all the way round and Jerry's line too, but you had your job to think of, you weren't there to daydream or sightsee. Jerry's anti-aircraft guns would pop at you but you generally knew the height you'd need, to keep out of harm's way. In the air the German pilots rarely engaged unless they had the advantage. In action you had to hold your fire, and that took some nerve; then you gave them a squirt with the Lewis Gun.

TO VICTORY

By midsummer, the German offensive was exhausted. Time and again they had sought to force a break-through and time and again they had been thwarted. Up and down the line, the Germans held salients penetrating deep into Allied lines that inevitably proved impossible to hold when Allied forces returned to the offensive.

During September, the Germans fell back on the Hindenburg Line. The outposts of this great defensive position were attacked one by one until the line itself, long deemed impregnable, was attacked on 27 September. In twenty-four hours, and after a million-shell bombardment, the line was fatally breached. The Germans had no expectation that they could make any sort of concerted stand. The war was in its last throws, although there remained much hard fighting until Germany finally capitulated

A/CAPTAIN NORMAN DILLON, MC, 20TH TANK BATTALION, TANK CORPS, 1896-1997

On 8 August, we made a big attack on each side of the Amiens-Peronne road. B Battalion was to lead the way, and my C.O. and I had a few hours' rest in a shelter, after seeing that all the tanks had arrived at their starting point.

Before dawn we set off and fell in with the tanks just before zero. The silence was broken by the roar of the artillery barrage, the Germans making no noticeable response. I accompanied the Colonel down the road so that I could show him the route the tanks would take. The attack was underway and we walked until we met a tank coming towards us, looking very menacing. It appeared that the officer in charge had not adjusted his compass properly and it was 180 degrees out. With some difficulty, we persuaded him that he was wrong and turned him about.

The leading tanks advanced so successfully that they quickly reached the German field-gun positions. One gun was still in place and was loosing off at point-blank range and a shell burst right between my legs. I got a piece of aluminium nose-cap in the left ankle, which lodged between the Achilles tendon and the bone. I also received sundry small wounds in the back. I was placed on a stretcher and carried by some German prisoners down the road to a Field Dressing Station. I was in hospital for three months, so it proved the end of the war for me.

PRIVATE TED FRANCIS, 16TH ROYAL WARWICKSHIRE REGIMENT, 1896-1996

There was a call for men with experience of car engines for a special job with the tanks. Like a fool, I stepped forward and volunteered. They wanted eight men in all, and as a group we were told to report to a tank battalion the following morning to meet the officer in charge, who would tell us our role in an attack. I was shocked. Our job, we were informed, was to walk behind four tanks with a special attachment fixed to our rifles firing smoke bombs over the top to create a smokescreen. Two men would be allocated to each tank. I said to the fellow next to me, another man from my battalion, "We've had it this time." He said, "What do you mean?" I replied, "It's a thousand to one on that we shall be killed, because the moment we go over the top of that ridge, every shell, bomb, rifle and machine gun will be at us and we shall be outside."

The first hundred yards were quiet but, sure enough, when we got to the top of the ridge the shells began absolutely flying over, as we tried to hide behind the tank. When all the smoke bombs had gone, the officer in charge of our tank, God bless him, saved our lives. "Have you used all the bombs?" he shouted. "Yes". "Well, don't just stand there, get inside." He was the only officer of the four tanks who asked the fellows to get in. The other six were left to themselves.

By this time the fellow with me was shell-shocked, his face was so contorted he could hardly speak, and we had to practically carry him to the nearest cover when the tank ditched in a trench. Most of the crew inside were injured and bleeding from the bumps, and they struggled to get out, because they feared the tank would be set alight.

PRIVATE TED FRANCIS, 16TH WARWICKSHIRE REGIMENT, 1896-1996

We were in a fairly quiet part of the line and taking turns on duty, looking over the top now and again, and a sergeant came to me and said, "There's a nice little dugout round the corner, enough for one; you're not on for two hours. I'll send somebody to call you." I got into this tiny dugout, just big enough for one man to lie down full length. On top were lumps of iron, railway sleepers, and wood that they put over the trenches to try and keep them bullet and splinter-proof.

I must have been sound asleep when a whizz bang hit it and the roof came down. I had one leg curled up but the other was outstretched and it was crushed. I screamed in pain. I knew immediately that my ankle was smashed, but of course I was in a fortunate position as only yards away were plenty of people, but it took them quite a considerable time to get me out, trying to pull me and jarring my ankle.

When I got to hospital, an American doctor came to me and whispered to the nurse, and this fellow in the next bed told me, "You lucky so-and-so, you're for England in the morning." I could have kissed that doctor. Those were the words that I'd longed to hear for

four years. I looked at my foot, and thought, surely even if I get well, I won't be sent to France again, and that gave me such a great relief. As far as I was concerned, I couldn't get out of the army quick enough, and here was a splendid wound, painful but splendid. I was overwhelmed with delight.

PRIVATE ALLEN SHORT, 1/8TH LONDON REGIMENT, 1899-2000

About 3 o'clock in the afternoon, Jerry started sending over gas shells and we got our gas masks on. He stopped shelling round about midnight; it was a bit breezy and the gas soon cleared. After eight hours of wearing these masks, we couldn't wait to get them off. All the time one's nose is pinched, making it difficult to breathe, while our temples were numb with the stretching of the elastic band round our heads.

A high explosive shell hit the parapet in front of my section, partially burying four of us. I remember a great clod of mud as hard as iron hitting my elbow and a piece of shrapnel grazed my forehead. A volley of gas shells followed and as we struggled to extricate ourselves we breathed in the gas. It was mustard gas, and it began to burn under the arms and between the legs, anywhere you were likely to perspire. I was anxious to get my gas mask back on, which wasn't easy as I wore glasses.

Our spell of duty ended and we climbed down from the firestep and dozed off, marvellous what you can do when you are tired. When I woke up, I was startled to see that I was bringing up green vomit; my sight was there but my eyes were all gummed as if by glue. I forced my eyes open to check that my sight was all right, while I discovered my voice had gone, all I could do was whisper. It was weeks before it came back.

A Welshman called Davies was swearing like anything, while another boy was crying for his mother. We were collected and taken down in a crocodile, each hanging on to the man in front. As we walked, everyone vomited over everyone else; I was lucky to be the last

"The leading tanks advanced so successfully that they quickly reached the German field-gun positions." Norman Dillon 20th Tank Battalion.

man in the line. My company, which had been sixty strong when we'd gone into the trenches, came out numbering thirty, that in normal times was meant to have a nominal strength of 250!

A/LANCE CORPORAL CECIL WITHERS, 17TH ROYAL FUSILIERS, 1898-2005

It was dark and we were sheltering from the shellfire behind a concrete pillbox when we were ordered to leave. To do so, we turned sharp left and down a little passageway and then made a dash for it. We were taking turns to go when the man ahead of me stepped out just as a time fuse shell burst over the entrance. He got the full blast and his head and body were flattened like a concertina. The force of the explosion flung me back bodily against the chaps behind who fell like dominos onto each other until the officer, at the end of the line, was dashed against the back wall with such force that it killed him stone dead.

I picked myself up. My turn. I went out to the edge of the St Quentin Canal close to the river Escaut where the engineers had constructed a narrow improvised bridge, on top of which they'd laid straw.

AIR MECHANIC HENRY ALLINGHAM, NO12 SQUADRON, RNAS, 1896-2009

We were going forward over the battlefield as the Germans withdrew. It was getting dark and really the only safe thing to do was to stay where you were, so I got my groundsheet and got myself ready to go to sleep. Before settling down, I went to look at something and fell in a shell hole. I couldn't get out and it was all crumbling at the sides. I got frightened, all sorts of dead things were in there. The more I tried to get out, the more the ground crumbled and I got deeper in the shell hole. The smell was awful for as I struggled, I disturbed the water. I moved a little to the left and the ground shallowed and I dug my feet in and got my belly on the ground and wriggled out. I sat there in the dark and waited for daylight. I didn't even dare to find my groundsheet again, I was so frightened. Well, that night I was stinking. Heaven knows what was in there. I wore that tunic until I got into Germany.

SAPPER ARTHUR HALESTRAP, 46TH DIVISION ROYAL ENGINEERS, 1898-2004

For the attack on the Hindenburg Line, we had a transmitter receiver, a trench set as it was called, in a wooden case with a carrying strap. Then there were batteries, which were very heavy cells, also carried in a wooden box with a strap. We had two tubular fifteen-foot steel masts in three-foot sections to sling over our shoulders with ropes and guys all together in a sack with a mallet and aerial wire. On top of this we had our own rifles, ammunition and field equipment, a knapsack, groundsheet, and gas mask, amongst other things, as well as six days' rations of bully beef, canned fruit, biscuits and bread, which had been placed in a sandbag.

We had been told a carrying party was coming to help us through the trenches, but we received a note from a runner to say that the infantry had no men to spare. The three of us struggled on but the job was impossible. We had to dump something and the only thing we could afford to lose was the sack containing our rations. When we finally got to the front line we found the infantry waiting to go over..

PRIVATE PERCY WILSON, 21ST MANCHESTER REGIMENT, 1899-2004

The Germans set booby traps on windows, doors, anything that could be moved. They knew men were looking for things, souvenirs and so on, and they rigged these things to blow. The officers used to lecture us. "Whatever you do, don't touch doors or windows." But the Germans were clever. We were clearing some old German trenches, making sure there was no one hanging back, hiding. There was a bottle standing on an old wooden box, with a glass beside it. Two men went over, and one got hold of the cork and pulled it, and bang, both men went up, we heard the crash.

Similarly, we came across a gun team of mules that had been shot. A group of us were ordered to dig a hole and bury them, to keep us occupied, I fancy. A Canadian, a Second Lieutenant, took us to a soft place where we could dig deep. He got down and was looking at the mules when all at once he came running back. "Get the hell out of there as fast as you can, those mules are booby trapped!"

TROOPER BEN CLOUTING, 4TH (ROYAL IRISH) DRAGOON GUARDS, 1897-1990

Increasing numbers of German prisoners could be seen, trudging back to our makeshift prison cages. Many were ridiculously young and looked as if their world had fallen to pieces. They looked dishevelled, their equipment dilapidated, for their lines of supply were breaking down, and many had been left to scrounge their own food. At one farmhouse where I stopped right at the end of the war, I found the owners in tears: the Germans had passed through, the previous night, and had eaten their old guard dog, cooking it at the farm.

I passed a cage with sixty or seventy prisoners. Most appeared very tired and hungry, and only seemed interested in swapping what bits and pieces they still owned for food.

PRIVATE SMILER MARSHALL, 8TH MACHINE GUN SQUADRON, MACHINE GUN CORPS (CAVALRY), 1897-2005

Just before the Armistice, the Germans started throwing their rifles away. They weren't going to fight any more, they told us that. One or two spoke English, one had been a pork butcher from York before the war, another had been a hairdresser in London, and they'd had enough. They were ambling along, without their rifles, walking towards Germany, accepting defeat. We believed we could go all the way to Berlin.

FIT FOR HEROES?

When demobilization came, the land fit for heroes was predictably absent; there were too many soldiers, sailors and airmen coming home to enable a nation to be grateful to them all, too many other pressing national and international problems to deal with for the government to care greatly for those who had fought.

For too many officers and men, the welcome home amounted to little more than an introduction to a hard life, with unemployment soaring and an economy driven into recession after years of free spending during the war. Those who had been granted demobilization quickly, realised that others who had extended their service in the army to peacetime soldiering were often far better off.

PRIVATE TED FRANCIS 16TH ROYAL WARWICKSHIRE REGIMENT, 1896-1996

It was difficult to get back into civilian life again. The Prime Minister had got on his feet and said, "Welcome home, lads, you've come to a land fit for heroes", and he was the best liar I've ever heard. When I got back, I naturally approached my old firm, the little factory, to get my job back. They looked at me like I was a complete stranger. There was hardly anyone I recognized and they almost pushed me out of the door, saying, "We've got no job for you."

Yes, I was bitter. What would anyone's feelings be, when the fellow who is walking up the gutter trying to sell matches has no arm or leg? It was two or three years before I landed a job.

HENRY ALLINGHAM
1896-2009

'In the RNAS we had it jammy compared to what the other fellows did. I don't know that I could have stood what those men stood in the trenches. Poor devils.

HARRY PATCH
1898-2009

'The day I lost my pals, 22 September 1917 – that is my Remembrance Day, not Armistice Day. The cenotaph service is all right – the rest of it is a military show. I'm always very quiet on that day and I don't want anybody talking to me. I shall never forget the three I lost.'

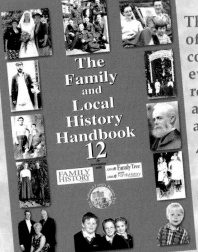